MUSIC FESTIVALS AND REGIONAL
DEVELOPMENT IN AUSTRALIA

Music Festivals and Regional Development in Australia

CHRIS GIBSON
University of Wollongong, Australia

and

JOHN CONNELL
University of Sydney, Australia

ASHGATE

Published by
Ashgate Publishing Limited
Wey Court East
Union Road
Farnham
Surrey, GU9 7PT
England

Ashgate Publishing Company
Suite 420
101 Cherry Street
Burlington
VT 05401-4405
USA

www.ashgate.com

British Library Cataloguing in Publication Data
Gibson, Chris
  Music festivals and regional development in Australia. 1. Music festivals–Australia.
  2. Music–Social aspects–Australia.
  I. Title II. Connell, John
  780.7'894-dc23

Library of Congress Cataloging-in-Publication Data
Gibson, Chris, 1973–
  Music festivals and regional development in Australia / by Chris Gibson
and John Connell.
      p. cm.
  Includes bibliographical references and index.
  ISBN 978-0-7546-7526-6 (hardback : alk. paper) — ISBN 978-1-4094-4367-4 (ebook)
1. Music festivals—Australia. 2. Music—Social aspects—Australia. I. Connell, John,
1946– II. Title.
  ML360.G53 2011
  780.78'94–dc23

                                                                              2011039527

ISBN 9780754675266 (hbk)
ISBN 9781409443674 (ebk)

Printed and bound in Great Britain by
TJ International Ltd, Padstow, Cornwall.

Contents

List of Figures

List of Tables

Preface

This book examines the changing role and significance of festivals in regional development. It draws from our own experiences conducting research on, and working with, festivals in rural and remote small towns in Australia, some very distant from metropolitan centres, where festivals contribute to local economies and to local cultural life.

We have organised the book in two parts. Part I discusses general themes concerning music festivals and regional development. The chapters draw on a range of case studies, illustrations and examples, some from outside Australia, that point to the role of festivals in a broad spectrum of regional development concerns, from direct economic impacts to less obvious benefits for community, social cohesion and well-being. We develop a perspective that seeks to integrate questions of cultural identity, belonging, volunteering and paid employment – for, as we explain throughout, a narrowly rationalist economic perspective on festivals and regional development at best only partially explains the significance of festivals. A purely economic perspective is not only ideologically indefensible in the context of discussing festivals; it would also run the risk of ignoring critical cultural, social and environmental issues. Without consideration of these, the true significance of festivals for regional development cannot be fully appreciated.

Part II is centred on particular places to provide detailed case studies of music festivals in the context of rural and regional development. Chapters tell the rich stories of individual festivals and, in doing so, the range of themes discussed in Part I come together in particular places. The case studies take up the important general themes in different ways: Parkes on economic success and struggles for identity; Opera in the Paddock and Bermagui's Four Winds Festival on 'bringing culture to the regions'; Tamworth on massive growth in a festival and on what is meant by 'country'; Byron Bay on community conflicts and questions of environmental management. The result is a perspective on a range of festivals of various types (classical, country, blues, alternative rock, opera) that have global reach and relevance.

This book also came together because of the involvement of the authors in a larger team of festival researchers (which at various times also included Gordon Waitt, Jim Walmsley, Chris Brennan-Horley and Andrew Gorman-Murray, whose involvement and insights we duly acknowledge here). The project, which was centred on the three southeast states of Tasmania, Victoria and New South Wales, was funded by the Australian Research Council (a Federal Government body), to systematically examine the range of social, cultural and economic dimensions of rural festivals. Anna Stewart, Elyse Stanes, Tegan Freeburn, Tristan Devitt, Brad Ruting, Jen Li, Shane Newton, Hanna Pelham and Robbie Begg contributed research assistance and ideas to that project. Thanks are also due to Deborah Davidson, who co-authored an earlier piece on Tamworth in *Journal of Rural Studies*, from which Chapter 8 draws inspiration (and likewise Chris Brennan-Horley for Chapter 6); to Kelly Hendry (formerly Atkinson) at Parkes for her on-going collaboration; to Peta and Bill Blyth at Opera in the Paddock; Sheila Boughen at Bermagui, and to the incalculable number of festival managers, performers, workers, home hosts, stallholders and audience members who gave their time to be interviewed or surveyed in the multiple times and places of our festivals research. We are most grateful to the Dorrigo Folk and Blues Festival and Marilyn Wall for the beautiful artwork for our cover. Thanks also to Kirstie Petrou and Naomi Riggs for research assistance for this book; to Jenny Atchison, Luke Della Santa, Rob Tacheci, and Rachael Somer for festival photos; to Kelly Allen, Vivian Lee and Kate Mirow for survey work at Splendour in the Grass, to departmental colleagues at both the Universities of Wollongong and Sydney for insights and open-mindedness (even when dealing with seemingly questionable, sometimes even bizarre, field work expense receipts and the like); and to Ali, Cara, Beth and Thantida for support and equanimity on the domestic front.

A final note: unless otherwise stated all quotes are from the official websites of festivals – there were simply too many and with addresses too convoluted to reproduce in the text or bibliography.

Sydney
August 2011

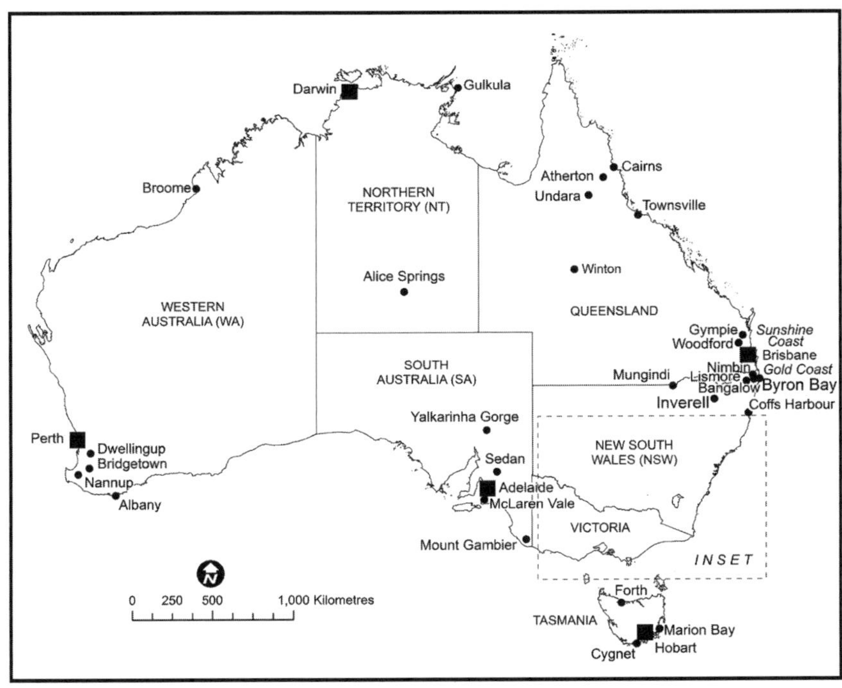

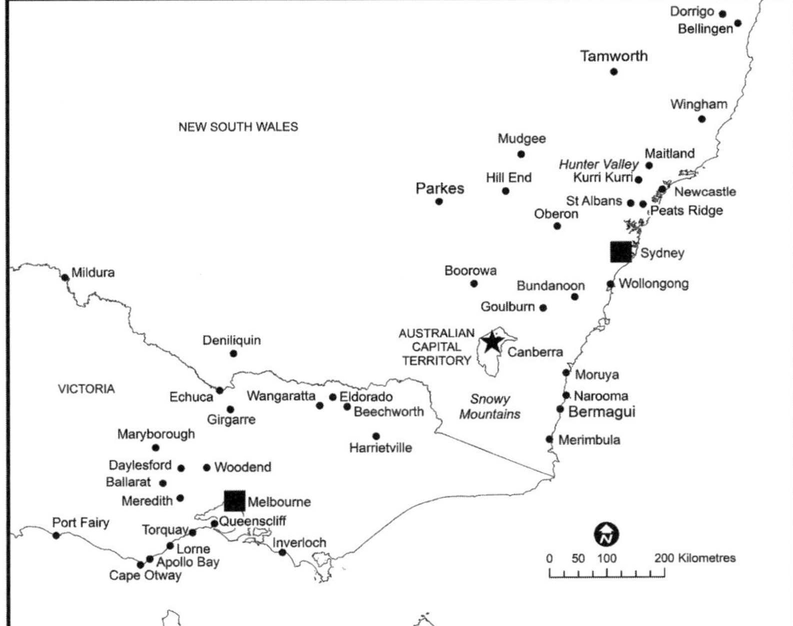

Figure 1.1   Location map of festivals discussed in this book

PART I
Music Festivals:
Promises and Predicaments

Chapter 1

Introduction

The Girgarre Moosic Muster is held annually to bring the community of Girgarre together. They are doing it pretty tough on the land and this gives them a free weekend, where they can enjoy all styles of music and let their hair down! It also gives them a chance to learn to play instruments and not have to pay for their first lessons. All funds raised over the weekend go back into the community to help them out. The committee that run the weekend are all volunteers, a mixture of Girgarre and city folk, that come together for one cause, the Girgarre community. (Jan Dandridge (Little Miss Country)'s Blog, 13 January 2009)

Throughout the world the number of music festivals has grown exponentially in the last two decades, as people celebrate local and regional cultures, as musical styles diversify, and as councils, business coalitions and non-profit groups use festivals to both promote tourism and stimulate regional development. This is scarcely new; as long ago as the 1800s European cities on the Grand Tour staged festivals to harmonise social relations as well as generate trade, and draw in people from outside. What has changed has been the proliferation of festivals of all types, often in quite small places, their increasing diversity and, in many cases, the sophistication of their marketing and management. And, as at Girgarre, a tiny farming settlement in Victoria (population 300), they play a valuable and sometimes unexpected role in rural and regional life.

Academic and applied consultancy research on the social, cultural and economic dimensions of festivals has concurrently expanded. Festivals have been shown to draw communities together to celebrate local cultures (Duffy 2000); to involve people of disparate geographical origins whose community is catalysed by highly specialised passions, shared pastimes or intense fandom (Mackellar 2009a; Begg 2011); or simply to entertain large numbers of people. Festivals can also include and exclude people by drawing boundaries around 'community', through subcultural affiliation, pre-requisite knowledge to appreciate narrow music styles, specialist knowledge required for entry (in the case of, for instance, raves) or meaningful participation. They can annoy local residents by generating traffic, pollution and congestion; and by attracting 'unwanted' types of people (often revealing as much about local residents' imagined picture of themselves as of the behaviour of the festival-goers). In places where tourism development has been rapid – and often linked to the rise of festivals – conflicts can ensue over local spaces, resources and the direction and meaning of regional development. This book seeks to discuss this range of issues, taking music festivals seriously as a regional development concern.

Debate surrounds what constitutes a 'festival'. Some are community festivals that emerge from dedicated local people and only in time come to attract audiences beyond the immediate locality. Others are primarily commercial – essentially full-blown open air concerts, organised by metropolitan promoters, that may even be foisted on places and play little role in regional development, despite high ticket costs. At high-profile commercial music festivals the roster of acts is crucial, compared with local festivals which place higher priority on community building and are keen to showcase local talent without need for big name imported acts. Each of these types of festivals has a different influence on regional development.

In our festivals research, conducted in Australia over a decade, demarcation was made between infrequent, usually annual, musical events, which were included (pending other criteria), and regular, recurrent events held throughout the year. Generally festivals had to meet at least one (and preferably more than one) of the following criteria: use of the word 'festival' in the event name; being an irregular, one-off, annual or biennial event; emphasise celebrating, promoting or exploring some aspect of culture (in this case music); or being an unusual point of convergence for people with a given cultural activity, or of a specific subcultural identification. Some lasted several days and involved hundreds of performers, others took no more than a long evening; the latter group were in many ways little more than concerts and have been included here only where they seemed to make some contribution to regional life. Festivals then were understood, following Getz (2007:31), as 'themed, public celebrations'. What makes festivals distinct is that they are usually held annually and generally have social rather than economic or political aims: getting people together for fun, entertainment and a shared sense of camaraderie. Most festivals created a time and space of celebration, a site of convergence separate from everyday routines, experiences and meanings – ephemeral communities in place and time.

At the outset it might also be queried what constitutes music – though we have chosen to ignore that as a stylistic consideration – and whether general community festivals that might have significant musical content ought to be considered for inclusion in this book. To take just one example, the Kurri Kurri Nostalgia Festival, New South Wales (NSW), focuses on the 1950s, and markets itself through appeals to nostalgia – cars, clothes, dancing and music. Music is not necessarily the main attraction, but is an important part of why people attend. In some places we have discussed such examples, because music is clearly a part of what makes these festivals successful, but this book primarily focuses on festivals where music was the primary component.

Although the field of festivals and special events research has blossomed (even spawning dedicated academic journals such as *Event Management*; see also Getz 2010), most studies have tended to be rather specialised. They suit specific needs (e.g. in consultancy research funded by festivals themselves); reflect the disciplinary backgrounds and perspectives of those undertaking the research (for example, focusing almost exclusively on the cultural and symbolic aspects, or on narrow modelling of economic multiplier impacts) or they have examined different dimensions of single festivals held in one place. Likewise, until quite recently the environmental impacts of festivals have been neglected and thus not linked into discussions of the economic and social impacts of festivals (Jones 2009; Gibson and Wong 2011). Debates have raged over the narrow economic impact of individual festivals (see Chapter 4), rather than discussing a broader set of interrelated regional development issues. Concerns such as how festivals cumulatively stimulate inward investment, link to local business networks, inspire potential migrants to move to regional towns, generate and (unevenly) diffuse fiscal and educational benefits and nestle within place marketing and tourism image construction campaigns have been rarely integrated – if at all. Little has been written about the *interrelationship* between economic, environmental and cultural dimensions of festivals – about how festivals could and are being used to promote local and regional development in the broadest sense, and what kinds of political and social issues are at stake. This book seeks to fill that gap.

That this sort of synthetic analysis of festivals and regional development is needed is borne out when listening to festival organisers and representatives of host communities. In the small town of Queenscliff (Victoria), annual tourism income from its music festival totalled over \$2 million[1] at the start of the century. For the festival's manager, Barbara Moss, beyond the direct impact,

> that economic impact is tied to the social fabric of the community. It's directly linked to the social health of the town and confidence is always a big factor in economic growth. A lot of local people become involved in the festival – up to 400 people volunteer to help out each year – and we've found that to be a big long-term stimulant to the economy. Some of those people might otherwise be lying in bed watching Oprah. Now they're out getting involved. That connectivity, the bringing together of diverse elements, is what social wealth is all about. (Quoted in Williams 2002:44)

These kinds of interrelated social and economic returns are particularly meaningful in small towns like Queenscliff and Girgarre, with limited labour resources and support infrastructure. In small places festivals can scarcely go unnoticed; large segments of communities invest money, time and emotion in them.

In rural and regional areas economic decline, rapid changes in the agricultural sector, and dwindling and ageing populations, have created a dynamic setting for the staging of festivals. Most of the festivals we discuss in this book are situated in what are in Australia called country towns – usually ranging in size from 5,000 to 30,000 people (though some, like Girgarre, are considerably smaller). Many small towns are struggling with a declining agricultural base, and relatively homogenous populations with little in-migration, where Indigenous people are a small numerical

---

1   All dollar figures in this book are in Australian dollars unless otherwise stated. At the time of writing, the Australian dollar was worth approximately US\$1.05, though in the past decade it has more typically fluctuated between US\$0.75 and US\$0.90.

minority. In some places – mainly on the coasts and in inland parts of Queensland and Western Australia – stagnation has been avoided by 'sea-change' in-migration from capital cities, resources and minerals booms, and the growth of tourism and creative industries. In such places there is a rather different, and dynamic, context of growth and prosperity. Festivals reflect such patterns of decline and growth, and the social and economic processes behind them. As we hope to show here, festivals have sometimes been actively incorporated into attempts by places to reinvent themselves, have helped turn around economic and population decline, or have played a substantial role in changing the character and distribution of benefits from the local economy.

In regional areas of countries as different as China and Australia, the tourism spin-offs deriving from the promotion of festivals are seen as one means of redressing rural decline (Walmsley 2003; Xie 2003). In 2003 an annual international music festival was argued to be the only viable means of rescuing the host Shoalhaven River Estate (NSW) from bankruptcy and mounting debts (*Sydney Morning Herald* 26 April 2003:5). Later that year the tiny former gold mining township of Hill End (NSW), with just 120 people, launched the inaugural Hill End Jazz Festival, which was expected to bring 1500 visitors and raise enough money to buy a defibrillator for the community (*Sydney Morning Herald* 24 October 2003:3). Regional places like Aldeburgh, Glyndebourne and Glastonbury in the UK, Bayreuth in Germany and Woodstock in the United States have been so successful that their festivals have substantially improved economic and social capital, and resulted in those places largely being known, even defined, through their festivals. The same is true for Tamworth and Gympie in Australia (Gibson and Davidson 2004; Edwards 2011). In such places, festivals have become a long-term place-marketing strategy rather than simply a short-term event (Hall 1989). Festivals are anticipated to bring multiple benefits to rural communities: to stimulate short-term employment; to improve the skills of residents and improve their chances of finding future work; to enhance social cohesion; and to re-invent places and their images. In short they can put towns on the map, and keep them there. And by and large they are an enjoyable way of doing so. In other places festivals are small and the real skill is in managing to marshal enough resources, to call on favours and make ends meet. Festivals fuel creative frugality.

For these reasons this book focuses on rural and regional contexts, excluding consideration of festivals in state capitals, such as Sydney and Brisbane. Although similar themes sometimes resonate with festivals in big cities (Waitt 2008), the different scale of the metropolis means that economic, environmental and social impacts are all more muted (Tindall 2011). By contrast regional festivals enable a particularly focussed discussion of the range of development issues and themes. Alongside the many cases of festivals putting places on the map, there are disappointments and economic losses, temporary benefits not sustained outside festival times, uneven distribution of profits (and aggravation of local conflicts), or concerns amongst local communities (and visiting participants) about the character, meaning and direction of festivals and their links to local economy.

There can be tensions between economic success and environmental degradation, as in Byron Bay (Chapter 9), and over what images are appropriate for regional towns (Chapters 6 and 8). Such challenges complicate the relationship between festivals and regional development. While rural and regional festivals have gained some attention academically (e.g. Long and Perdue 1990; De Bres and Davis 2001; Higham and Ritchie 2001; Chhabra et al. 2003; Moscardo 2008), their treatment pales in comparison to that lavished on mega-events in major cities, and the complexities surrounding festivals and regional development remain largely unexplored. Such complexity is a central part of our story here.

Why choose music festivals in particular? Music is in the broadest sense the oldest and most common element of festivals. Musicians have always been present at community festivities around harvests, equinoxes, village fairs and Mardi Gras. In the Middle Ages musicians, often travellers themselves, added a soundtrack to the relaxation of social norms that accompanied seasonal celebrations. In more modern times, the proliferation of professional music festivals is remarkable – big, small, conservative, radical, alternative – every demographic and niche audience is catered for, from children's music to speed metal, opera to techno. Music festivals are some of the largest festivals in the world – Berlin's Love Parade, Roskilde, Lollapalooza, and in Australia, the Tamworth Country Music Festival (Chapter 8) – but, in their proliferation, they also fill some of the smallest and most specific niches: in the case of the Roy Orbison Festival in Wink, Texas or the Elvis Presley Festival in Parkes (Chapter 6) dedicated to the music of a single (dead) musician; or at Herräng, in Sweden, an otherwise small and largely anonymous village ('a sleepy one-horse town in the outskirts of nowhere but still fairly easy to reach by car or public transportation') that hosts the world's largest annual gathering of jitterbug (swing jazz) dancers. Individual instruments too can be rationales for music festivals, often located where regional traditions are strong (or are revived in the face of cultural globalisation), where competition for hotel space and visibility is less fierce or where specialisation gives a small town festival a unique niche. Examples include the Cape Breton International Drum Festival (Nova Scotia, Canada); the Welsh International Harp Festival (in Caernarfon, Gwynedd); Australia's International Guitar Festival (held in Darwin in the country's remote tropical north); the Yosemite Flute Festival (held on the edge of the national park, and which specialises in Native American flutes); and the International Clarinet Association's annual Clarinetfest (in 2012, in Lincoln, Nebraska). For violins alone there is an international network of events, most of which are in regional towns or rural locations. Beaulieu-sur-Mer in the French Riviera hosts an annual Violons de Légende Festival (Legendary Violins Festival), which is aimed

> at all those interested not only in top quality concerts but also the history of musical instruments, in these violins that have crossed the ages. The Festival aims to become a meeting place for the world's major violin collectors, who would meet here once a year, to compare and have their acquisitions listened to.

For bagpipes there are festivals in Glasgow (Scotland), Malahide (Ireland), Strakonice (Bohemia, Czech Republic), Mihovljan (Croatia), Gela (Bulgaria), Mont Cassel (France), New Jersey (USA) and Minsk (Belarus), far beyond where bagpipe festivals might have been expected. Since 1996, Oulu in Finland has been the site of the annual world air guitar championships, a festival coined as a joke, and meant only to be a side attraction for a music video festival, but which became the major event. In Australia, Cairns (Queensland) has a ukulele festival (as, more predictably, does Waikoloa in Hawaii) and Hawkesbury (NSW) hosts the National Fiddle Festival (which 'celebrates the Fiddle from all cultures in all genre of music'). Perhaps indicative of just how specialised such music festivals may be is the Australian Gumleaf Playing Championship. Held annually in Maryborough (Victoria), with its coveted Golden Gumleaf Award, it has become a focus for enthusiastic Aboriginal and non-Aboriginal players from around Australia. Gumleaf playing started as an Aboriginal tradition but by the 1920s was highly popular in the wider Australian community, trained in the ancient art of whistling using eucalyptus leaves. The music festival scene has expanded and specialised perhaps more than any other segment of the special event industry – hence a rather more sophisticated discussion of regional development issues is possible for this one type of event.

This book emerged from some degree of frustration with the current orthodoxy in regional development research and practice – an attitude which seemed to privilege particular industries and perspectives (often fixated on agriculture, big business and transport infrastructure), at the expense of smaller scale, seemingly transient phenomena such as festivals. In one example, in an otherwise impressive scholarly textbook on regional development in Australia (Beer et al. 2003) tourism barely rated a mention, and 'festivals' was completely absent from the index. Nor does it appear in the indexes for Gradus and Lithwick's *Frontiers in Regional Development* (1996) or Pike's (2006) *Local and Regional Development*. Even in Giaoutzi and Nijkamp's *Tourism and Regional Development* (2006) there were no chapters or extended discussions dedicated to festivals. This book seeks to play some role in redressing this imbalance. As Whitford (2004) observed in her analysis of public policy-making, festivals are simply not acknowledged as part of the regional development equation; where festivals policy-making does emerge, it is only intermittent and within 'insular' circles in cultural planning or community services.

A handful of events are exceptions, and have been directly linked to regional development, but usually by their organisers rather than from regional development agencies. Thus the not-for-profit Wingham Akoostik Music Festival in NSW has been organised, like many others, by a small group of Wingham residents for the benefit of the town and to give musicians the chance to play their original music live, but it has also been supported by the Foundation for Rural and Regional Renewal, a non-government organisation (NGO) whose role is 'to promote for the public benefit rural and regional renewal, regeneration and development in Australia in social, economic, environmental, and cultural areas'. At the state level the NSW

Government in 2007 developed a major government corporation, Events NSW, to create and attract large-scale festivals. Initially its focus was metropolitan ('it will drive a more aggressive approach to attracting big name events to Sydney' (Premier of NSW 2007a)) and geared towards international place marketing ('It will also help cement Sydney's status as Australia's global city' (Premier of NSW 2007b)). The focus was squarely on 'spectacle' (cf. Quinn 2010). Only much later – after criticism of its city-centrism and obsession with mega-events – did it broaden its scope to include regional festivals and adopt a broader development focus.

Festivals, and particularly small regional festivals – seemingly ephemeral, concerned with fun rather than job creation, often not explicitly commercial, and largely invisible other than when actually being staged – have been overlooked by regional development academics and practitioners, in the face of obvious examples of successful transformations they have catalysed. Even in the most visible cases, regional development agencies, local council managers, town mayors and economic planners have taken years to be convinced of the value of festivals, despite obvious empirical evidence to the contrary (Chapter 6), because few seem to make much money. But as Australia and other countries move towards a so-called 'post-productivist countryside', where agriculture is of declining significance relative to other sectors, notably service provision, so the role of festivals becomes more important.

Festivals are worthy of examination in a regional development framework not just because they are growing and becoming more commercially significant, but because they invite a more critical perspective on regional development (Gibson et al. 2010). Analysing festivals as regional development initiatives necessarily requires consideration of social and cultural perspectives, and a particular kind of theorisation of regional development that moves away from narrow, neoclassical economic interpretations. To truly understand how festivals contribute to regional development, qualitative theorisation is needed on the character and meaning of local economic transactions and networks. Festivals are sometimes straightforward commercial affairs, organised by private companies for profit – but rarely are they so simple. Usually they bring together segments of the capitalist economy with local government, non-profit organisations and informal, unregulated sectors of the economy. They are hybrid economic affairs – less like single investments or enterprises emanating wholly from one industry, and more like a kind of central meeting place for different parts of local economies. Festivals act like 'glue', temporarily sticking together various stakeholders, economic transactions and networks. This hybridity and temporality make a profound difference to whether festivals generate benefits for local communities and how they might be critically analysed in a regional development context. Beyond regional development themes (and beyond the scope of this book), music festivals are also potent sites for ethnomusicological, historical and psychological research. Such themes – although of great interest – rarely surface here for fear of diluting the book's focus; they are covered by others through a diversity of perspectives (see for example, Duffy 2009 and various chapters in Gibson and Connell 2011).

Because this book stems from a research project, at various stages we refer to data generated from that project between 2005 and 2010. That project itself had evolved from work previously undertaken in Parkes, Byron Bay and Tamworth. Our aim was to comprehensively document, and map, the extent and significance of festivals in rural Australia. It involved the compilation of a database of festivals, for three Australian states – Tasmania, Victoria and New South Wales – including information on the name, aims, organisers, location, marketing material, date and frequency of every rural festival that could be found through internet searches and collection of flyers and pamphlets (Gibson et al. 2010). A total of 2,856 festivals were found across non-metropolitan areas of these three states, evidence itself of the extent of the proliferation of festivals in rural and regional areas. Some 288 of these (about 10 per cent of the total) were music festivals, and music festivals were amongst the most common types of festivals (see Chapter 2). Information specific to these music festivals is discussed at various stages in this book.

We also sent a detailed survey to festival organisers where an identifiable organisation or address was publicly available, to examine the extent to which festivals were incorporated into economic development and regeneration strategies. We asked organisers a range of questions on their event's aims, history, crowd size, stalls and stages, the geography of festival-goers and inputs, target markets, organisational structure, employment, volunteerism, sponsorship and advertising, community attitudes, and estimated economic impacts. A total of 480 completed surveys were received from festival organisers (overall a 28 per cent survey response rate). Some 92 surveys (or around 20 per cent) were from music festivals. Findings from these surveys with music festival organisers are also discussed here. Both before and during this project we pursued a series of more detailed case studies of festivals, through face-to-face and phone interviewing with festival organisers, more detailed analysis of economic impacts via visitor and business surveys at single events, and analysis of community development themes via interviews with various stakeholders in specific festival places. These became the main case studies in the book.

We have consciously sought to avoid parochialism. The book draws on studies of music (and other) festivals and regional development from across Australia and around the world. At the same time the Australian examples presented here have wider, global relevance for regional development themes and our analysis seeks to scale-up from the specific to the general based on these insights. We have sought to achieve a balance between coverage of the detail of individual festivals and places and more synthetic discussion of festivals and regional development themes.

Consequently the book is structured in two parts: the first discusses broad issues affecting music festivals globally, especially in the context of rural revitalisation – and draws on a mix of international and Australian case studies. The second part provides detailed discussions of festivals of types commonly found throughout North America, Europe and Australasia, such as country music, opera and alternative music festivals. We hope to show how festivals are more than mere frivolity or escapism; they are relevant yet difficult to theorise in a regional development sense. That these two points alone are true gave us good reason to write this book. Hopefully too we have been able to preserve at least some sense of the fun and pleasure that music festivals generate; after all, without these qualities no music festival could hope to be viable. In the end, despite various political interpretations and social conflicts over ownership and identity, festivals are a form of travel, education, escape, temporary transgression and even hedonism. They reflect and embody the contradictions of wider society, and sometimes allow for a negotiation of these, but ultimately they are about a temporary release from the everyday, from the mundane, enabling both pleasure and fulfilment, while also contributing to economic change and development.

Chapter 2
The Rise of Music Festivals: A Means to Regeneration?

Music festivals have been around for centuries. Just when they began is impossible to trace; the title of 'Europe's oldest festival' is claimed by England's Three Choirs Festival which dates to 1724 (and still continues) in the cathedral cities of Hereford, Gloucester and Worcester. Before then, music was central to the maintenance of culture in innumerable indigenous, village and peasant societies, and very much part of occasional seasonal gatherings, and in Australia was part of frequent Aboriginal and Torres Strait Islander ceremonies. In northern Europe maypole dancing was long part of celebrations of seasonal cycles. Established in England by the early Middle Ages it became increasingly popular throughout the ensuing centuries, with the maypoles often being seen as 'communal symbols' that brought the local community together – forever linked with picturesque fantasies of 'Merrie England'. Somewhat later morris dancing performed a similar function, so that some of the earliest European festivals, to celebrate the seasons and fertility, were in some respects also music festivals.

Most of the first deliberate celebratory festivals in Australia were agricultural shows, where music played a secondary role to bringing a scattered farming community together, publicising agricultural production advances, and celebrating the mastery and harvests of nature (Darian-Smith 2011). Music was more of a presence in early Australian rodeos, Wild West shows and travelling circuses – each firmly aimed at entertaining audiences rather than informing them. Country music especially became globalised in the 1930s through the popularity of singing cowboy movies (Hicks 2001) and was performed in Australia between exhibitions of buckjumping, campdrafting, whip-cracking and gun-trickery.

Music festivals, as they are now conventionally known, only emerged in developed countries in Europe and North America after the Second World War. They were pioneered by jazz festivals such as that at Newport (Rhode Island), which began in 1954, and in the 1960s were linked to the rise of the countercultural 'hippie' scene, youth rock music cultures, and the maturing of jazz and classical music audiences seeking experiences beyond one-off performances in opera houses and concert halls (Rawlins 1986). Music festivals were an alternative space for social and sexual interaction, drug consumption, musical expression and relaxation. Their beginnings often comprised part of social revolutions, motivated by desires to invert orthodoxy and moral conservatism, rather than commercial imperatives. Internationally famous examples, such as Woodstock, Montreux, Monterey and the Isle of Wight, were complemented by lesser-known, but equally innovative festivals such as Nimbin, Australia's Aquarius Festival in the mid-1970s. The 1970 Pilgrimage For Pop festival at Ourimbah, just north of Sydney, with 6,000 participants, is argued by some to be Australia's first rock festival, and a 'milestone in an unspecified movement away from the stresses of a purely consumerist society' (Rawlins 1986:10; Elder 1999). Establishing an early link with rurality, countercultural folk and rock festivals were usually held outside capital cities on large pastoral properties that handled the crowd sizes, promised bucolic charms and offered retreat from the tedium and oppressions of suburban life.

The late 1960s and 1970s, a period of unprecedented affluence and new leisure time, also marked the expansion of mass tourism, both domestically and internationally. Even avowedly countercultural festivals, such as Woodstock and Monterey, sought to attract visitors from across the country and around the world. Countless music festivals have subsequently been started as quasi-promotional investments for regional tourism campaigns. Democratisation of tourism through accessibility to motor cars, working-class family holidays, and the emergence of new kinds of tourism for backpackers, retirees and students, all resulted in feasible new markets for music festivals. Music festivals were viable in otherwise small beachside towns in summer months (and hence became useful opportunities for record companies to spotlight that year's new pop bands to mass audiences, hoping that their tracks would become the 'soundtracks of summer'). Rather than festivals for hippies most were 'driven by booze and an ambience that teetered on the chaotic … the summer festivals of what would eventually become known as "pub rock"' (Elder 1999:2). Festivals also became important in ski-fields, where they generated the requisite 'party' atmosphere. In the cases of both country music and classical music, festivals became anchors for retiree/recreational vehicle (RV) tourism for hundreds of small rural towns in the United States (and in Australia, where the parallel 'grey nomad' phenomenon emerged), often later spawning the construction of focused, purpose-built music venues for year-round tourism (Gibson and Connell 2005). The emergence of mass tourism also coincided with a global era of ethnic revivalism, which created a demand for Celtic music festivals in Wales (where Eisteddfod festivals were revived), Scotland, Ireland, France, Canada and the United States. On a smaller scale such ethnic revival festivals also began in Australia, amongst migrants from particular parts of Europe, but usually in the metropolitan capitals where migrants lived.

Blues and country festivals emerged in the United States celebrating American national heritage, held in famous music towns closely linked to rural music practices in the early twentieth century, such as Memphis (Tennessee) and Clarksdale (Mississippi). In a typical example, The Mississippi Valley Blues Society hosts its annual blues festival in Davenport (Iowa), aiming 'to educate the general public about the native art form of blues-related music through performance, interpretation and preservation, thus enhancing appreciation and understanding'. Folk music revivals in the United States and Britain also brought similar festivals (Connell and Gibson 2003). The resurgence of ethnic identity and renewed interest in national heritage generated new markets for music festivals.

In the 1990s, a second phase of more commercial festivals grew in many western countries linked to the increased mobility of consumers, more sophisticated marketing in the music industry (where festivals were seen as an advertising opportunity to spur record sales), the emergence of 'alternative' music scenes (centred on large festivals such as Lollapalooza in the United States, Roskilde in Denmark, Glastonbury in the UK, and in Australia the Big Day Out, which had originally been an antipodean Lollapalooza), and an increasingly internationalised touring circuit controlled by oligopolistic and territorially organised promotion companies. A shift in the perception of music festivals accompanied this, as commercial motives triumphed over community orientation. Indeed such large festivals often provoked community antagonism.

From the 1980s onwards, however, a multitude of music festivals had begun to appear in small towns, many for no special reason other than for entertainment and because local authorities wanted to enhance local cultural life. Others started because of desires to promote particular musical genres, because of the efforts of enthusiastic fans and local musical clubs looking for a focal point on their annual calendars of events, or because musicians themselves sought outlets for performance where few previously existed. Many music festivals in small towns happened just once, or lasted for a few years depending on the enthusiasm of the local organising committee or local government-employed festival organiser. Others survived, gained reputations and developed their own heritages and traditions, rising from small beginnings to national and even international prominence. The more well-known have included the Tamworth Country Music Festival (and competitors in Gympie and Mildura), Maleny/Woodford Folk Festival, Byron Bay's East Coast Blues and Roots Festival, the Wangaratta Jazz Festival and Goulburn's Blues Festival. All these are now known as leaders nationally in Australia in their respective genres, having grown steadily from modest local beginnings in country towns.

Predictably, major festivals in big cities dominate the commercial musical festival scene, although several, such as Glastonbury in England and Australia's Falls Festival, remained in the country and sought to stay true to original aesthetic and philosophical sentiments. The Falls Festival website declared in 2011

> In an era of increasing globalization, capitalism and commercialism, The Falls Music & Arts Festival is one company that has its primary focus firmly on benefiting others. Despite costing literally millions of dollars each year to stage, the budgets are tighter than a rusted lid on a jar of nanna's homemade jam and cut just enough slack to keep things going from year to year.

Outside the corporate music industry, the burgeoning rave scene supported 'underground' techno raves – known in Australia as bush 'doofs' (an onomatopoeic term for their distinctive 'doof, doof, doof' music) held in secret locations in state forests and on pastoral properties in urban hinterlands. These reached their zenith in the late 1990s – at the height of popularity of the techno music style – before drug raids and burnout led many ravers to seek more mellow alternatives, such as reggae and dub festivals, which subsequently grew in the 2000s, as raves faded. Other festivals, such as the Gympie Country Music Muster (in Queensland) began as modest affairs organised by enthusiastic individuals, but outgrew their original facilities and moved to dedicated premises outside towns (Edwards 2011), where extra space for stages, audience, camping and stalls could be found in a rustic setting that helped evoke notions of community and simpler rural lifestyles. Music festivals pitching themselves to a politically-active, environmentally-conscious audience (such as the Falls Festival and NSW's Peat's Ridge Music Festival) also chose settings on 'idyllic' farm properties or near prized 'wilderness', to hint at the potential for communing with nature.

Since the 1980s, in Australia and elsewhere, some music festivals have been linked to local tourism strategies, their growth nothing short of dramatic and their economic potential considerable. At the start of the 1980s pop festivals had become a 'regular feature of the British countryside in summer' (Clarke 1982:1), and by the end of the century various estimates suggested that in the United States there were more than 4,000 music festivals every year, over 520 in the United Kingdom, and over 800 in France (Waterman 1998; Hughes 2000). In the early 1990s Frey (1994) counted between 1,000 and 2,000 classical music festivals alone in Europe every summer; moreover 'hardly a genre or a geography has been left untapped' (Delaney 2003) so similar numbers of festivals probably existed for devotees of other forms of music. Festivals had assuredly arrived and, as in Sweden, were remarkably evenly distributed throughout countries (Aldskogius 1993). Every part of every country sought at least one, as their economic and social value became more evident. Music festivals were well established throughout the developed world and were extending far beyond that.

A similar situation had emerged in Australia. In 2007 we found 288 music festivals in regional areas of the three south-eastern states (Tasmania, Victoria and NSW), confirming earlier estimates of several hundred music festivals taking place outside capital cities every year in Australia (Gibson and Connell 2005). Although music festivals were not as numerous as agricultural shows, community festivals or sporting carnivals (Table 2.1) they were more common than other popular festivals such as arts and food and wine festivals. Although many of the more prominent regional music festivals (as at Tamworth, Goulburn and Gympie) have existed for well over a decade, most of the music festivals were relatively new. Over 80 per cent had been established since 1990, of which over a third were first staged less than five years previously. Music festivals were both expanding and evolving extremely quickly.

Of the 288 music festivals, the most common types were general music festivals tagged to place names (for example 'the Lismore Music Festival') and country music festivals – the most popular single genre. Some festivals, like the Tablelands Folk Festival (Atherton Tablelands, Queensland), offered an extraordinary variety of musical genres ranging from 'Traditional Australian Folk, Celtic, Irish, Country Folk, Lap-slide Blues, Bluegrass, Hot Swing Jazz, Latin Gypsy, Punk Folk, Middle East and Indian, Tropical Swing, Reggae, and plenty of Contemporary

Table 2.1   Numbers of festivals by type. Tasmania, Victoria and NSW, 2007

Type of festival	TAS	VIC	NSW	Total	%
Sport	86	485	488	1,059	36.5
Community	45	216	175	436	15.0
Agriculture	19	146	215	380	13.1
Music	**13**	**116**	**159**	**288**	**9.9**
Arts	12	73	82	167	5.8
Other	7	87	71	165	5.7
Food	10	53	67	130	4.5
Wine	7	49	32	88	3.0
Gardening	20	43	14	77	2.7
Culture	2	21	11	34	1.2
Environment	1	8	12	21	0.7
Heritage/historic	4	8	7	19	0.7
Children/Youth	0	10	5	15	0.5
Christmas/New Year	0	10	2	12	0.4
Total	226	1,325	1,340	2,891	100

Note: The 'other' category includes small numbers of lifestyle, outdoor, science, religious, seniors, innovation, education, animal, beer, car, collectables, craft, air shows, dance, theatre, gay and lesbian, Indigenous, and new age festivals. The total for this table is slightly more than the total number of festivals in the database, due to counting of some festivals in more than one category (for example, 'food and wine festivals').

Source: authors

Folk'. The extent of country music festivals might seem surprising (country music normally being associated with American culture), but country music has long been prevalent in rural Australia and with strong lyrical links to 'the land' is now considered a music of 'country' Australia (Gibson and Davidson 2004; Edwards 2011). Indeed, country music festivals in Australia play a prominent role in maintaining myths of Australian nationalism and frontier masculinity, ironically using an American music style as the basis for festivals that celebrate an idealised Australian rural heartland (Chapter 8). Following country music in popularity were jazz, blues, rock, classical and opera (Table 2.2), contrasting somewhat with nationwide consumption patterns for recorded music, where jazz, folk, blues, classical, opera and country have much smaller 'niche' audiences. Moreover the widespread popularity of 'pop music' has not been translated into music festivals,

Table 2.2   Music festivals by genre. NSW, Tasmania and Victoria, 2007

Type of music festival	Total number	Percentage
General music/ not specified	90	31.3
Country	56	19.4
Jazz	50	17.4
Folk	31	10.8
Blues	20	6.9
Rock and/or pop	11	3.8
Other	11	3.8
Classical	9	3.1
Opera	8	2.8
Bluegrass	4	1.4
Rock 'n' roll	4	1.4
Scottish	4	1.4
Alternative rock	3	1.0
Indigenous	2	0.7
Irish	2	0.7
Rhythm and blues	2	0.7
World music	2	0.7

Note: The total in this table is greater than the 288 festivals in the database since about 10 per cent of festivals listed multiple genres (e.g. jazz and blues, folk and country). In such cases genres were counted separately. Hence figures in the 'percentage of all music festivals' column equal more than 100 per cent. The 'Other' category includes single festivals of the following types: metal, reggae, dance music, busking, rockabilly, Celtic, Christian, German, hip hop, Indian, contemporary and Latin.
Source: authors

other than in a small number of large, commercial pop festivals – suggesting its more ephemeral nature.

The spread of music festivals outside capital cities (Figure 2.1) reflects a mix of cultural, demographic, social and geographical trends. In Tasmania, beyond the Falls Festival in Marion Bay, music festivals cluster along its northern corridor of towns including Launceston, Evandale and George Town – following a well-trodden tourist route. Western Australia (WA), so distant from the eastern states, has its own distinct circuit of festivals, mainly in the south-west. In NSW and Victoria, larger regional centres predictably have more music festivals (in towns like Wagga Wagga, Mildura and Ballarat that have the critical mass to support them), as do 'festival places' such as Port Fairy, Bellingen and Deniliquin (towns increasingly known through their proliferation of festivals), and old river port towns such as Barham and Echuca, located on the Murray River and integrated into a network of inland heritage tourism – hence the popularity of jazz festivals associated with 'river life', paddle steamers and celebrations of early twentieth century culture. Specialisations, from folk festivals to those for specific instruments, have accompanied rising numbers. Busking at festivals is widespread, culminating in an annual international busking festival in Coffs Harbour, on the NSW coast. There is also a curious concentration of jazz festivals – around that seemingly most urban, late night, inner-city music – in some of the smaller towns in Australia, like Moruya, Bellingen and Wangaratta. The latter, now known as Australia's premiere jazz festival, is particularly successful because it is located in rural Victoria, outside the usual inner-city cliques. According to jazz pianist Barney McAll,

> You get a fantastic beautiful confusion of inner city bohos and farmers and freaks and drunkards and yobbos and intellectuals and international super stars … it is the master stroke that stirs the fires of creativity and is just downright more interesting. Cities are boring on their own, as are rural places. But mix 'em up and you get the Wangaratta Festival which is testimony to the crucible appeal. (Quoted in Curtis 2010:101)

Very large rock and country music festivals take place in Byron Bay, Lorne (Victoria) and Tamworth where organisers decided to start them decades ago, for personal and commercial reasons, and where festivals have thus had sufficient time to grow large and loyal audiences. Beyond these places – where music festivals are now often supported by local councils who employ full-time staff and are geared towards regional economic development and tourism – they are widely scattered and ever-present. Just about every rural town in Australia now has a music festival and they have become a generally accepted and popular feature of the annual calendar.

The increasing 'niche' marketing of music, and the rise of nostalgic tourism associated with particular eras and individual artists, has contributed to a growing diversity of festivals in both urban and rural areas. For each niche – from folk to opera to rave – festivals have emerged to meet demand, often catering to fans of specific artists, not all of whom are alive. Some festivals may be short-lived; the 2009 Peter Allen Festival, for 'The Boy from Oz', lasted just one year in Armidale (NSW), where he grew up. The proliferation of festivals has also meant that fewer have obvious musical links to place, but have emerged from local attempts to develop a valuable cultural and economic activity. Indeed only in a handful of places are there particular claims to some form of musical place authenticity.

Settings have however proved important, especially in Europe, with festivals often being situated in picturesque locations from natural landscapes of mountains, lakesides and beaches to heritage cities and castles. In Australia, a country without such extensive constructed heritage, natural landscapes play a significant part. The Kowmung Festival in Oberon (NSW) presents chamber music in unusual

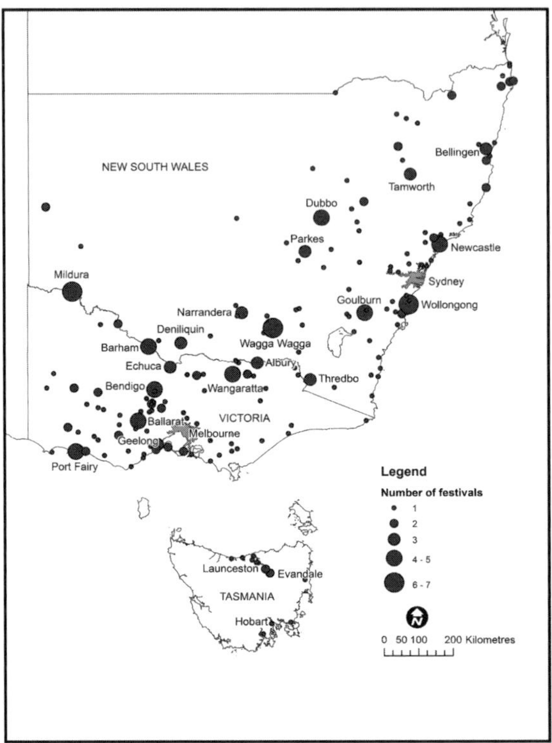

Figure 2.1　　Map of music festivals. NSW, Tasmania and Victoria, 2007

venues including limestone caves and cattle sheds. The combined role of music and landscape is exemplified in numerous festivals in wineries, where jazz and opera festivals amidst the vines create income and sophisticated identities for rural regions. Commercial concerns have led to both local competition and diversification, with events restructured to cater for more diverse populations and parallel attempts to extend the duration and impact. Growing diversity has also meant linkages with non-musical activities such as food, wine and the visual arts. Festivals have become valuable promotional devices, even in places without connections to music scenes.

Music Festivals as Revitalisation

Many contemporary music festivals are explicitly commercial, either from the point of view of tour promoters looking for fruitful markets in which to stage festivals, local planners and tourism officers seeking ways to boost local economies or participants wanting to earn incomes. None want to run at a loss. This growing economic role has been accompanied by more comprehensive marketing, such that by the 1990s the major festivals were institutionalised, as part of formal tourism campaigns, and sought increasingly national and even global markets. In contrast smaller festivals in smaller towns have rarely intended to do more than make a modest profit. Nonetheless some small towns have been so successful that festivals have substantially contributed to economic and social development, and resulted in those places being known through their festivals. Meredith (Victoria) was once a sleepy highway town of 1,100 people until three friends decided to throw a gig for alternative bands on a parents' family farm, 12 kilometres away. In subsequent years the Meredith Music Festival, held every December, became renowned for alternative rock music, its quasi-anarchic rural atmosphere, laid-back security and non-commercial format. Hence,

> Basically everyone camps on site. You can bring a tent, a marquee, sleep in the car, bring a caravan, campervan, motorhome, old bus, make a loungeroom in the back of a truck, get a chartered bus and driver, build The Tarp Mahal, do almost anything you like.

However, according to one founder, Greg Peele,

> When we started Meredith there was no other festival like it. We had no real model to work with. It fell into place. Each year something new was added and there was never any forward plan. We didn't have a three-year strategy. We just said "what did we do poorly last year?" and one of the key aspects was we wanted to get better before getting bigger. It wasn't about getting more people and it wasn't about making lots of money. It didn't make money.

But it did bring vital incomes to local caterers, petrol stations and the general store, and firmly established Meredith as a festival destination. Warren Ellis from alternative rock bands Grinderman and The Dirty Three has described it as 'simply the best festival in the world' (*The Age* 9 December 2010). On the same site a sister event, the Golden Plains Festival, began in 2007 every March. From obscurity Meredith became an iconic place for alternative music fans. Likewise, Port Fairy (Victoria), once a tiny fishing and farming village, and now dependent on second-home owners and tourists to thrive, has been boosted annually by its folk festival, one of the most famous in Australia. That success had enabled it to build a series of other festivals, which have included a Koroit Irish Festival, Rhapsody in June (mainly for local music), a Spring Music Festival and a Singing Up Country Festival (of Aboriginal music).

Music festivals can therefore be serious components of local economic development and regeneration strategies (Table 2.3), especially via their link to tourism and its direct economic benefits – through visitor expenditure, both at the festival and en route, for such obvious things as petrol, accommodation, food, drink, tickets and souvenirs. The Murraylands Music Festival, for example, in the tiny river town of Tailem Bend (SA, population 1,400), gained sponsorship and financial support from its local council as well as the South Australian Tourism

Commission and and the non-profit organisation Foundation for Rural and Regional Renewal. The Falls Festival is, according to its website, 'deliberately located in regional areas far from typical touring routes, ensuring more isolated communities have this rare opportunity to receive maximum benefit from such a major event', bringing both culture and revenue to the periphery.

Table 2.3   Summary of potential local benefits and costs of hosting music festivals

Tangible benefits	**Tangible costs**
Increased revenue to local economy Job creation Positive media coverage and images Sponsorship opportunities Networking opportunities Improved viability for niche musical genres (e.g. jazz, blues, bluegrass) Revenue generation from charges Increased volunteerism Skills acquisition (e.g. management, musicianship) Subsequent tourism Encourages participation in activities	Essential services (police, cleaning etc.) Costs of promotion Direct costs of staging the event – e.g. performers, PA hire Eroded markets for other forms of entertainment locally (e.g. cinemas) 'Burnout' of paid and volunteer staff Infrastructure costs for subsequent tourism
Intangible benefits	**Intangible costs**
Improved quality of life Enhanced or maintained community pride Puts places 'on the map' Tool for regeneration and renewal Increased interest and investment Place promotion and marketing Development of human capital Increased cultural awareness/ appreciation Enhanced sense of belonging and community (whether to the host place, or to a community of fans or specialists) Rising property values (benefit to property owners) Intercultural contact Morale boost	Detriment to quality of life Perceived loss of traditions Crowding and inconvenience to residents Noise and visual pollution Poor reputation and image if badly organised Alienation of local residents through inappropriate or elitist place marketing Environmental degradation Social exclusion and exacerbation of existing socio-economic and cultural divides Rising property values (cost to renters and low-income earners) Potential for intercultural misunderstanding Can trigger greed (e.g. price-gouging)

Source: adapted from Woods and Thomas 2009:152 and Reid 2008

The music itself is obviously important, and while many festivals might be described as generalist or even 'middle of the road', in some places festivals deliberately promote a particular kind of music, often classical music in one form or another, in areas where this is less likely to be accessible. Thus the principal aim of the North Wales International Music Festival, held in St Asaph Cathedral, was to bring classical music to the community and promote Welsh music and artists (Wood and Thomas 2009). Likewise the Blackwood Festival brought chamber music to Bridgetown, a small town in WA. A feature of many festivals, including those at Bermagui and Inverell (Chapter 7), is bringing international quality performers to places where the opportunity to hear their music – even their genre of music – is non-existent. Many festivals stress the presence of distinguished performers and, like Opera in the Paddock, an opportunity for regional musicians to interact with them, and enable career development. Festivals may directly be musically innovative.

Place Marketing and Place Identities

Employment and the contribution of tourist expenditure are only the most obvious impacts of music festivals. Even when events create few full-time jobs, and only briefly support the local economy, they have intangible and usually positive effects on places. The elusive impacts of image may be equally or more valuable than the hard currency of immediate economic success. Place marketing has become commonplace and discussed largely in terms of the rise of entrepreneurial governance, neoliberal ideology, and as campaigns that commodify place and identity (Gibson and Davidson 2004). Place marketing is not new: colonialism involved extensive campaigns aimed at enticing 'free settlers' to Australia in order to establish rural growth industries, fill certain shortfalls of skills and encourage entrepreneurial activities. While tourism itself remained largely a domain of the elite throughout the nineteenth century, the deliberate positive depiction of places in marketing efforts was well established. More recent phases of place marketing have sought to redirect public policy away from the provision of utilities, infrastructure and 'safety net' services, towards various corporate activities, such as 'place-branding' exercises aimed at attracting mobile investment capital and tourists. Local communities can either become increasingly repulsed by place promotion and tourism (including festivals), becoming resistant to festivals in the process (Chapter 9), or they get used to the 'image' projected from their place to the wider world, and come to adjust to life in the tourist spotlight, so long as the gains are substantial enough (Chapter 6).

The more subtle indirect benefits from music festivals – in the context of attempts to regenerate regional economies – stem from their particular ability to create and disseminate images and associations with place. Towns become known through festivals, particularly if they attract national media attention, play on a quirky theme, or establish a reputation as a quality festival for a certain genre or musical niche. The particular associations between regional festivals, music and place are thus somewhat different from the kinds of place marketing regularly discussed in cities. Festival place marketing entails a whole range of different agendas, strategies and limitations. As we discuss throughout this book, in Tamworth, Parkes, Bermagui and beyond, place marketing through festivals is principally enacted through constructions of rurality, community, creativity, frivolity and escape. Rather than alienate by appealing to an inner-city elite, many music festivals in rural contexts market places as quaint, honest and laid-back. Although development and alterations to the built environment have been outcomes (Chapter 8), they have had quite different impacts and implications from urban and metropolitan contexts.

In Australia Tamworth was a somewhat anonymous regional centre in the wool, sheep and transport industries, until it created a major country music festival. Now it is synonymous with that music, hosts the annual (televised) national country music awards in a purpose-built entertainment arena (Chapter 8), and has permanent infrastructure to remind visitors of the association with country music (from a giant guitar at the town entrance, through country music museums to guitar-shaped swimming pools in motels). In Parkes (Chapter 6), kitsch, quirkiness and nostalgia combine to give its Elvis festival national media coverage every year. After fifteen years of steady growth, the event's success has enabled local tourism staff to mount an additional campaign to attract conventions and conferences during the other weeks of the year, while Elvis is used by the council in other forms of place promotion (Connell and McManus 2011). Wangaratta is home to Australia's most credible jazz festival – not because the town had any pre-existing, cutting-edge jazz scene, but because the festival there was the first, and it has carefully cultivated its reputation over many decades (Curtis 2010). In Australia's jazz scene there is no better known place – simply because of its festival. The National Blues Music Festival in Goulburn is so synonymous with the town that in blues circles it is simply known as 'Goulburn' – a definitive place association only reserved for the very best, much like Wimbledon for tennis. At Narooma on the NSW South Coast, the success of its annual blues festival had put the town on the map to the extent that its organiser could successfully run for office as the local mayor – a post he continued to hold while running the festival. Inverell touts Opera in the Paddock as a symbol of the good life in the country, and advertises it widely, though not necessarily providing infrastructure or other support (Chapter 7).

Woodford, a small, once declining agricultural town of no more than 5,000 people, in the Sunshine Coast hinterland of southern Queensland, is perhaps the most celebrated festival place in Australia. It is one of the more established, having begun in 1987. The first Maleny Festival, which sold 900 tickets and ran for three days, became the week-long Woodford Festival in the mid-1990s, as it outgrew the Maleny site. It regularly draws over 100,000 visitors to its 200 hectare site, which unusually was bought by the organisers, and the festival is still organised by the not-for-profit Queensland Folk Federation. Queues form three days before it opens. It is also large enough to have a core of long-term staff, with some 140 managers coming in at particular times of the year, and 2,400 volunteers prior to and during the festival. Woodford has traded on its alternative tag, and introduced a mid-year Festival of the Dreaming, but rapid growth has meant some management struggles, and a perceived exploitation of volunteers and musicians despite the festival's claim to be a place for those with a social conscience (Sorensen 2007a).

The small northern NSW town of Bellingen first attracted people seeking alternative lifestyles in the 1970s, turning it into one of the livelier rural towns as the newcomers developed markets and festivals. The long-established (1989) Bellingen Jazz Festival and the subsequent Global Carnival celebration of world music, alongside smaller musical events (such as Stamping Ground, a two week long festival of dance, and Dorrigo Folk and Bluegrass Festival), and a recent Readers and Writers Festival, have played significant parts in revitalising, and giving a new image, to a valley where agriculture was languishing, so contributing to bringing in new residents. Alongside an eclectic range of markets, shops and restaurants, festivals turned Bellingen into a place of entertainment and alternative culture. That atmosphere is evoked in its standard tourism publication, a rare example of festivals being formally regarded as prime attractions:

> Magic thrives on belief. And the people of the Bellinger are great believers – in maintaining the beauty of their stunning environment, in a close knit and friendly community, and in creativity, whether it is artwork, music, festival or food. Welcome to a world where magic can and does happen. (Tourism Bellinger 2006:3)

The first Global Carnival in 1995 sought merely to fill a gap by being the first world music festival in Australia: a boutique festival in a small town, intending only to involve 'global' musicians resident in Australia. The core vision was to 'create an experience to reveal our common humanity'. The first festival had just two 'international' acts: the Tibetan singer Yungchen Lhamo and the shakuhachi player Riley Lee, both of whom fortuitously happened to be living in Australia at the time. The festival made a small profit and has subsequently steadily grown; by 2009 it was attracting 15,000 people (5,000 for each of the three days) to a town of about 2,600 people. Even the most prominent performers are hosted by local families, contributing to a relaxed and intimate atmosphere, that spills over into traditional storytelling, workshops (for lantern making or mosaic tiles), multicultural foods, puppetry, acrobats and buskers (Sorensen 2007a; Elder 2010). That number of visitors has reached around the limit that the infrastructure of a small town can absorb with festival venues not far from the town centre. Its organiser has said:

> We are committed to staying small enough for the group of prime organisers to keep an overview. We believe in trying to be authentic, in a sincere way, not saying one thing and doing another. That could be construed as a cliché but it's also the truth. (Quoted in Sorensen 2007a:14)

In none of these places, from Tamworth to Bellingen, was there any obvious connection between the music genre and the place but good luck, good timing and good management enabled each of them to be success stories in different ways. In time they became fortuitous place marketing assets.

More broadly, as in each of these places, festivals are an important means through which tourism destinations become known, and longer-run tourism economies can be built. Festivals are 'medium-long term' tourist resources (Quinn 1996) in that they bring repeat visitors, spread word of mouth, provide positive images of places in the mainstream metropolitan press and constitute a lively tourist product. The long-running Moyneyana Festival in Port Fairy (a play on the local river name, the Moyne) is claimed by organisers to have been a major factor in that town becoming a summer holiday destination. Even the smallest festivals play some part in putting and keeping small towns on the map, in the absence of anything else distinctive.

Nonetheless, not all festivals succeed and 'putting a place on the map' can be a challenge. Both Tamworth's country music festival and Parkes' Elvis festival occur in January, Australia's summer holiday period – a quiet time when stories on popular, fun or bizarre festivals fill empty news slots in metropolitan newspapers and television broadcasts, and suit the relaxed season. Conversely, a certain amount of 'crowding out' occurs in key tourist periods of the year: long-weekends in Easter, June and October, when multiple festivals are held around the country on the same days. Moreover a degree of conservatism has crept into how towns decide what kind of festival they wish to stage. Inspired by Tamworth, country music festivals are now ubiquitous; as are blues festivals (after the success of Goulburn and Byron Bay's East Coast Blues and Roots Festival) and jazz festivals (in the wake of Wangaratta). Jazz has become increasingly popular in regional centres, notwithstanding its inner-city image. For these styles of music, product differentiation has become increasingly difficult. The surfeit of blues, jazz and country music festivals has meant that they became commonplace, with new festivals struggling for a unique profile and media attention. In Mildura (Victoria), which belatedly sought to stage a country music festival, a conscious decision was made to make it the 'alternative' country music festival to Tamworth, concentrating on independent music labels, up and coming artists and fringe styles. It could not compete with Tamworth's budget, scale and reputation; instead, it cultivated an image as the 'credible' alternative and now the town is well known in country music circles as *the* place for industry insiders as opposed to the more commercial festival at Tamworth.

Classical music and opera festivals have been linked to tourism and place marketing campaigns, as much for their contribution to image as specific revenue-raising ability. This is particularly true in metropolitan Europe, where cities have some association with a composer or work that can be exploited, such as Vienna's Haydn Festival, Nuremberg's Wagnerian Ring Cycle and Verona's Opera Festival, but has little resonance in Australia where such connections are absent. In England however classical music and opera have triumphed in rural locations from Glyndebourne to Aldeburgh, Brinkburn and Oundle (Gibson and Connell 2005:224). In Australia opera and classical music have also succeeded in rural locations (Chapter 7) although, for some, opera and classical music have been a means to support tourist branding of wine regions, exemplified in both Jazz in the Vines and Opera in the Vineyards (Hunter Valley, NSW). In such places many promotions emphasise landscape and culture (and buying wine) as much as music. Such festivals have often been marketed in a way that appeals to a more elite and discerning market with some degree of sophistication (and the ability to pay high prices), suggesting that regional towns and their hinterlands are far from divorced from what was once called 'high culture'. At the same time, in a number of places accessible to metropolitan areas, notably the Hunter Valley, festivals – or at least grand open-air concerts – have been commercially presented. Numerous places and people have thus sought to stage festivals that might seem to be almost the antithesis of the Parkes Festival (Chapter 6), in their elitist or commercial orientations, and in their absence of an obvious sense of fun and frivolity.

Festivals in Place

Because many festivals are quite small they have chosen and been able to take advantage of natural landscapes, such as paddocks (rather obviously, for Opera in the Paddock), rivers and their banks, occasionally caves, deserts and the 'outback'. The Kowmung Festival in Oberon presents chamber music in caves, community halls and cattle sheds; its artistic director has stated 'It is utter magic to take contemporary music and the traditional Western canon out of the concert hall and into a cave or shed'. The Abercrombie caves, with a stream flowing through, enable musical contributions from distant crickets and birds. Nearby Jenolan caves host regular concerts and small festivals, so that 'Jazz lovers can swing into Jenolan (the world's oldest caves), for 'Hot Jazz in the Cool Caves' … a twilight jazz concert in the Devil's Coach House Cave, followed by a hot and spicy menu in award-winning Chisholm's Restaurant. As in previous years, concertgoers will bring a folding chair or cushion, and lounge amongst the huge boulders as they enjoy the concert'. Distinct acoustics and the unusual ambience are central, as they are at the Naracoorte Underground Music Festival (SA), literally held in underground limestone chambers. In Tyalgum, at the annual Festival of Classical Music, 'each year we hear the rustling of leaves on the roof and the local bird calls, so this year we are bringing them into the concert hall with an especially commissioned new work, *Tyalgum Dawn,* by composer Ann Carr-Boyd'. The 2011 WOMAD Earth Station Festival, staged under the stars in South Australia's Belair National Park, featured a composition called Sun Rings by Kronos Quartet's David Harrington and Terry Riley that incorporated sounds of space recorded by NASA Voyager missions (Shedden 2011a). Outside noises are not always as welcome: at the Huntington Estate Music Festival (Mudgee, NSW) bird and traffic noise is problematic, and in 2006 the local airport was even requested to prevent light aircraft – actually carrying water to nearby bushfires – from banking over Huntington while concerts were on-going (Westwood 2006).

The 1997 Opera in the Outback in South Australia used a variety of natural sites, and especially the Yalkarinha Gorge, but also linked the event to 'typical outback' activities such as campdrafting and sheep shearing (and, incidentally, flash flooding). In the tiny and remote town of Broome (WA), Opera Under The Stars has been held under palm trees next to Cable Beach, a place its website describes as

> Famous for its fiery sunsets … a breath-taking backdrop for the presentation. The relaxed and less formal ambience of this unique event is perfectly complemented by the tropical beauty of the Cable Beach Amphitheatre and surrounds, with a star filled Kimberley sky above providing the finishing touch to this truly sublime setting.

Both Alice Springs and Kalgoorlie's Desert Festivals are actually in the middle of these large towns. The annual Opera in the Outback, at Undara, a township on the edge of the Undara Volcanic National Park, some 300 kilometres south-west of Cairns, is one of Australia's more remote festivals (with an audience of around 300 people). Access and logistics have made deserts more challenging for festivals in Australia than in North America or Africa.

Jazz in the Tops (Coolah, NSW) takes place in the Coolah Tops National Park, some 32 kilometres outside tiny Coolah, while the Cygnet Folk Festival, in a small township on the banks of the Huon River in Tasmania, is in a bird sanctuary. The Meredith Music Festival takes place in a 'supernatural amphitheatre' on a farm, and the 2011 event was timed so that the headline act, Nick Cave, finished performing just as a total lunar eclipse took place. In tropical climes the annual Top Half Folk Festival alternates between a resort outside Alice Springs and the Mary River Park between Darwin and Kakadu, where optional extras include tour boats for bird and crocodile spotting. Fairbridge Festival in bush land at Pinjarra (WA) largely takes over the historic village using many of its cottages and the chapel as venues, alongside the festival marquee. Norfolk Island's Opera in the Ruins partly takes place in the ruins of the nineteenth century convict compound, while its Jazz in the Pines Festival does take place amidst Norfolk pines, and in the same convict ruins, on the edge of a coral lagoon. The Queensland Music Festival runs for two weeks with events scattered through regional Queensland. The 2007 Festival opened in the Bladensburg National Park outside the tiny central-west Queensland town of Winton. The Festival Director observed that

> It was logically complex to set up out in that landscape, but so much of this festival is about place, and I got the feeling that whatever we're doing this is working. It was quite mysterious to be in this incredibly beautiful park, unchanged for millions of years, with the mountains in the background and to remember that music is the language we all share. (Quoted in Sorensen 2007b:8)

Perhaps predictably, Mud Bulls and Music, a four day festival that 'combines the thrill of rodeo, 4x4 action and the best of Australian country musical talent', takes place in a regional landscape. As the website states:

> Set on a beautiful rugged working cattle property near Jimna in South East Queensland, and surrounded by natural State forests, the spread is transformed for four unique days in November to bring you all that opitimises [sic] Australian bush life. Watch the big bulls roar in our Bucking Thunder Rodeo or see the 4x4's battle it out in the Super Rally Cross and the Go-to-woe events. Then enjoy some of Australia's finest Country bands, singers and stars.

Not surprisingly most rural festivals have some reference to the countryside and the rural ambience, in both a social and physical sense.

More frequently, since most festivals are in populated areas, they have employed distinctive agricultural landscapes (notably wineries) and distinctive human creations, such as churches, winery barrel rooms and, in the case of Byron Bay, an ex-abattoir. Bellingen uses its Old Butter Factory. Few festivals tout the ambience of prosaic leagues club concert rooms, town halls, racecourses and urban parks, the location of most festivals. For several festivals the small size of event and location, and the intimacy, community and authenticity that these are said to involve, are important. The Blackwood River Chamber Festival is a private venture, directed by its founder, that brings chamber music to Bridgetown in the Blackwood River Valley, some 300 kilometres south of Perth,

> a verdant district of rolling orchard, vine-growing, forest and farming country settled in the late nineteenth century, on the northern edge of the giant karri and jarrah forests. The Festival is a restorative meeting of kindred spirits that takes place in a largely unspoiled country town redolent of early post war Australia.

The primary venue is St Paul's Anglican Church, capable of holding just 140 people, thus the Festival is limited to 140 participants. One concert takes place on the Saturday afternoon in a 'rustic setting away from Bridgetown': a tree nursery in 2011. The Bangalow Music Festival (NSW), similarly small-scale and oriented to classical music, is equally constrained by the size of the town's lone hall, which holds about 300 people. Such festivals are distinctive yet tiny, positive images for places seeking an exclusive audience.

Consuming Passions: Music Festivals, Food and Wine

In a growing number of other places music festivals have become part of local and regional attempts at new forms of branding, to promote tourism and even migration. As that has happened directly or indirectly they have become linked in to a wider elite countryside. Hence gourmet food, wine and music have combined to shape a more Tuscan countryside in the Hunter Valley, a new Mediterranean has been hinted at in the olive growing areas of northern Victoria, and the Barossa has frequently reinvented and accentuated its German heritage (Peace 2011), and in every case music festivals have played a part. The Hunter Valley first transformed itself into 'Wine Country' in the early 1990s, a process which subsequently involved further transformation and diversification into a gourmet region. In 1997 the Wine Country tourism brochure announced the inaugural Wyndham Wine and Food Festival (replete with 'the music of wandering songsters and musicians'), arguing that 'The Hunter Valley, renowned for its world famous wines and award winning restaurants is fast becoming renowned for its hedonistic indulgence each October at Jazz in the Vines'. Opera in the Vineyards was similarly established, and Jazz by the River took its place in the Upper Hunter.

By 2006 cheeses and olives were increasingly important (a Gourmet Cheese Festival had arrived), farmers' and growers' markets thrived, new festivals were established, some that also linked into cuisine (a Thanksgiving Festival, A Taste of Tuscany) and others that offered diversity (a Film Festival, a Rodeo, Steamfest) and multiple music festivals, including a Buskers Challenge (and others where music played merely a part, such as the St Patrick's Weekend Celebrations, the Festa del Vino and the Lovedale Long Lunch – 'wine and dine your way around 7 participating wineries over the weekend enjoying a glass of wine, gourmet food, fabulous music and art'). In certain selected parts or rural and regional Australia, local councils, vineries and restaurants were steadily transforming the countryside, in a degree of fortuitous collusion with magazines such as *Australian Gourmet Traveller* and *Country Style*, to fabricate a heritage that conveyed regional distinctiveness, a legacy of small farms, wineries and farmers markets, and an artisanal tradition that was to be celebrated in festivals.

Many music festivals have subsequently taken on some incorporation of superior cuisine. As its website intimates, Opera in the Otways (Victoria) is 'synonymous with good food and wine, and this year people will be spoilt for choice. The region's best produce, wine, beer and handmade gourmet delicacies will be served at a Paddock to Plate celebration during the gala'. The Opera ran in conjunction with the adjoining day-long Paddock to Plate Festival, celebrating local gourmet food and wine. Other festivals have taken similar approaches. The Mildura Jazz, Food and Wine Festival has existed for thirty years, combining four days of jazz in clubs, bars and cafes, and also in restaurants, churches, streets, with the main events using Murray River settings and all the events showcasing regional food and wine. The Festival sought to combine traditional jazz with contemporary and quirky sounds, catering to hardcore jazz enthusiasts and more general music lovers, 'not to mention those that just enjoy sitting back to the music, soaking in the ambience of one of Mildura's paddle steamers, riverside wineries and parks, taking in the gourmet food and locally produced wine'. Multiple festivals have similar orientations and aspirations, including the Riverboats Jazz Food & Wine Festival, where

Echuca's historic riverboats will once again host some of the most memorable performances of the Festival weekend. Having traversed Australia's inland waterways since the 1860s, today Echuca boasts the largest operating fleet of paddlesteamers in the world. One of the most popular ways to start the Festival weekend is by securing a seat on the Riverboat Ramble, and The Pride of the Murray and PS Pevensey will both embark on two-hour river cruises whilst passengers enjoy drinks, nibbles and a superb performance by a quartet of jazz musicians.

Dingo Creek Jazz and Blues Festival, in southern Queensland, is a little more low-key, in allowing visitors to camp out in the Dingo Creek vineyard 'described as one of the prettiest wineries on the Sunshine Coast ... Held over two days and nights, a relaxed community atmosphere prevails, where it's common to ask your favourite musician to "pass the sauce" for your breakfast snags [sausages]'. The lure of rivers has been consistent and seemingly unavoidable. The Murray River International Music Festival, also in Mildura, similarly focuses on 'regional food and wine along with outstanding international musicians in beautiful Murray River locations'. Once again the website extols the beauty of the music and regional setting: 'Held in one of the most beautiful gardens you'll ever see in regional Australia, along with the food and wine of the region, audiences will be graced by the sounds of the finest Australian players performing the pinnacle of baroque chamber music'. And as the website records: 'A patron from Toorak, Victoria [an elite Melbourne suburb] summed it up well in 2008 by exclaiming "World Class Food, World Class Wine and World Class Music – all here in Mildura – who would have believed it"'. And, yet again in Mildura, Opera by the Lock (Lock 11 on the river),

> offers patrons a chance to indulge their senses in glorious music and fine regional food and wine which will be sold through outlets prior to the commencement of the concert. For those seeking something very special, the Premium Package which comprises a two-course pre-concert dinner followed by dessert at the interval is available on board the historic paddlesteamer the Mundoo.

Canberra's Wine, Roses and All that Jazz Festival, held in wineries and restaurants outside the city as much as inside, simply describes itself as promoting 'liquid geography' where the music is almost an afterthought.

Music, place and food are also drawn together in the McLaren Vale's Coriole Music Festival,

> a weekend of fine music, food and wine in the beautiful McLaren Vale winery region of South Australia. The 13th Coriole Music Festival brings together some of the finest chamber musicians from around Australia and overseas to present music by the great Russian composers. The annual Coriole Music Festival is a weekend celebration of outstanding chamber music performed in Coriole's

acoustically superb Barrel Room. Following each concert Tina Llewellyn from The Rolling Pin will present a delicious three-course meal created from local South Australian produce and accompanied by a selection of Coriole's own highly awarded wines. The informal meals in the Coriole courtyard are an opportunity for the musicians and the audience to get to know each other in a relaxed and social setting.

In each of these contexts, the festivals themselves promote a sense of place. Tourist boards in such regions have usually included similar promotions, which focus more on the region than on the music, but are rarely less enthusiastic. In some contexts festivals have been deliberately used not simply to promote but to change the image of the region. Maitland, a large town of 60,000 people in the once-industrial Hunter Valley, has specifically and deliberately used festivals to influence its image, with a distinct 'city centre' strategy:

> The image changing process of Maitland CBD has been showcased with the introduction of two new Festivals for the City Centre this year: The Maitland Taste Food, Wine & Jazz Festival held the last weekend of March each year where celebrity chefs, wine master classes and horse and carriage tours are features of this event. The Maitland Aroma Coffee, Chocolate and Fine Food Festival is held in the middle of August each year and features fabulous blues and jazz music together with outstanding entertainment, as well as guided history walking tours. Both of these inaugural events held in the Maitland Heritage Mall attracted huge crowds and proved a great boom to local retail businesses and will now become annual events.

Maitland also hosts a long established annual Steamfest Festival centred around the heritage Maitland railway station; Bitter and Twisted (an annual international boutique beer festival held at the historic (and closed) Maitland jail, that celebrates beer, food and music – where 'festival-goers were treated to a diverse range of international gourmet cuisine from Turkish Gozleme to Beef Jerky to complement the large selection of wine and beers') and Groovin' the Moo, an annual music festival held at the Maitland Showground (a commercial event featuring prominent Australian and international popular musicians and attracting as many as 75,000 people). Like other larger towns, and with somewhat more diversity than Mildura, Maitland has promoted a variety of festivals that seek to harness the virtues of heritage, music and regional cuisine.

A Commercial Countryside

In contrast to those festivals that have grown from local communities, and stress their local connections, and especially their donations to charities, a new genre of festivals has emerged with primarily commercial goals, that just 'happen' to be in or near similar small town locations. Probably the first concert in a winery was in 1985 when Leeuwin Estate (WA) hosted the London Philharmonic Orchestra. In the 1990s as wine and music increasingly came together, wineries took on broader roles that developed into wine and cheese tasting and meals, then accommodation, and subsequently concerts. A glut of wine on the Australian market for more than a decade has meant low prices and necessary diversification, hence the promotion of festivals.

The flavour of such events – and flavour is often a key theme – is well expressed in the website of the Huntington Estate Music Festival in Mudgee (NSW) discussing a relatively small classical event with an attendance of about 350 people:

> The Huntington Estate Music Festival is held each year in the Barrel Room of the winery in Mudgee, a fantastic space with 'one of the greatest acoustics on the planet' (Richard Tognetti) and a unique atmosphere. All concerts include generous interval refreshments and are followed by gourmet meals and a selection of the best Huntington wines. All evening concerts are preceded by a choice of aperitifs, with the full service of Huntington wines continuing throughout the concert interval and afterwards. The musical content is devised by Artistic Director Carl Vine and managed by the world's largest chamber music entrepreneur, Musica Viva Australia. In keeping with the long and distinguished history of the festival, each year features a stunning collection of prominent international performing artists alongside Australia's finest musicians, in stimulating programs that run the full gamut of the chamber music experience.

As one visitor observed: 'An exciting blend of musical styles, performed by a wide range of top-class performers. Meals under the trees, and drifting in and out of the cool winery with its wonderful smells and amazing acoustics'. Its artistic director has even argued: 'The Huntington Festival is an unrivalled experience for serious lovers of chamber music. Even for us seasoned professionals it's an unparalleled sensual immersion that uniquely fuses great food and wine with brilliant music into some sort of hybrid experience that defies categorisation'. Several themes are evident. The festival is promoted by a commercial wine company (anticipating increased sales beyond the event), with no evident community goals. While the winery is close to Mudgee, Mudgee has no obvious role in supporting the festival, though it benefits from it in standard ways. 'Festival' may thus be a way of branding what is essentially a commercial venture. It offers sophisticated music from 'prominent international performing artists' in acoustic excellence, with gourmet meals, fine wines and aperitifs: a combination oriented to discerning patrons whose numbers are limited by the dimensions of the venue. High prices emphasise that elite orientation, while all commercial activities are owned by the festival. More attention is devoted to the food and wines than to the content of the chamber music, which effectively provides the aural backdrop to the acquisition of cultural capital.

Numerous other commercial festivals have developed in similar ways but involving some local component. Opera in the Vineyard at Ballandean Wines, Stanthorpe (Queensland) is held in conjunction with the local Rotary Club, and with its partner event, Jazz in the Vineyard, has raised thousands of dollars for charities (principally the local Wesley Hospital). The Stanthorpe Shire Council has both promoted the district's scenery and horticultural products, and helped the Opera in many ways – from providing a grand piano each year to shifting landfill when the new site was constructed – as a means of place promotion.

Most of the more commercial concerts have assumed and attracted a metropolitan population willing to travel some distance for a unique (and expensive) performance usually without any particular local musical content (though there may be supporting acts). Concerts therefore used the ambience of wine-producing regions such as the Hunter Valley, McLaren Vale and Margaret River, although some wineries developed particular genres, usually jazz and opera, or staged the 'return' of 'heritage' stars, such as Leonard Cohen. Thus in the Hunter Valley the Wyndham Estate Winery developed Opera in the Vineyards, whose 2006 brochure advertised 'The sun setting over the vines will be your cue to adjourn to a magnificent open-air amphitheatre for a gala concert under the stars with a full orchestra. Indulge in a Food and Wine Fair from 2pm'. Tickets ranged from $72 to $148 (in 1998 it was $39 to $89). The musicians and the pieces were not named. In the following year,

> Wine, food and song will combine with the breathtaking views where you and your friends will be seduced by Opera Australia's finest and most exciting singers. Thrill to best loved works by Mozart, Puccini, Verdi and famous love songs from all-time great musicals on the banks of the Hunter River … concluding as the night sky is illuminated by a spectacular firework finale.

By 2008 the Opera was naming its leading singers and advertising 'Top 20 Hits of Opera' from such operas as La Bohème, Carmen and Tosca. Identifying the singers, if not the pieces, continued, though by 2010

> Flattery and flirtation, lust and intrigue … few events can rival an evening of Mozart at his seductive best. Artists in period costume will take you on an enchanting journey though the life of this musical genius, set against the stunning backdrop of the vineyards. Fall in love under the stars!

Elsewhere in the Hunter Valley, Tyrrell's Estate promoted its annual Jazz in the Vines which, by the late 1990s, had become a weekend event. As its 1997 brochure suggested:

> Be picked up from the Sydney Coach Terminal Saturday morning, travel to Jazz in the Vines with luxurious accommodation in either Newcastle or Port Stephens including breakfast. On Sunday enjoy a delightful Jazz cruise across

beautiful Port Stephens complete with lunch, before returning to Sydney. There is a wide choice of accommodation available in the Hunter Valley from cabins and cottages to four star luxury resorts. Jazz in the Vines is a celebration of colour and movement, sight sound and taste.

By 2011 its repeated success was assured and its website reflected on this:

> It's a combination of a lot of things. A fantastic site that has plenty of space for you to spread out and is set in such a pretty, natural setting – Music that you can groove to and sing to – A great choice of wines from not just one winery but four or more – Fantastic food from five of the area's best restaurants – Friendly, happy people enjoying the day with friends – It all adds up to such a great atmosphere! So come along, bring a picnic and some friends, sit back and relax or party hard, the choice is yours. The Hunter Valley's longest running annual party is on again!

While opera and jazz suggested a degree of elitism and cosmopolitanism, most events in wineries are large-scale celebrations of pop and rock music, rather more commercial concerts than festivals, but oriented at nostalgia rather than contemporary stars. The wholly commercial A Day on the Green emerged in 2001 as a means of creating a new niche in the Australian concert circuit, initially by targeting people over forty, a group who had grown beyond the pub-rock environment, but still enjoyed rock music. Until then 'while more genteel jazz and classical concerts in wineries had worked, no-one thought you could do the same with rock and pop shows' (Zuel 2005:4). The first concert was in 2001 on the Mornington Peninsula (Victoria), with James Morrison and Renee Geyer, well established Australian performers, followed by another in Bendigo, with Paul Kelly. In the next seven years A Day on the Green held almost 150 concerts, with 18 wineries under contract (including some in New Zealand), while other promoters developed their own winery shows. By 2010 A Day on the Green was running 40 concerts a year, and had become 'the Big Day Out for grown-ups'. Performers often combined indoor and outdoor shows, though some 'heritage artists', such as Meatloaf, Eric Clapton, Lionel Richie, John Mellencamp and Leonard Cohen, have engaged in tours exclusively of wineries (Shedden 2008), and retained a profile that might otherwise have faded.

Wineries concerts have also resuscitated the careers of Australian performers like Richard Clapton:

> Rock gigs for my generation [Clapton was then 57] are getting increasingly difficult. The atmosphere in those older venues [clubs and pubs] doesn't always suit older audiences. I do get a lot of older people who get frustrated because they can't bring kids to the shows. The whole mood and attitude of winery shows is different … It is almost tailor-made for me because the age-groups seem to be

> mainly people approaching middle age who bring their children and are turning them on to my music. (Quoted in Shedden 2008:6)

Likewise, other performers such as Stephen Cummings welcomed concerts as an opportunity to play to audiences who could not see them on television or hear them on the radio because their music was no longer played to what was assumed to be an under-25 audience (Zuel 2005). Jazz in the Vines and Opera in the Vines had established a context and market for 'heritage' acts, most of whom were no longer able to obtain slots at younger festivals like Homebake and Big Day Out. Their audiences were not only unwilling to stand in pubs, but were willing to pay substantial sums, typically between $100 and $400 by 2005 (Zuel 2005), and more by the end of the decade (see Chapter 4).

So successful have winery concerts been that those estates able to accommodate rock concerts have prospered so much from them that many replaced vines with seats. At Bimbadgen Estate in the Hunter Valley

> At the moment in Australia there's an oversupply of wines. So we pulled out vines for a good commercial reason: to increase the size of the amphitheatre. We can always buy grapes down the road somewhere. Small operators have to have a tourism oriented business that brings people to their site. It's important for us to be able to sell at the cellar door. (Quoted in Shedden 2008:7)

One of the venues for A Day on the Green, Bimbadgen Estate, has an amphitheatre capable of accommodating 8,000 people. It also hosts an annual Funk 'n' Groove Festival (with Australian acts), claiming to 'epitomise Bimbadgen's philosophy – that it's not just all about the wine, but the experiences you have whilst enjoying it'. In practice most wineries saw the concerts as 'a break-even branding exercise'; as the manager of Centennial Vineyards in Bowral has stated

> We get 7,000 people in who otherwise haven't heard of us. We don't make any money from tickets. The promoter finds the artist, approaches us, sells the tickets, we provide the venue. What we and all the wineries get is branding and great publicity. To get you in the face of people like this would otherwise cost a fortune. (Quoted in Morrison 2008:11)

Such events allowed only food and bottled water to be taken in, to maximise local sales of alcohol. In 2008 Hope Estate in the Hunter Valley completed a $3 million, 19,500 seat amphitheatre, a clear indication of the growing market size. Concerts were thus a collusion between wineries seeking custom, especially at a time of glut, and promoters (and performers) seeking new (and old) markets. In 2011 the two principal performers at the Hope Estate were Elton John and Dolly Parton, undertaking two concerts each, with prices descending from VIP tickets at $699 each. More generally a successful concert was good publicity for the winery 'if the punters leave here with a smile on their face'. Like festivals concerts bring expenditure into the regions, and increase their exposure to people who would not ordinarily have gone there. In areas like the Yarra Valley (Victoria) commercial concerts have become a crucial part of the local economy, not least because the audiences are older and wealthier. Concerts at the Rochford Estate are 'the biggest contributor to GDP in the region' since 35 per cent of all visitors 'make a weekend of it' (quoted in Shedden 2008:7). Such concerts are very actively promoted by local tourism boards, because of their scale, the affluence of many visitors and their contribution to regional image. Nonetheless, wineries, promoters and performers are the principal beneficiaries.

Place Promotion and the Limits to Growth

Many regional Australian towns are stagnating, the smallest are losing population, and most have adopted various development and marketing strategies, to stimulate new migration and growth. Potential new migrants are concerned about amenity, and the quality of life in smaller communities. Attracting people to move to small rural communities requires both economic and lifestyle attractions – employment and housing, but also a sense of a welcoming community, a cinema, sporting facilities, even a decent cup of coffee (Connell and McManus 2011). Festivals are one means to add vitality, generate a sense of community and market a place as caring about fun, pleasure and quality of life, where the arts are present. Large festivals especially draw thousands of visitors, many from metropolitan areas, create employment and effectively promote regional Australia. In the case of the Harboursound Festival in Albany (WA) it was itself established by a sea-change migrant 'to bring another layer of cultural, social and economic impact for Albany' (Rod Vervest, personal communication 2010). Festivals are part of a suite of possibilities that places have at their disposal to create the impression of amenity, potentially one factor in turning around declining places.

Festivals have long been an important part of place marketing, partly because towns are often seen at their best at such times, often deliberately choosing a particular season, and hinting at the various forms of cultural life and activity that exist even in small towns. In NSW and Queensland annual Expos bring local councils into Sydney and Brisbane respectively to market their towns in an attempt to encourage urban-rural migration and stimulate regional economic growth. Metropolitan residents who show some interest in relocation are encouraged to visit the towns at festival time: towns, festivals and tourism are promoted simultaneously. Inverell, for example, takes flyers promoting its annual Opera in the Paddock – which draws over a thousand visitors to Inverell for the one-day concert (Chapter 7). Conversely Parkes, which has one tourist officer specifically engaged in developing and promoting the annual Elvis Festival, always brought a life size cardboard Elvis Presley to draw visitors to their Expo stall (Connell and McManus 2011). Potential residents become familiar with towns and regional areas through festivals; are better informed when making decisions about relocation; and many return, some even permanently.

Music festivals in particular have been the preferable option for communities with limited resources since, as one promoter phrased it:

> they are a much easier festival format because it basically comes down to box office receipts to cover the costs of the event. It's a much harder gig to try and charge for visual arts … When I was at Albury-Wodonga [a small city on the NSW-Victorian border] they got big dollars to do a big visual arts thing and it was pretty amazing but it was just a huge amount of money. When the grant money ran out it just sort of stopped.

Music festivals have proved to be an option for small towns and rural shires forced to look at different ways of attracting tourists. In Boorowa on the NSW south-west slopes, music has been combined with its main agricultural pursuit to create the weekend-long Irish Woolfest. The festival, which culminates in the 'Running of the Sheep' (where 'full wool merinos rampage down the main street in a woolly reminder of the Running of the Bulls in Pamplona') takes place in a tiny community greatly affected by drought in the past decade. To its organiser Barbara Manion, it has been invaluable in 'generating community spirit – a great bonding exercise giving pride in the town' (personal communication 2007). In Nimbin local cannabis growers support the Mardi Grass festival, where the central icon, the Big Joint, is paraded through the town to the sound of 'jungle drums'.

There are however dangers in seeing festivals as part of a strategy to attract new residents. Aspen, in the Rocky Mountains, which has had a music festival for more than fifty years, and which by 2002 lasted over nine weeks, was so successful that 'the music festival is partly responsible for the high level of property values. It's made Aspen a desirable place to live. People come to Aspen for the winter but stay because of the summer' (Peters 2002:36, 39). However some such affluent newcomers were resented for their conspicuous consumption and wealth. English festivals at places such as Aldeburgh and Glyndebourne have similarly stimulated migration to nearby areas of Suffolk and Sussex respectively. In Australia the small Victorian town of Daylesford sought to respond to rural decline in the 1980s by stimulating tourism, especially through festivals. Within twenty years it had been transformed by festivals, tourism, in-migration and gentrification. On weekends festivals brought Melbournians escaping the city for entertainment and gastronomic indulgence. But success and growth brought other problems: Daylesford became so expensive that locals could no longer afford to rent housing or shop there, and resented crowds, traffic congestion and the sense of weekly invasion from Melbourne (Gorman-Murray et al. 2008). Some local residents chose to shop for groceries in towns up to an hour away to avoid festival congestion. Festivals can thus prove to be a key component of strategies to revitalise places, and to attract new migrants, but such gains are not unlimited or uncontested.

The rise of music festivals has not therefore been without criticism. Proclamations of festivals as panaceas for economic decline can involve overblown estimates of direct economic impacts. Music festivals can make money, and catalyse spending in small places that need the income, but how much of this translates into new job creation, and how it is distributed within a community, is highly variable (Chapter 4). The resources required of local councils to assist in managing and promoting music festivals may sometimes come at the expense of other, more worthy avenues: resources that could be used on social welfare or other essential services and infrastructure on the basis of social need or equity. It is a hallmark of entrepreneurial governance that fiscal decisions based on principles of essential and equitable service provision come to be supplanted by motivations to increase local economic competitiveness through place branding and event hosting. When councils become more concerned with stimulating tourism and promoting a place through advertising campaigns and heavily-underwritten festivals, other institutions and members of the community may suffer through dwindling public financial support. If only certain groups (tourist businesses, local service suppliers and already-wealthy small business owners) benefit from festivals staged with public support and some people are disadvantaged by festivals, debates can quickly emerge about funding priorities and local needs – although this is often more so in big cities and in the funding for mega-events like Olympic Games and Grand Prix than in rural and regional areas, where investments are smaller. In many respects the key to the success of festivals is their ability to attract visitors, and to persuade them to part with at least some of their income as they do so, and it is to these themes that the next two chapters turn.

Chapter 3
Who Goes? Audiences, Fans, Fanatics

In large part the ability of any kind of festival to contribute to regional development depends on how many people attend, who they are and what they do there – and what they spend while they are there (and getting there). Various factors influence attendance at festivals, including the musical genre, the quality of the programme (the line-up of 'names'), accessibility (accommodation, transportation, ease of purchasing tickets), flexibility of movement through a festival and its various events, and additional attractions in the surrounding district or city: loosely the ambience. Simply knowing that a festival exists is crucial, hence most festivals stick to a rigid timeframe. Location and timing are crucial. The weather can, literally, be a dampener even if everything else is planned to perfection. Crowds are unpredictable.

Large festivals with particular themes and in beautiful locations logically attract more people and more distant audiences. Few festivals in Australia rival such overseas festivals as Glastonbury or Roskilde for their size, and their ability to attract international visitors. Australia is much more distant from most overseas markets. Even so, the small Glenelg Jazz Festival in Adelaide (South Australia) gained 3 per cent of its audience from overseas, and the larger Adelaide Festival 13 per cent (Hughes 2000:217–18), despite its isolation from international airline routes, compared with most other state capitals. About 3 per cent of the audience at the Tamworth Country Music Festival (NSW), and 2 per cent of those at the Elvis festival in Parkes, are from overseas – but few if any came to Australia specifically for these events. Even the famous week-long Woodford Folk Festival draws only 2.5 per cent of its visitors from overseas. For good geographical reasons most Australian music festivals have an almost exclusively national audience.

Most festivals are patronised by local people and the bulk of festival-goers usually come from nearby. Indeed most festivals are oriented to a local market, and advertising beyond the range of the local media is difficult, expensive and rarely worthwhile. Visitors travel great distances only for specialised festivals or superstar performers, meeting particular niche markets. Thus the 1997 Opera in the Outback, on the edge of the Flinders Ranges National Park 200 kilometres north of Adelaide, featuring Kiri Te Kanawa, had as many as 40 per cent of its visitors from outside South Australia (half of these from New South Wales) although only 3 per cent were from overseas (Richard Trembath Research 1997). Out-of-town visitors are much more numerous in tiny places such as Woodford, Peat's Ridge and St Albans, at numerous raves or various concerts 'in the vines' (Chapter 2) where there are few participants from nearby, since the festival is literally out of town. Even the Woodford Folk Festival draws about two thirds of its visitors from within 100 kilometres (Woodford Folk Festival 2010). On average just under half of visitors across the music festivals we surveyed were from the host town (slightly lower than the 58 per cent for all festival types); 15 per cent were from the state capital (Sydney, Melbourne or Hobart); 24 per cent were from elsewhere in the state; 11 per cent from interstate and a tiny 1 per cent were international visitors. At least a fifth of festivals reported that 90 per cent or more of the audience were from the host town.

Who are They?

Remarkably little has been documented about who festival visitors are, despite widespread – and correct – assumptions that participants at open-air raves and rock festivals are more likely to be younger than those at more sedate classical music festivals where, as at Bermagui, the website states 'We ask patrons to observe the usual concert courtesies of not moving in and out of their places while musicians are playing'. The socio-economic status of visitors is largely unknown, though some festivals can cost several hundred dollars especially where they extend over several days, and accommodation, food and travel must also be purchased. Many, like that at Parkes (Chapter 6), have a combination of free events and ticketed ones, hence ticket costs at least should not inhibit visiting.

Classical concerts of various kinds certainly attract audiences of higher socio-economic status. The 1997 Opera in the Outback was particularly attractive to 'older persons from higher economic strata possibly in the "empty nest stage" of the family lifestyle [with] both necessary time and disposable income to attend special events'. Some 68 per cent of the audience were managerial, professional or retired and almost none were from 'blue-collar' occupations (Richard Trembath Research 1997). At Opera in the Paddock well over half the visitors were over 50 (Chapter 7) and at the Opera in the Outback some 67 per cent were over 50 (Richard Trembath Research 1997), despite the main accommodation being tents. Where nostalgia was an influential factor on attendance, notably at the Wintersun Festival (Coolangatta, Queensland), centred on rock 'n' roll, at least 80 per cent of the participants were over 40 and most were rather older (Mackellar 2009b), as at they are at the Kurri Kurri Nostalgia Festival and at Parkes. At Opera in the Paddock and the Four Winds Festival (Bermagui, NSW) audiences were significantly older than average, grey nomads were not unusual, very few were blue collar workers and almost all the 'unemployed' had retired. Indeed at several such festivals, and similar events, the distinction between the visitors and the local population is often considerable and has produced debate over supposed elitism and failures of 'belonging' (Chapter 7). Survey data from the Tamworth Country Music Festival suggest that 60 per cent of visitors were over 60 (Pegg and Patterson 2010) while at the much smaller Nanga Music Festival (Dwellingup, WA) in two successive years the proportion of those aged over 45 never fell below 56 per cent (Nanga Music Festival 2009). At Apollo Bay (below) visitors were reportedly gracefully aging. By contrast at the Woodford Folk Festival only 23 per cent of visitors were over 50, though that proportion was slowly growing (Woodford Folk Festival 2010). The evidence suggests that most festivals attract a middle aged population and that average age is increasing.

Australia appears not to hold any women's only music festivals unlike some parts of North America (Gibson and Connell 2005:249) and most festivals have a relatively even gender balance. Nonetheless some two thirds of the audience at the Opera in the Outback were women, as were 58 per cent of those at Woodford (but that may partly be the outcome of equating survey respondents with participants). However at a community festival in rural Indiana and a series of festivals in small town New Zealand, with the single exception of an air show, participants were similarly dominantly female, with the Gore country music festival having more than 75 per cent female participation (Li et al. 2009, Nicholson and Pearce 2000). Data from Tamworth similarly suggest that 59 per cent of visitors are female (Pegg and Patterson 2010). Jazz festival-goers are more likely to be male, at least in the UK (Oakes 2010).

The social composition of music festival visitors varies considerably. While social elites are supposedly more likely to attend classical music or opera festivals, distinctions are subtle and far from rigid. Festival-goers at classical and jazz concerts may be of more elite employment status, and potentially contribute more to the local economy than those at popular music festivals, but the absence of credible data means that generalisations may rest as much on prejudice as fact. However if such statements are valid, the attraction of certain festivals for income generation is obvious. Evidence from overseas jazz festivals does suggest a somewhat elite attendance. At the Saskatoon Jazz Festival in Canada in 1993, 65 per cent of visitors were employed in professional/managerial occupations, earned high incomes and held graduate or postgraduate university degrees, and a broadly similar situation was true of the Cheltenham International Jazz Festival in England (Saleh and Ryan 1993, Oakes 2010), though both were in large cities where costs are greater. While classical music, jazz and opera festivals may to some extent still be a pursuit of the elite, many have become more widely popular, and perhaps amongst those with ambitions to upward social mobility, especially when on holiday: 'attending, for example, an opera at Verona's Roman amphitheatre needs very little psychic effort by a visitor booking a trip to Northern Italy, but the same person might not dream of visiting an opera performance during the normal course of the year' (Frey 1994:32). Likewise attending Jazz in The Vines or Opera in the Outback places few demands on even those with no prior knowledge of either genre.

Despite assumptions that visitors to pop festivals are not from the elite, that is now demonstrably untrue. In Britain, by the 1990s, the image of British pop festivals had been transformed from their being 'disreputable events attended by quasi-criminal low-life to major cultural events with an increasingly mainstream appeal' so that the market constituted employed people mainly aged between 25 and 44 and drawn from 'upper middle class, higher managerial, administrative or professional' social groups (Stone 2009:212). Part of the more affluent nature of pop festival audiences is a function of rising ticket prices. Glastonbury attracted an older crowd than other pop festivals, to the extent that there were even concerns that it had become too middle aged and respectable (Gelder and Robinson 2009:188), just as the average age at the Woodford and Byron Bay Festivals (Chapter 9) is steadily increasing. Increasing age is a function of growing baby-boomer participation in festivals, rather than their inability to attract newer younger visitors, as overall festival numbers have also increased. Young people are more reluctant to pay to travel or be in the country and prefer large commercial festivals in metropolitan centres (Davey 2011), and may simply enjoy a style of listening more active than at most festivals. Visitors to the Woodford Folk Festival in Queensland during the 1990s had relatively low incomes, reflecting the large number of students and teachers, but over half were undertaking or had completed university studies (Raybould et al. 1999). A decade later that had changed significantly, with the largest group of visitors being 'management/ professionals' (30 per cent) with few blue collar workers; although students still made up 18 per cent of the numbers. Nearly two-thirds had completed or were engaged in some form of post-secondary education (Woodford Folk Festival 2010). In other words, most festival visitors are from relatively high socio-economic groups, and increasingly so, even among the young, and thus can be expected to have greater than average spending power.

Festivals naturally want visitors to return, not least since it saves advertising costs and marks the success of the event. Many do. In Gore (New Zealand) some 75 per cent of country music festival visitors were returnees (Nicholson and Pearce 2000). The 1997 Opera in the Outback, while a one-off event, had been preceded a decade earlier by a similar event. Some 10 per cent of those who had been there in 1988 came back, but especially those who came from nearby (Richard Trembath Research 1997). Likewise large proportions of visitors to the quite different Parkes and Opera in the Paddock also returned. At Woodford as many as 71 per cent of visitors are returnees, and over 20 per cent had been more than five times (Woodford Folk Festival 2010), a measure of its success. At the Wintersun Festival some 70 per cent of visitors returned every year and, as at Parkes, many had booked accommodation over a year in advance (Mackellar 2009b). Indeed a large part of the success of all these events came, in an economic sense, from having some significant degree of assured market and, in a social sense, from the pleasure that visitors got from familiar performances and meeting up with friends and relatives.

Listening to the Music?

Exploration of the motivations of music festival visitors is sparse, perhaps because there are simple assumptions that music festivals are enjoyable and that the kind of music performed there will be a significant influence on visitor numbers and types. Logically those who enjoy folk music tend to go to folk festivals while jazz lovers go to jazz festivals (Formica and Uysal 1996). And so they invariably do, but for most festivals a significant element of participation is related as much to relaxation and escapism as to the particular nature of music (though heavy metals fans are unlikely to attend opera festivals and vice versa). While visitors might be expected to be at music festivals to experience the music, many participate for reasons that do not necessarily have much to do with music at all. They are there as much for relaxation, passing the time, an escape from the mundane routine world, spending time outdoors, something different to do, partying, drinking or taking drugs, an opportunity to be with family and friends, new experiences, and general passive entertainment as much as an appreciation of the particular music, performance or place. Not all visitors to Scottish festivals appreciate the inevitable bagpipe music but are there to be nostalgic about Scottishness. Ambience is crucial to enjoyment, and ambience extends beyond the musical performance, especially when it takes in vineyards, paddocks and open spaces. As the *Sydney Morning Herald*'s music critic, Bruce Elder, has observed of WOMADelaide, the World Music Festival: 'Lying on the grass in Adelaide's beautiful Botanic Park, surrounded by huge and ancient fig trees and listening to great music is as close to heaven as we can hope for in this lifetime' (2003:18). The social context is equally important. There is a world of difference between that enjoyable yet passive experience and the more active participation that results in others dancing spontaneously, or developing fringe concerts, busking sessions, technical demonstrations and poetry readings. The longer the festival, the more that social activities play at least some role, as eating, drinking, sleeping and conviviality become necessary. The music and the social context – the whole point of a festival as opposed to a concert – become intertwined, as the scope for involvement and interaction expand. Likewise the scope for local expenditure is even more considerable.

Almost all those who attend music festivals of any kind come with someone else, often in quite large groups; hence it is very much a social experience. Many come simply because they are accompanying others. At the Parkes Festival some visitors were even taken 'kicking and screaming' by partners who were more enthusiastic. Some had little knowledge of the musical context; many visitors were simply too young to know much about Elvis Presley's music, life and times (Chapter 6). Visitors to the Woodford Folk Festival were there out of some desire to escape their normal environment, relax, and be involved in self-discovery and social interaction: that is 'entertainment', 'experience of an authentic performing arts festival' and 'a break from normal routine or environment' while authenticity and uniqueness were most sought by return visitors (Raybould et al. 1999:201). So much is festival-going a social experience that many visitors are not easily able to explain why they are there: they have no specific reason for being at a particular festival, have tagged along with other family members or friends, welcome a day out that promises enjoyment but know relatively little about the festival or the particular kind of music. At the Brigadoon Scottish Festival many visitors vaguely referred to the overall atmosphere and their enjoyment of bagpipe music (which was inescapable) or 'simply having a day out with family and friends'

(Ruting and Li 2011:270). Large concert-format festivals such as Byron Bay's Splendour in the Grass attract a crowd who 'go to festivals to "get hectic", to be seen rather than to see … the line-up is seen as a bonus' (Davey 2011:30). Not only does the basic idea of 'a day out with family and friends' permeate many responses to surveys – much more than the specific context of festivals – but it also explains why there are so many successful festivals in attractive towns that are relatively close to metropolitan areas, from where a day out is enjoyable and the distance no disincentive.

For many visitors to the four-day long 1997 Opera in the Outback, sought-after features had little to do with the music, but included being able to visit the Beltana Races, a so-called picnic race meeting, usually associated with an Outback Ball and country and western music (which had resulted in Beltana, once a mining town, becoming described in Wikipedia as being 'known for continuing to exist long after the reasons for its existence had ceased'). The race offered an attractive package of 'animals, dust, dirt, heat and the race caller'. Other enjoyable features included the landscape (and especially the staging of one part of the Opera in the Yalkarinha Gorge), Aboriginal culture (primarily an Aboriginal choir), campdrafting, shearing and even flash flooding. Rain and mud actually added to the pleasure for some (Richard Trembath Research 1997:60–61). While many visitors had previously experienced musical concerts of various kinds, and 45 per cent had been drawn to hear Kiri Te Kanawa sing, the musical experience was muted, in comparison with the excitement of races and other less predictable 'outback experiences'. The setting and the atmosphere were the most frequently mentioned reasons for satisfaction. Visitors to the Festival were thus categorised as either 'indulgers', 'discoverers', 'time out' or 'adventurers'; only the 'indulgers' (just 25 per cent of the total) were rated as having any significant interest in classical music and opera (and also food and wine) while members of the other groups were more likely to be interested in non-musical motivations for being at the Opera and also more likely to enjoy jazz, blues, country or pop music (Richard Trembath Research 1997:10–12, 23). Opera music was not near the front of most visitors' minds.

Based on many similar situations, an American study has posed the question: 'does the music matter?' and, in the somewhat obfuscatory language of market segmentation, concluded, for a several-day rock music festival in Virginia, that cluster analysis of the reasons for participation revealed four groupings of visitors, based on their patterns of motivation: 'Just Being Social', 'Enrichment Over Music', 'The Music Matters', and 'Love It All' (Bowen and Daniels 2005). More simply, some participants were there for loosely social reasons, such as friends and family, others for the wider ambience of the festival, wandering around the site and meeting other fans, and some for the music. Socialisation and non-musical experiences were as important as the right combination of bands on the main stage. A similar set of motives drew visitors to the 2001 Sidmouth Folk Festival in England, resulting in them being divided into four groups: fun, family, friends and folk (Mason and Beaumont-Kerridge 2004), just one of which therefore prioritised the music, while at the Störsjoyran Rock Music Festival in Sweden, there were four similar generic motives for attendance: to socialise, to party, to experience novelty and excitement and to enjoy the festival program (Tomljenovic et al. 2010). For a group of festival-goers in Queensland the festival experience and atmosphere were most important, followed by the music itself, the social experiences and 'separation' (doing something new and/or different) (Packer and Ballantyne 2010). At the Bermagui Festival of the Four Winds even the leading organisers recognised that music was just one of several reasons for being there, alongside personal connections in a small community and especially the ambience of a natural amphitheatre in a scenic setting (Chapter 7). Whether the ambience suggested fun and frivolity or links with a benign and beautiful natural landscape it had a critical role.

Fun and Frivolity

Everyone attends festivals because they anticipate pleasure and enjoyment and, as the previous discussion indicates, for some the music is almost irrelevant. For those who are not committed enthusiasts the social experience outweighs the music, and festivals are simply an enjoyable escape from routine, providing a range of sensory experiences and a relaxed, holiday atmosphere. No festivals are meant to be entirely serious and even – perhaps particularly – the most narrowly focused are about renewing old friendships and socialising. Others are primarily about enjoyment and escapism. At various festivals a sense of carnival and the inversion of daily life means a complete escape from routine: 'a boys' weekend, to get on the beers', dress up and dance (Chapter 6). All sense of seriousness and sobriety are to be eschewed. Hence Meredith Music Festival features an Arch of Love (under which festival-goers must pass to get around the site, with tradition that if two people walked under it simultaneously they must kiss); an old tree painted red (Red Tree) at which redheads are to gather; and a nude sprint race, The Meredith Gift, contested for the prize of a case of cold beer. Intensely loyal fans are referred to as Meredithians and are known to bring their own couches and coffee tables, and even erect pergolas in camping areas given suburb, country, personal and/or 1970s car names ('Kevin', 'North Kevin', 'Kingswood', 'Belmont', 'Mongolia', 'Outer Mongolia') to which allegiances built up over successive years. In the words of co-organiser Greg Peele,

> The beauty was: turn up, find your own patch, go and watch bands, fall asleep, get up, watch some more bands. Nobody telling you "you have be quiet now" or "you've had enough to drink" or "the pub shuts at ten". No "you can't drive home you're too drunk". It was a freeing experience, something people in Melbourne weren't used to. And it was wild.

Beers and dressing up (or down), even in medieval or Celtic garb, are part of the fun. A majority of visitors went to Parkes for fun and relaxation, with a musical backdrop. Indeed, since Elvis Presley has long been dead (or so most believe), for many it would have been hard to take his impersonators – even the best tribute artists – entirely seriously. Yet many of the most dedicated enthusiasts of Elvis were there too and their participation in the Festival took a somewhat different form (see below). Fun comes from the musical background, and the wider ambience, the food and company, the ability to spend time with friends, acquiring new friends, escaping suburbia, sampling unusual substances and simply being there in the midst of a realm of sources of entertainment. For some it may be no more than an excuse for anticipated bacchanalian orgy.

The East Coast Blues and Roots Festival markets itself to 'discerning' music lovers, as a 'serious' music festival not just about drinking; even there, however, most visitors come for the 'atmosphere' or 'vibe' of the festival, rather than specific acts. Loss of a headline act would not topple it. In 2006 out of a sample of 40 visitors at the East Coast Blues and Roots Festival, 60 per cent came largely for the overall atmosphere rather than the music itself, with comments such as 'I don't know, I came for the vibe of it'; 'festivals get under your skin, man. You just have to do it, be a part of the experience. It's a buzz'. Less than half said their interest in music was 'fanatical' and only one said they would not have attended had their favourite act cancelled.

Some visitors are simply festival fans. Various visitors to the Parkes and Tamworth festivals, and to Opera in the Paddock, had linked these events to wider travel plans. Opera in the Paddock drew 'grey nomads' particularly, while Byron Bay was part of a much more youthful backpacker circuit and participating in a festival was part of an overall hedonistic Byron experience (Chapter 9). A large number of visitors to Parkes were on their way north to Tamworth for the Country Music Festival a week later. Others went from the Summernats car festival ('Australia's Biggest Horsepower Party' and 'a festival of the street machine lifestyle') in Canberra to Parkes and then Tamworth in succeeding weeks. Festivals were fun and the music was background rather than foreground.

Indeed festivals do not always take themselves too seriously and certainly enjoin visitors to have fun, evident from the website of the Apollo Bay Music Festival:

> The Apollo Bay Music Festival is like a breath of fresh sea air; a gentle reminder of how cultural get togethers should be. Punters usually begin to suffer from major festival lethargy around this time. Summer is traditionally dry, but musically, it's saturated. Each weekend seems to host yet another festival. And most of them have a familiar ring, as line ups are often dominated by the same old, albeit talented, names … Then there's the overpriced food and drink … But thankfully the Apollo Bay Music Festival is a pleasant detour on the music festival road map; a touch more unique, and of course, a bit more mature – mosh pits are mere rumour, while bald spots are in greater number than baseball caps, around these parts. Its blueprint is simple: cordon off both ends of the main street, fill with entertainers and punters, and mix vigorously … an exciting, relaxing, toe tappin', loose limbed experience … around mid afternoon, the

typically quiet main drag transforms into a major thoroughfare of music and culture … Around sun down, it all began to resemble Glastonbury with a middle aged spread, as the beer sunk in and the mud got stickier … The Apollo Bay Music Festival is a step back in time, to when festivals were a truly moving and intimate experience.

Somewhat similarly the flyer for the 2007 Mungindi Music Festival in a small town 500 kilometres west of Brisbane, offered 'five good reasons' to visit the festival:

1. Mungindi has never had a traffic jam
2. There are no terrorist alerts out for the Mungindi Music Festival
3. Peter Beattie and Morris Iemma [then Premiers of Queensland and NSW] are not trying to force high rise development on us
4. The sky is wide and blue and the sunsets are divine
5. Fun, fabulous music, fantastic week-end

In the even smaller opal mining town of Lightning Ridge, further west than Mungindi, the 2010 White Cliffs Art and Music Festival combined all possible regional activities into the festival, from auctions and photo competitions to plant sales and sausage sizzles, centred around a Saturday Night Concert featuring 'White Cliffs' own Bush Poet and Country Singer' and the Lonely Horse Band, described as 'Well loved by one-horse towns'. Fun was surely implicit.

Fun was central to the era of bush raves. At Mount Victoria in 1999, and no doubt enhanced chemically, 'Five thousand are there simply to meet and dance … There is an atmosphere of care, both in the night and particularly in the morning, when everyone seems to be getting hugged' (Konkes 1999:1). At the first Glenworth Valley Festival in 1998,

By the end many were feeling like throwing in their jobs back in the city and spending the rest of their lives moving from festival to festival. A lot of people who had never been to a festival before were amazed at the friendly, laidback atmosphere and the sense of camaraderie that sprung up amongst complete strangers in the camp sites. There was a lot of people coming together to make their own fun. (Bowen 1999:24)

At its sequel, the Peat's Ridge Festival,

Going feral is all part of the fun. To spend three days in a muddy field, eating hot chips and being blasted with decibels, and sleeping in a leaking tent next to a portaloo. People were sliding through the mud, playing around in it, and then they simply wore it. By the last day … people were just rolling in mud; they'd given up on any sense of looking decent. It's what I love about those long festivals – you enter this other world for several days. It's almost like an endurance test. (Bilton 2010)

The organiser of Big Day Out has likewise said of rock festivals:

> When you've got people coming out for a four-day event, the pace is totally different. It's an older crowd and they're going to something to get away from their job or their uni or whatever. The music becomes auxiliary to that. The four-day thing is a survival process. You stand around for four days; even if it doesn't rain, you go 'I stink, I'd like to change my clothes, I'm sick of this food. I just want to have another joint and sit out in the park'. (Quoted in Shedden 1998:11)

But endurance and survival bring their own pleasures, alongside the acquisition of social capital. While fun-seekers are more likely to be young, many of the visitors to the Elvis Festival, even of a certain age, emphasised that frivolity was a priority. Multiple festival facebook pages attest to fun, but rarely in great detail:

> The Nannup Music Festival was a blast! I was a spectator and I had a great time … such a relaxing chilled out vibe.

> I went to Port Fairy Folk Festival. It was awesome.

> A huge thank you to the performers, volunteers and Cygnet community for creating a spectacularly vibrant event which will stay in our minds and hearts for a long time.

Earth Freq, in South-East Queensland, was described on its website as

> not just a festival or party, but a gathering of different tribes and a weekend of connection, intention and inspiration. The focus is on creating a meaningful space to gather, where we can raise awareness and share useful information on environmental issues and sustainable lifestyle choices, consolidate community bonds with creative and fun activities, and provide a positive and transformative festival experience in the beautiful Australian outdoors, with a full range of music, performance, talks and workshops and creative activities.

Yet fun was still central, especially in contrast to urban musical scenes:

> The thing I love about earthfreq is the music, atmosphere but mainly the people. There are no drunk retards stumbling around causing fights and problems or all the posers trying to act tough like you get in the clubs. It's just friendly people and good vibes.

> I like the fact that girls can't wear high heels on the grass. I reckon the doof chicks r far more interesting than club girls. Oh and the fact that you can actually hear enough to be able to talk to people helps.

> Loved this party! Loved that we could camp away for some space, and loved
> that it was a really family friendly event.

Ambience was never far away. At the Nanga Music Festival, 'What really appealed
to me was the marvellous setting. I loved the fact that we had to walk through the
beautiful jarrah forest to get to the venues'. At the Dorrigo Folk and Bluegrass
Festival 'the music is fabulous and the campgrounds very beautiful. Everyone
talks about the food, of course, and it's all delicious!' Woodford Folk Festival
simply summarised the comments from a sample of over 2,800 visitors at the
2009–2010 Festival as 'amazing, awesome, brilliant, brilliant, chilled, community,
cool, diverse, enjoyable, entertaining, excellent, fabulous, fantastic, fun, great,
hot, inspiring, magical, muddy, rejuvenating, relaxing, stimulating, wet wet wet,
and wonderful … to name just a few!' (Woodford Folk Festival 2010:iv). Similar
comments occur over and over again, emphasising that the overall ambience was
at least as significant as the particular musical experience.

Fun and frivolity, and a memorable context, are not solely the preserve of
audiences. Festivals are usually fun for the musicians, perhaps especially where
they are small and more intimate, and repeat visiting is common. At the Harrietville
Bluegrass Convention in Victoria:

> We had an amazing time. There are some incredible musicians there and you get
> to play with them – sitting around and picking. It's a real musicians' paradise.

> It's always such a letdown coming home after such a good festival. Back to the
> daily grind of normal life. We had a blast and by the applause and comments we
> received the crowd loved it too.

> It was another great festival dampened by a lot of rain but not enough to stop
> everyone having a great time … Along with a few others we ended up singing
> ballads and playing tunes into the night, which was a lot of fun. So – high points
> – seeing the bands, getting the chance to play onstage at this great festival,
> seeing a lot of familiar faces again and meeting some new ones.

Or at the Kelly Country Pick (Beechworth, Victoria),

> A collective yee-haa to say how much we enjoyed the festival … We'll definitely
> be back and are keen at this stage to come earlier for the camp pre-festival. We
> were all impressed by the level of musicianship in the jam sessions – there are
> some really great pickers down in Vic!

At the Dorrigo Festival

> Over the years I have definitely come to appreciate the music that flows from
> the campgrounds. Whether the musicians are performing in the official line-up

or not, the talent hidden in festival campgrounds are always worth avoiding the comfort of motels for.

And at the Cairns Ukulele Festival,

> OMGosh – I wish I was still there!! All the members of Ukenasia (from South Coast NSW) had an absolute blast at the festival. Great venues, super, super inspiring artists and an awesome reception to our performances. Yeah – go Cairns!

or the Huntington Estate Festival where fun may elide into a deeper sense of enjoyment over time:

> More than anything else the opportunity to get to know an audience over a few days. In our normal lives we give one performance and move on seldom getting a chance to meet more than a few members of the audience. At Huntington, we perform, and then we eat and talk with the audience, and over the course of the festival the relationship changes from performers/audience to one of a group of friends sharing a feast of the senses.

> The music I played, the Chopin, pulled me right into the abyss of my inner world of emotions. I could not stay indifferent. The Huntington audience received me with an open mind and warm heart … And most importantly we shared the world of communication where so much can be said without words.

Many festivals depend and rely on the return of musicians from earlier festivals. One of the characteristics of various festivals, such as Parkes, is not just the return of popular performers but also the return of the buskers, for the pleasure of performing to receptive audiences. Jazz and folk festivals too are characterized by performers returning to enjoy jamming and socialising (Begg 2011; Curtis 2010) and the wider shared ambience.

Finally, local residents too invariably enjoy the experience, even at Parkes where many residents were initially deeply sceptical: 'It gives everybody a good time whether they like Elvis or not', 'The festival brings the town and community together at times when things are hard', 'It makes people aware of each other and makes kindness come to the front of people's minds', 'The Festival is the best thing that's ever happened to the town. I love seeing all the people around the town' (quoted in Jetty Research 2010). At the Charters Towers (Queensland) Ten Days in The Towers Festival residents similarly welcomed the break from routine and the chance for celebration. 'It's a good atmosphere … that buzz down the main street, music out in the open air, it's a lovely atmosphere it really is. The town loves that part of it. People say it should be like this every week' (quoted in Moscardo et al. 2009:16). Even when a rave was staged near the tiny South Australian town of Sedan, not only were almost all the goods in the village store sold, but 'the locals loved it. The pub was packed with local afterwards who wanted to discuss the fact that *something* had happened in their town' (Kirstie Petrou, personal communication 2010). Here, as in so many other places, festivals are carnivalesque, everyday life is temporarily abandoned for novelty, and pleasure replaces duty, even as many residents work hard to make the festivals successful.

Fans and Fanatics

The majority of visitors to music festivals are there to socialise and have fun, as much as for the musical genre, but all festivals have a certain percentage of dedicated fans and regular, repeat visitors – the fans and fanatics (McKellar 2009a, 2009b). Fans and fanaticism are more evident at lengthy festivals, where on-site residence is possible (and sometimes necessary), at more esoteric and specialised festivals in remote locations, and where audiences and performers intermingle and are sometimes interchangeable. Relatively rare bluegrass festivals are usually for aficionados. The Kelly Country Pick 'commenced in 1999 as an annual picking meet between a few pickers and families from Victoria and NSW, with a view to spending a relaxed music weekend in a lovely historic country town'. Nowadays it attracts 300 to 500 musicians and visitors, and 'joining in some of the many informal picking sessions is one of the highlights', alongside an on-site teaching program and the presence of acoustic instrument makers. Lismore's annual national swing dancing festival is both an opportunity to socialise and dance at night, and an essential rite of passage for dancers improving their skills during eight hours of daily workshops, across a full week, training with some of the world's best instructors. Jazz festivals particularly include competitions with prize money at stake. Fun certainly, but frivolous scarcely.

For many the music is important and certainly explains why visitors choose particular festivals. Country music has definite fans. Some 52 per cent of those at the Tamworth Country Music Festival were there primarily because they loved country music, and especially the variety of events and the atmosphere that this entailed, while in New Zealand at least 45 per cent of those who were at the Gore Country Music Festival were there for the music and, significantly, for the line dancing (Pegg and Patterson 2010; Nicholson and Pearce 2001). Those who dislike country music (and there are many who dislike it intensely) are unlikely to attend, no matter how good the party vibe. The Wintersun Festival characteristically attracts rock 'n' roll enthusiasts, and also veteran car enthusiasts ('rodders'), many of whom are also members of clubs in their hometowns, and who welcome the opportunity to meet and perform with others and participate in 'show 'n' shine' car displays, both 'celebrating a generation and more narrowly focussing on an interest (or hobby) which they can master' (Mackellar 2009b:90) or at least actively engage in. Performance and participation, in dance, song or more passively in dress, are marks of fandom.

Festivals necessarily attract genuine musical enthusiasts for whom the music and also the camaraderie, centred on that music, are everything – and the place may be quite incidental (even if it creates the 'right' context for a successful experience). Festivals obviously provide places where fans of particular styles and performers can get together, meet and perhaps get to know each other, re-unite, perform, drink and eat together, purchase relevant merchandise, exchange memories and songs and so on. The Goulburn Blues Festival, which bills itself as the annual national blues festival in Australia, brings a scattered and fragmented music scene together – a rare event given the tyranny of distance. For Karin Grant, from the Launceston Blues Club: 'you get to see so many wonderful young and old Aussie acts you would normally never have the chance to see or know, plus one of the few festivals where you can mix with someone from just about every Australian blues club or society'. For John Durr of Black Market Music,

> I think that it is most important that such a festival, serving as a meeting place for Blues musicians, fans, music industry people, exists and thrives. Goulburn is an ideal town for such an event, being accessible to attendees from all the states of Australia. The fact that it features only Australian artists, especially the young and up and coming, gives it a real relevancy to the Australian music scene. Throw in the awards, Australia's only national awards for Blues music, and you have a festival that is a real feature on the Australian artistic landscape.

In this way festivals turn virtual communities briefly into real communities, and are an 'alternative universe' for 'true fans'. Such fans, who may develop their own websites and blogs, or are on particular fanbases, may be atypical, yet their experiences are widely shared, even more so when festivals seek to create a particular social and musical ambience. They are also the most likely to return. Those returnees, and the most frequent festival visitors, for whom the experience is obviously the most intense, stress the significance of the music and its performance as much as the broader social experience (Packer and Ballantyne 2010). That performance enables visitors to enact an identity, as dancers, singers or musicians, not merely in a supportive context but where, in the words of one participant at Wintersun, 'it's the one time when I can feel normal' (quoted in Mackellar 2009b:96), amongst other serious fans and fanatics.

At the Hawkesbury Folk Festival visitors were there to meet old friends, relax in the countryside, enjoy the experience of camping out (or caravanning) or escape a weekend in suburbia. But for a significant proportion festival going was part of a way of life. Some 38 per cent of the participants had attended the Festival more than six times, many others were regular returnees and most expressed a considerable commitment to the folk scene, whether in festivals or clubs, even lasting over fifty years. They were most likely to stay for the five days of the festival, compared with the less committed who were there for shorter times. For particularly committed festival-goers, who took in several festivals in a year, sometimes following a distinct circuit (Begg 2011), festivals provide 'a space and time away from everyday life in which intense extraordinary experiences can be created and shared' (Morgan 2008:81; Packer and Ballantyne 2010:172–3). For such enthusiasts fringe events were often more important that headline acts on central stages and some of the more 'extreme' fanatics even participated in folk festivals without actually witnessing any of the main events (Morgan 2008; Begg 2011). Somewhat similarly at Parkes some self-proclaimed real fans of Elvis Presley denounced the lack of respect for Elvis, and tried to avoid what they perceived as the trivialisation of his name and fame (Chapter 6). The organisers of Opera in the Paddock likewise resisted the views of a handful of visitors who sought Gilbert and Sullivan light opera (Chapter 7). A proper respect for music and history was important.

Some genres are more likely to inspire devotion, respect and fandom. Folk festivals may enable people 'to connect with their authentic cultural heritage and to fulfil perceived needs' (Raybould et al. 1999:204) especially where such needs are loosely linked to desired 'alternative lifestyles' (Lewis and Dowsey-Magog 1993). The Woodford Folk Festival sought 'to create a village atmosphere where a community of strangers would come together into a community of friends' (Cameron 1995:205). Camping on site emphasises the social and committed context. Folk music and varied notions of 'traditional' music seem most likely to draw visitors into what have been described as sub-cultures, or 'neo-tribes', as at a Celtic music festival in Scotland (Matheson 2005), or at least be involved in some celebration of and enjoyment in group identity. For many the group identity assumed at festivals is more real and vital than anything possible elsewhere.

Festival 'families' or sub-cultures emerge at festivals as regular visitors become re-acquainted, stay in adjoining camp sites, exchange news, music, food and drink, and perform together, according to particular shared interests and values. At most festivals distinct sub-groups are evident. Thus at a range of music festivals, from folk festivals even to the Elvis Festival, one such sub-cultural group are bush poets who often perform and exchange poems at poets' breakfasts, many 'with romanticised notions of the Australian bush, settlers and farmers' (Begg 2011:256). Dancers also form regular groups at many festivals – from rock 'n' roll at Wintersun and Parkes, to bush dancers and morris dancing at folk festivals. For some such groups the conventions differ from ordinary life, partly through the intensification of experience in what can be all-night sessions, and partly as senior group members blood newcomers on what is expected of them, such as appropriate 'session etiquette' on the rules and conventions of when to take one's turn to sing or dance (Morgan 2008:90; Begg 2011). Festivals are thus learning experiences, for visitors and performers.

Jazz festivals, more than others, invite improvisation and change so that festivals like Wangaratta become the lifeblood of Australian jazz music, an incubator for new talent (Curtis 2010). The New England Bach Festival has an improvisation concert where the audience provides 'themes to festival musicians to see what they can make of them. It will be music you've never heard before'. The Nanga Music Festival (Dwellingup, WA) restricts the number of participants to 300 so that artists and visitors can mingle, six 'emerging artists' are given short slots, and others participate through 'blackboard sessions', with scope for intimate workshops which include the development of artistic skills (songwriting, instrumental and vocal skills) and dance skills (Nanga Music Festival 2009). At the Kelly Country Pick free entry is given to visitors under 18 since the festival 'focuses on 'picking', sharing music, and teaching technical skills, with instrument workshops over the weekend including fiddle, mandolin, double bass, guitar, dobro and banjo', and organisers were anxious for young people to acquire such skills. The Wintersun Festival held workshops that enabled 'skill progression' as participants refined their dance moves (Mackellar 2009b:94). At some jitterbug festivals dancers are graded, en masse, at the first event, and put into 'streams' of skill-level for the remainder of the festival's workshops. Many music and dance festivals have separate spaces for such workshops where visitors can learn from each other and from leading exponents. The Wangaratta Jazz Festival holds a series of youth workshops designed for secondary school students and other festival visitors, which provides a critical structure for the exchange of musical ideas (Curtis 2010) and a means of binding the festival closer to the local community. Most festivals offer impromptu opportunities for visitors to be involved – some in karaoke and sound-a-like competitions, as in Parkes – others through a separate venue where aspiring performers can take their turn. A particular feature of the Denmark Festival of Voice (on the south coast of Western Australia) has been the Festival Club, which offers a 'ten minute open chalkboard' where any act (from individuals to choirs) can have a turn. Many festivals are about entertainment, active participation and learning.

Serious festival participation exemplifies the involvement of 'those for whom cultural pursuits are an active form of identity creation, an extension of general leisure and a serious pursuit' (Stebbins 1996). Serious visitors could also be involved in a 'festival career' involving a number of achievements such as being involved in performance (playing or dressing up) and social group identification, marked by detailed knowledge of relevant personalities, events and genres. Knowledge, performance, return and repetition enable participants to graduate to an inner circle of devotees. As one long-time participant at the Hawkesbury Folk Festival, and on the festival circuit, said: 'these festivals are my home, they're what I do and pretty much the reason I exist'. Another saw 'festival participation as a bonding opportunity for like-minded people – it's like a family reunion' and a third 'It's all about meeting people and stimulating my mind. Every festival is a learning experience for me, whether it be about the music, learning a new set of chords or simply learning more about me and life … these things open up your horizons' (quoted in Begg 2011:254). As one musician at the Wangaratta Jazz Festival phrased it,

> All the camps come together for one beautiful long weekend. The traditionalists,
> the conceptualists, the scientists and the heretics. The prophets and the preachers.

> The protagonistas and the provocateurs. Musicians from all around the country
> get to share music, food, drinks and stories. (Quoted in Curtis 2011:287–88)

Perhaps unsurprisingly, devoted and repetitive festival-going has been likened to pilgrimage, perhaps more evident at rural sites like Woodford, with its long history (Cameron 2005), although elements of pilgrimage – seasonality, ritual performance, attire, sense of release and commonality of purpose – may be ubiquitous. The most ardent fans live for their festivals.

Many primarily music festivals have linked up with other creative arts to diversify festival experiences (though perhaps initially for children, or when festivals last for several days). At the 2011 Woodford Festival, like its predecessors, all manner of creative arts workshops were available (and demand was such that they had to be booked three months in advance). That year had a particular Balinese flavour: 'sign up to create your own batik silk, papier-mâché an *ogoh ogoh*, or construct a spirit house lantern to appease the spirits, or learn to perform the 'chak-chak' monkey chant of the *Kecak*'. Workshops covered a multiplicity of activities, from live wire sculpture and Persian wood carving to decorative 'slumped glass' and aluminium etching, that complemented the folk music context. Skills and education might be acquired quite separately from any musical experience.

Most festivals focus on a particular musical genre, sometimes extremely specialised, where visitors may be highly focused purists, dedicated to the preservation of that style. The music, and its performance, certainly matter. Beyond the music, some participants at folk festivals, where much Australian folk music has been shaped by Anglo-Celtic traditions, regard festivals as means of strengthening this ethnicity. One regular visitor to the Hawkesbury Folk Festival stated: 'The concentrated Anglo-Celtic flavour present at most [folk] festivals is maintained through our strong values of preserving tradition and as a result the festivals become a celebration of our ethnicity' (quoted in Begg 2011:261). The Brigadoon Scottish Festival gave enthusiasts opportunities 'to dress up and act "Scottish", to watch distinctly Scottish events and listen to particular types of music, and to act out forms of cultural pride' (Ruting and Li 2011:270): to enact Scottish identity and ancestry. Just as some participants at the Hawkesbury Folk Festival sought to learn more about folk music heritage and style, so some visitors at Brigadoon sought to learn about clan histories and genealogies. At Wangaratta musicians came to learn from each other and develop improvisation so that the festival became 'a temporary neo-tribal meeting point for performers where they can talk together, listen to and hear sounds together, make sense of sounds together, perform together and drink and eat together' (Curtis 2011:286). The Bridgewood Chamber Music Festival involves national and international artists, and young local musicians, playing as soloists and in ensemble. The Festival thus enables serious aspiring musicians to work with seasoned visiting artists over the weekend; the intimate venues, the informal arrangements, the meals and the travel in common, bring the artists and the Festival audience together in a way not possible in a concert hall. For all such participants the festival scene is characterised by a set of values and styles that contribute to strengthening particular social groupings, even 'neo-tribes', and perpetuating a conservative order. For serious participants the rewards of attendance are different from those of more casual visitors: an experience of self-renewal, self-expression through music and performance and the acquisition of status symbols ('sub-cultural capital') by obtaining such material products as t-shirts and new instruments (Begg 2011:254). Frequent participation strengthens an enduring commitment to a genre and a group, which may become more important than the everyday world of employment and domesticity.

At the core of most festivals, are 'a large number of enthusiasts, who actively shape and construct the festival, give it direction and vitality and for whom it is a significant part of their lives' (Begg 2011:263). It is these serious participants, whether at Hawkesbury, Parkes or elsewhere, and in quite different ways, who are not merely passive visitors but actually core participants in establishing both the musical scene and the wider social context of the festival. Dressing up, whether as Elvis in Parkes, in a dinner jacket for Opera in the Paddock or a kilt at Bundanoon, or spontaneously dancing, give festivals their aura. Expert swing and rock 'n' roll dancers with national and international reputations dazzle newcomers with expert displays and set the benchmark for what is possible for the most committed fans. At Brigadoon, as one visitor described it, 'Bagpipes are very emotional. The sounds send shivers up the back of your spine', while the massed bands display at the closing of each festival provided visitors 'with a sensual and engaging representation of Scottish traditions' (Ruting and Li 2011:275). It is these participants who take festivals most seriously, but alongside those who take them most frivolously, who add diversity and make festivals what they are.

Bums on Seats and on the Grass

It is certainly not only, or even primarily, music festivals where people participate for diffuse and diverse forms of pleasure rather than for the underlying rationale of the event. At a community festival in rural Indiana most visitors were identifiable by six factors: escape, novelty, nostalgia (and patriotism), excitement, family togetherness and socialisation (Li et al. 2009) and 'avoiding' was at least as important as 'seeking'. Such multiple and diverse reasons for attendance indicate that music festival planners may need different marketing tactics to broaden a festival's appeal and that it is risky for event managers to rely on the music itself or a specific artist to draw large festival crowds. The atmosphere is at least as important. Indeed by the late 2000s visitors to the pioneer pop festival Glastonbury were there for its atmosphere, to socialise with friends and family and because of its reputation; the music and artists came a poor fourth. Women and older festival-goers were particularly likely to stress socialising as the main motive (Gelder and Robinson 2009). Exactly the same is true in Australia, especially at youth rock festivals, where partying was as important as the music. Some minimal participation and socialisation are essential.

Compared with the various dedicated and committed festival participants for whom this was 'serious leisure', evident in the mobile sub-cultures that reassemble at folk festivals or in the bagpipe bands at Scottish festivals (Begg 2011; Ruting and Li 2011), the majority of festival visitors were there for a day or weekend out, where both place and music were not necessarily of great significance. Notions of community, cultural meaning and shared performance of identities at festivals are important, but can be exaggerated and are less likely to be evident at some commercial events, which can promise, but fail, to deliver a sense of communality. In the end, festivals are quite diverse and so are the visitors to them, all of whom have their own values and identities, their own knowledge and experiences, and their own ways of experiencing the festivals. Some may be escaping from some components of everyday life, others seeking to participate in some mildly liberating experience, some are there with families and others with neo-tribes, but most are there simply because the festival is there.

The content of the musical performance and programme are nonetheless relevant, even to those with limited interest in the music. Large numbers of visitors to the Parkes Elvis Festival had only limited knowledge of, or much interest in, his music, though it often provoked nostalgia, but enjoyed the festival and intended to return. But 'quality' and 'content' usually extended beyond the music. What visitors saw as important to the success of the Saskatoon jazz festival primarily involved factors such as 'quality of the programme', 'high-quality product', 'clean facilities', 'quality hotels' and 'good local restaurants' (Saleh and Ryan 1993; cf. Thrane 2002). Here, as at many cultural festivals, the facilities were at least as important as the musical content (Van Zyl and Botha 2003). In other words festival-goers were drawn both by the content of the festival itself and its wider context. Locations were usually important, but reasonable accessibility could be as welcome as the music or the specific ambience. While people attend festivals for many reasons, and engage in a range of activities, the single most consistent feature is that they spend some money (usually more than they anticipated) and thus make at least some contribution to local economic development, however inadvertently and unintentionally. That economic contribution can now be examined.

Chapter 4

What's it Worth? Economic Dimensions of Music Festivals

This chapter discusses the economic dimensions of regional music festivals. Economic benefits are crucial – since it usually these (and the number of visitors) that stimulate local council support (financial and otherwise), the interest and sponsorship of local companies and ultimately the support of local people. The most obvious contribution of festivals to regional development is their link to tourism and the direct economic benefits this can bring. Visitors typically spend money on transport, petrol, accommodation, concert tickets, souvenir t-shirts, festival programs, food, drink and sunscreen. At very large festivals, the accumulated benefits of this for host communities can be enormous. Other economic dimensions of music festivals include employment generated, the extent of volunteerism, work for musicians, and linkages and networks that festivals generate within rural and regional communities. Particularly relevant are the organisation, management structure and aims (Getz et al. 2010), and links between festivals, local authorities and economic development strategies, as well as with non-profit organisations, charities and clubs. This recognition of complexity emphasises the difficulties of estimating monetary benefits, and the need to understand festivals as nested cultural and economic activities producing a range of regional development impacts. Other impacts extend beyond local settings. Market vendors come from quite distant places, and their produce and profits move long distances. Lighting and sound engineers may similarly make a living through travelling between festivals. Companies hiring portable toilets and tents likewise benefit enormously from festivals. The economic impacts of festivals can be both quite diffuse and geographically extensive.

Many general accounts of festivals, especially in the media, are replete with simple statements concerning their economic benefits. Thus the 1998 Woodford Folk Festival was reported in the local *Sunshine Coast Daily* to have injected about $3 million into the local economy (Kither 1998). The Australian Festival of Chamber Music in Townsville apparently brings in about $4 million (Morgan 2003). In 2003 A Day on the Green in Mudgee was said to have returned around $500,000 to $600,000 to the town in actual financial returns (Zuel 2005). The Falls Festival, which takes place twice each year in Tasmania and Victoria, was claimed by the festival to have generated $27.2 million and $22.5 million in 2008 in the two locations. In Victoria's Yarra Valley commercial concert-format festivals are said to have become a crucial part of the local economy: concerts at the Rochford Estate are 'the biggest contributor to GDP in the region' (quoted in Shedden 2008:7).

Such estimates are invariably unexplained and whether they are any more than crude calculations from ticket sales and full accommodation is quite uncertain. While they naturally suggest that large festivals generate considerable income, how much that is, where it is spent and what later happens to it is unclear. This chapter seeks to provide more depth and clarity to such estimates. We also discuss a broader range of economic implications including employment, volunteerism and musical work, contributions to place promotion and the geographical patterns of economic activity festivals generate – including links, networks and capacities not accounted for in simple monetary measures of visitor spending or ticket sales.

Accounting for the Economic Impacts of Music Festivals

Studies of the economic dimensions of music festivals are uneven and somewhat contradictory. There are few studies of the profitability of festivals, partly because such information is often zealously guarded. Where studies have been published (or made publicly available from consultancy reports), the most immediate concerns have been estimating monetary impacts, based on visitor expenditure. Most simply, economic impact can be thought of as a net change in an economy, in dollar terms, resulting from the staging of an event (Lee 2001). This view of the contribution of festivals is thoroughly embedded in a market economic paradigm. The most common method used is a survey of visitors (Ritchie 1984; Crompton et al. 2001), in which questions are asked about the amount spent in various categories (e.g. accommodation, food, services) during a defined time-period (usually the previous 24 hours). 'On-the-spot' surveys tend to be simpler and more quickly administered than other alternatives such as in-depth interviews and expenditure diaries (Davidson and Schaffer 1980). However, it is widely known that visitors do not accurately estimate spending while at a festival, and spending is usually under-estimated (Irwin et al. 1996), depending on the timing and location of survey administration, length of festival, and categories of spending included.

Some festivals are held over a single day in one specific place with purchased tickets and easily estimated attendance levels; others are a mass of various activities, usually free, over a wide area, lasting several days, where attendance is not easily estimated (Davidson and Schaffer 1980). Since average spending figures generated from surveys of visitors are routinely multiplied by estimated audience sizes, the estimated audience size matters enormously. There is no easier route to boost a festival's apparent economic success story than to nudge estimated audience figures, especially if an event is free or involves multiple sub-events across numerous venues (at which none, or only some, are ticketed). Other technical considerations hamper efforts to estimate economic impact. Most festival-goers may have been locals or were visitors in that place anyway, and attended a festival as part of their holiday, meaning that it technically did not generate 'extra' income (Crompton et al. 2001). Hence at the Darwin Festival in remote northern Australia, only 4 per cent came from outside the city, and visited Darwin with the festival as their prime motivation (NT Treasury 2007). Accordingly, when visitor expenditure impacts for this festival were calculated its total impact was comparatively modest, even though 12,000 people attended. Other visitors, 'time-switchers' (Gelan 2003), may have come specifically for a festival, but would have travelled to that place instead at another time when the festival was not held. Their expenditure is sometimes excluded from economic benefit estimates.

Some patterns are clear. In an absolute (and obvious) sense, larger festivals generate more money than smaller ones, and require larger investments (Allen et al. 2008; Tindall 2011). Hence the Tamworth Country Music Festival, held over 10 days with an average of 60,000 visitors per day, generates something in the order of $90 million in direct visitor expenditure; the Parkes Elvis Festival, held over three days with an audience around 10,000, generates approximately $5–6 million, while the much smaller Opera in the Outback, with only 300 participants, generated just $100,000 (Moscardo et al. 2009). A big factor in what proportion of this goes into local hands is how much is swallowed up in ticket prices. Some are free community events where money is spent predominantly on accommodation, food and souvenirs. The largest commercial music festivals, with camping incorporated, can involve major outlays but mean less money left over for discretionary purchases. The Wangaratta Jazz Festival makes about $300,000 at the box office, having grown steadily from $25,000 initially in 1990 (Wilson 2008), equating to approximately $100 per person spent on tickets. Tickets at Splendour in the Grass in Byron Bay (Chapter 9) by comparison earned organisers $13 million in 2010, with camping tickets costing $461 and day tickets $360: 'it's our most expensive music festival' (Whyte and Connellan 2010:28). Indeed, that particular festival is one of the world's most expensive rock festivals, in 2008 compared to Glastonbury (£195 or $338), Coachella (California) US$324 ($358); Roskilde 1675 kroner ($324) and Reading (£192, $333). Only the Fuji Rock Festival in Japan was more expensive (42,800 yen, or $547). One author distinctly remembers his first visit to Splendour, in 2003, being the only one of a party of five with enough discretionary money to indulge in buying a souvenir t-shirt, after purchasing tickets.

If monetary benefits are crudely a function of duration and size, then music festivals are slightly more likely to deliver results than other festivals. In our survey of festivals, the average crowd size for all types of events was 7,020, but 8,688 for music festivals. Actual results were variable. Twenty-four music festivals had audiences of 10,000 or more, but twice as many had audiences of less than 5,000. However, music festivals were less likely to be very small: for all festival types 29 per cent had audiences of fewer than 1,000 people; for music festivals it was 19 per cent. Four of the eleven festivals of any kind with audiences of more than 50,000 (only 2 per cent of all festivals) were music festivals. Music festivals were rather longer (on average 5.5 days, versus 3.3 days for festivals of all types), and had more stallholders, performers and venues. Music festivals were thus somewhat larger and slightly more significant for monetary impacts than other festivals.

There are, however, enormous differences in the format, length and layout of festivals that influence visitor expenditure: at single ticketed events within a bounded venue most visitor expenditure occurs within the confines of the site. Whether such festivals contribute significantly depends on the incorporation (or otherwise) of local interests. At some, the presence of stallholders from outside the region, and food, drink and catering suppliers from elsewhere, can reduce regional visitor expenditure impacts, because profits will leave the area after the festival is finished. Yet at winery concerts (Chapter 2) spending on alcohol is captured solely by the winery and exclusion of external vendors means less distribution of benefits locally – beyond the cellar door. This 'leaking' of visitor expenditure is particularly pronounced for festivals that are owned by private companies that are based elsewhere, and for festivals held in farms and fields in rural areas, away from any notable population centres, where money flows to outsourced suppliers, performers and even out of area accommodation: 'This leakage problem is particularly obvious in remote and rural communities where the current levels of service-oriented infrastructure and industry are not adequate to capture visitor spending' (Yu and Turco 2000:147). Location and size are simple factors.

At large concert-format festivals in pastoral locations there are simply few opportunities to spend money other than within the festival site. By contrast the Parkes Elvis Festival, held in the centre of town, with the main shopping street barely a hundred metres away from thousands of visitors, delivers immediate benefits not possible at festivals such as the Hawkesbury Folk Festival or the Nanga Music Festival (held in a bush camp where food is cooked on site) which are deliberately located in remote settings, where the ambience is valued, but the ability to spend quite limited. In some instances such as at Splendour in the Grass and the Peat's Ridge Festival at Glenworth Valley organisers have even established luxury tents, tepees and yurts available for hire (at up to $1,250 each) for those that want a 'classier' experience, and to avoid having to take their own camping gear – further obviating the need to find local hotels, and consolidating expenditure within the festival site.

Even very large festivals can deliver few local expenditure benefits if the region merely provides a stage for an event organised by others, for others. This is even more so if organised and catered by outside companies, but with audiences made up mostly of locals (and not outside visitors) and with local councils footing the bill for infrastructure and post-event clean-up. Nevertheless, as some raves have shown, expenditure can still be significant by people in transit, and much in demand. Before the Enchanted Forest rave, held near Sedan (population 400), party-goers literally bought everything available from the general store and all the pub's accommodation was booked out. Publicans and the general store owner were ecstatic, and the Mayor was forced to back down on his opposition to festivals.

The idea of a simplistic positive association between festival audience size and scale of economic impacts is also undercut when festivals are understood as relative to the size of their host communities, to the scale of infrastructure investment required to stage them, and to the levels of wider media interest (and thus marketing effect) they generate. Predictably, large festivals in big cities generate impressive total visitor expenditure, but it remains within big cities. Thus within big cities even an enormous festival can deliver only slight benefits to the economy – because multiplier effects filter through only some parts of a big place (Tindall 2011). In smaller places the *relative* boost to the regional economy may be far more influential, with a greater proportion of the resident population benefiting from increased trade and visitor expenditures.

Major festivals in modest regional places, such as Tamworth, and the Deniliquin Ute Muster (a car festival in inland Australia with a substantial music component), deliver even more sizeable daily, per capita returns than metropolitan mega-events – from an audience base decidedly blue collar in origin. At the Ute Muster more than 60,000 cans of alcoholic drink are sold at each year's festival – making it the single largest outlet in the country for one major national alcohol brand (Bundy Rum). Alcohol sales are exclusively licensed by inter-state companies, who have constructed a purpose-built, permanent pub on the Ute Muster festival site only used once a year for the festival. But even then there are paradoxes: the Ute Muster is run by a non-profit committee, so there is no leakage of entry fees to distant commercial interests, but it takes place on a site out of town, a limitation on maximising local expenditure benefits. Organisers have sought to ameliorate this by bringing selected events into town. Ultimately what matters most is the size of the event in relation to the host community, the duration, location and format, who attends and what they tend to spend money on (see below, and Chapter 2), and whether profits leak from the region.

Income Distribution and the Trickle-Down Effect

Most festivals, local councils and residents are concerned with the tangible benefits delivered to people within their host communities – the actual dollars earned rather than per capita modelling of visitor expenditure. Exactly how incomes are distributed and earnings circulated through a host community is critical – but difficult to measure. At some festivals, event organisers consciously recruit local suppliers for food and drink, and favour local stallholders over those from elsewhere, in an attempt to maximise trickle-down. At Splendour in the Grass (Byron Bay), the very large demand for alcohol purchase was met solely by a local publican, who had the exclusive rights (Chapter 9). Local pubs and clubs in the main part of Tamworth are conversely the key live music venues at its country music festival, hence some proportion of monetary benefits stay 'in town'. Not everywhere though are pubs and hotels owned by local people – especially in larger centres that have hotel chains rather than independently-owned and operated businesses.

At the Goulburn Blues Festival, losses in 2006 forced festival organisers to rethink its planning. Market stalls were set up centrally in town to add to the atmosphere and catalyse trade for local shops (rather than detract from them), and proceeds were raised for the local Rotary Club. At the Meredith Music Festival, a hot food 'community tucker tent' is organised and staffed entirely by volunteers from local community groups, who share the profits. The much larger Glastonbury Festival in England sought to purchase all goods used at the festival from within twenty kilometres of the site, to support local businesses (Wheat 2000). Such policies frequently respond to local political debates about festivals and the legitimacy of support given to them by local councils and communities.

A high degree of local reliance appears in community rather than profit-seeking festivals. The geography of economic links between festivals and places was traced in our festivals survey by asking organisers about the source of inputs to their festivals, and what proportion came from the host town, the state capital, or beyond. It was then possible to calculate how 'local' the festival was in terms of connections to the regional economy. For certain inputs, such as staffing, catering and staging and public address systems (PAs), local reliance was very high; only very small fractions of these inputs were sourced from outside the local economy, hence the multiplier effects were also high. For all but one input, the performers (see below), at least three-quarters came from the host locality (Table 4.1). We also asked about organisational structure and whether festivals were profit-seeking or not: 75 per cent were run by non-profit organisations, many very small (Table 4.2). Only seven festivals were operated by profit-seeking, private sector companies. Somewhat counter-intuitively, non-profit festivals contribute relatively more local monetary benefits than large commercial ones. Hence the Woodford Folk Festival, organised by a non-profit organisation dedicated to maintaining folk music culture, makes about $300,000 (US$210,000) a year on ticket sales (Roberts 2003) – a small margin given its size – yet brings over 100,000 visitors who spend literally millions of dollars in the region.

How much extra business is generated can also be estimated by surveying local businesses – especially relevant in small communities where the task of identifying extra trade is much easier for shopkeepers than in big capital cities. Some businesses do better or worse at music festivals than at other events, and local businesses are well-placed to estimate this. Industries that generally reap the greatest rewards are retail trade, local transport, printing, hotels and restaurants and the creative industries (Chhabra et al. 2003). Hotels and restaurants are inevitably primary beneficiaries, since festival-goers must eat and sleep, whereas undertakers fare badly, even at nostalgia festivals. Likewise most festival-goers travel by car, and local service stations benefit. Many beneficiaries are also en route, especially selling food, petrol and accommodation and other goods and services, and when the towns are 'full' for the festival there are many regional beneficiaries. Larger festivals are increasingly expected to deliver returns for a wider region. Hence an on-going concern for the Tamworth Country Music Festival is whether visitors go to other nearby places: in 2007, according to festival surveys, about half did,

Table 4.1   Sources of inputs: music festivals in NSW, Victoria and Tasmania, 2007 (%)

	Local region	State capital	Elsewhere in state	Interstate	Inter-national
Staff	92	1.9	1.3	1.3	0.2
Catering	87.1	1.3	8.3	3.3	0
Stall holders	75.4	3.3	13.5	7.4	0
Staging/PA systems	74.3	7.7	12.8	4.8	0.2
Performers and musicians	41.3	17.5	15.9	25.1	4

Source: authors

Table 4.2   Organisational structure: music festivals in NSW, Victoria and Tasmania, 2007

Management structure/ organisational type	Number	%
Non-profit organisation	69	75
Local council	10	11
Private company	6	7
Other	4	4
Committee of local business leaders	2	2
Public company	1	1

visiting five much smaller towns outside Tamworth. The necessity to stay out of town because of limited supply of accommodation enhances this wider regional trickle-down.

Within types of businesses there are also variations: restaurants, takeaway food, accommodation providers and retail shops benefit depending on audience age, disposable income, length of stay and festival timing in relation to seasonal variations in tourist numbers. At Tamworth visitors pay double the normal rates at local hotels. Folk festivals and raves in remote settings may necessitate BYO accommodation, such as tents and campervans, with little local impact. Festivals in Parkes and Tamworth have long since filled up all the formal accommodation, and have expanded into camp sites and homestays. Even Opera in the Paddock has established its own camping ground. Where accommodation is in homestays – that is in the homes of local people – the benefits to the local community are considerable and expenditure is more likely to be retained locally (Li and Connell 2011). In

Parkes, the homestay program involves local residents receiving paying guests (earning several hundred dollars for a long weekend). Even between music festivals in the same town, variations are apparent – a function of audience demographics and event timing – as comparison of Splendour in the Grass and the East Coast Blues and Roots festivals in Byron Bay demonstrates (Chapter 9).

The microgeography of a festival matters enormously: where the site is, how separate it is from the town, who owns and manages it. When the Parkes Elvis Festival was held at a park near the edge of town, beyond walking distance from the centre, shopkeepers closed at midday on Saturday and did not open on Sunday – the traditional operating hours in country towns. When the festival shifted to the town's civic park, adjoining the main shopping street, opening hours were extended, with worthwhile financial rewards. When the Woodford Folk Festival left Maleny's traditional agricultural showgrounds – nested neatly within the town and thus of benefit to shopkeepers – Maleny suffered, and Woodford became the food and supply station. By contrast other comparable rural festival sites within striking distance of capital cities – such as at Peats Ridge, in Glenworth Valley near Sydney – are nowhere near as lucrative for nearby settlements because of the particularities of freeway routes, so that festival-goers mostly bring their food and supplies with them. A good proportion of the expenditure related to the festival thus remains elsewhere, usually in Sydney, though the festival is on a rural property.

Yet expenditure extends much further than might be expected. While local suppliers of food and accommodation most obviously benefit, restaurants, clubs and pubs are direct beneficiaries. So too are local taxi and bus services. Visitors at most festivals in or near towns spend money in many shops – from newsagents to clothing stores – especially music stores, but even hardware and homewares, because the opportunity and the mood are there. The WHO Tattoo Studio in Tamworth doubles its trade during the Country Music Festival (Olding 2010a:9). Umbrellas may sell well in one year, sun screen in the next. Solicitors make out contracts for performers; electricians and plumbers maintain halls, performing spaces and public toilets. While some stores claim, with some justification, that festivals hardly benefit them – festival-goers are unlikely to buy furniture or carpets – they may be belated beneficiaries. The income that others accrue more directly may later be spent on just such goods.

Distant businesses also benefit from festivals. A well-established network in regional Australia takes many itinerant stall-holders festival-to-festival, earning a living selling food, clothing or other items. Much of what is sold in fact has nothing much to do with music – clothes, bags, trinkets, garden furnishings; at the Parkes Elvis Revival Festival itinerant stallholders sell everything from national football club merchandise to Harley Davidson gear, woven rugs, garden gnomes, local goat cheese and hand cream.

Much larger companies are involved in similar circuits. The tent providers at Parkes, Tent City Hire, are the same as at Tamworth, from where the idea came. Based in Gympie, that company increasingly dominates the market for tent accommodation at outdoor music festivals in regional Australia – providing tents at the Gympie Muster, Woodford Folk Festival, Tamworth, Dingo Creek Jazz Festival, Narooma Blues Festival, and Splendour in the Grass. Their format of establishing temporary tent communities on festival sites is convenient for patrons and provides helpful order and predictability for organisers, but the monetary benefits return to Gympie. Portable toilets too are very big business – as evocatively portrayed in the hit Australian film *Kenny.* These 'portaloos' tend to be rented through hire companies (such as the evocatively named '1300 Dunnys') that are organised territorially: for obvious reasons carting empty (and full) portable toilets around by truck can be both expensive and messy, so the market is broken up into regional providers. Conversely, at Woodford the scale of the festival and the keenness of organisers to be environmentally conscious meant seeking Federal and State Government money to build seven new permanent amenity blocks containing toilets and showers, eliminating the need for portable toilets altogether. Better facilities for festival-goers now equates to less business for portaloo operators, but improves waste management on site.

Some festivals such as the Goulburn Blues Festival have made decisions to deliberately exclude outside stallholders, to protect local businesses and charities (such as schools and boy scouts, who run the cake stalls, merchandise sales and BBQs) or to exert greater control over what food and merchandise items are offered for sale. The Wangaratta Jazz Festival, an event which depends on maintaining a highly credible reputation geared around musical experimentation and quality (Curtis 2010), lists strict instructions for stallholders: vendor stalls must be

> vital, varied and associated with high quality goods that are produced locally. With this in mind, we will use our discretion to choose vendors according to the type and quality of their products … All goods must be handmade and/or relate to the High Country Tourist Region (either directly, socially or culturally); Priority will be afforded to Community Fundraising Initiatives; Commercial or second hand goods are not allowed; Franchises, Party Plan or 'Pyramid' businesses are not welcome. Only quality items will be sold at the market. Decision of inclusion is made by the Market Coordinator and is final.

Opera in the Paddock has gone one step further, excluding all stalls, so that even bottled water is unavailable; the only things that could be purchased in 2009 were programs and DVDs of previous events. Meredith Music Festival bans market stalls and all commercial signage, encourages bring-your-own (BYO) alcohol, and free drinkable town water is made available from giant water tanks. Such detachment from the commercial world is otherwise rare. In these examples cultural considerations (outsiders versus insiders, alternative versus mainstream, perceptions of itinerant stallholders as 'tacky', an abhorrence of commercialism) drive decisions of a commercial nature. Festival organisers are aware of the importance of retaining dollars locally for political and economic reasons – hence they encourage local food vendors and carefully choose from where equipment, printing and legal services are hired. But in the tiniest of places, much of this may simply not be possible even with the best of intentions. In the case of the Enchanted Forest rave at Sedan, organisers attempted to use local suppliers and contractors wherever possible – and 'anyone from Sedan who wanted a job, they employed' (Kirstie Petrou, personal communication 2010), but in such a tiny community, necessities such as fencing and portaloos were simply not available and had to be imported. Even though the visitor expenditure impact was enormous in relative terms, with the local pub and general store doing unparalleled business, leakages via infrastructure suppliers were inevitable.

Finally there is the issue of fungibility: clearly there are no economic gains if people simply switch from spending on some goods and services to others (the source of some businesses' antipathy to festivals), with no net expenditure increase. This is more problematic in big cities where festival-goers are mostly from that city anyway, and would otherwise be spending money on those days in shopping malls, cinemas, pubs and cafes. In some country towns, simply getting people out and about and spending money, and giving shopkeepers a reason to stay open longer, can be worthwhile achievements.

Costs and Outlays

Visitor expenditure – and its flow through to local businesses – provides one means of understanding the economic impacts of festivals, but costs are borne by organisers, local authorities and communities. Money must be spent on facilities, invested by councils in infrastructure and marketing, and required to clean-up and minimise pollution and congestion. There are costs in paying musicians (who can command six-figure payments for headline acts at large concerts). Organisers of the Deniliquin Ute Muster estimated that paying musicians – at an event where music was not the sole attraction – constituted at least 15 per cent of total costs (Department of State and Regional Development 2008). In 2011 the Big Day Out offered U.S. rapper Eminem $6 million to headline the festival but that was not enough money (he reputedly earned $5 million per show during his own separate concert tour that year). There are costs hiring stages, lighting rigs and PAs; printing costs for tickets and posters; and contracting specialist event logistics companies to handle traffic, security and waste management; and advertising. Tamworth spent $700,000 in 2005 on a single block for its tent city camping site. The promoters of the 2009 Blueprint Festival in regional Victoria initially stated 'We're just a group of young guys who love music and don't care about the money', but immediately after the festival went into hiding when their debts far exceeded the income. From hiding they observed: 'We expected the ticket revenue to pay for everything, and then the money we made from the food and beverage sales to go into the bank … We knew it was going to be a bit tight. We didn't think far enough though: sound, lighting, stage, toilets, water, electricity, security, staff, food, marquees, the list keeps going. We didn't really think about any of that stuff. It just blows your mind the sort of costs involved' (quoted in Sarahanne 2011).

Large music festivals are increasingly required to complete environmental management plans, secure planning approval and undertake safety and risk audits to comply with public liability insurance rules (the cost of which constantly rises). All such costs have to be recouped through sponsorship, ticket sales, merchandise sales (usually high profit margin), food and drink. Outlays can be substantial. Byron Bay's Blues and Roots Festival costs an estimated $1.24 million to stage. The Falls Festival, staged in two locations in Victoria and Tasmania, costs $3.2 million to run, leaving only a 3–4 per cent return (Kazi 2006). According to organiser Simon Daly: 'When we know we are going to sell out each year, we're not trying to make a cream off it … for the tenth year bar prices have not risen – it's the only place where you can still get six beers for $20' (quoted in Kazi 2006:16). Such restraint on profit-maximisation is atypical for fully commercial events. Yet in our surveys, festivals generally had small funding bases, limited turnovers, and frequently only just broke even or made very modest profits (Tables 4.3 and 4.4). Only two festivals made more than $100,000 in profit, even though twenty-four had audiences of 10,000 or more – suggestive of the slim margins involved. Going into the red was not uncommon – and many nascent festivals are never staged again. The Forth Valley Blues Festival (Tasmania) kept 'rainy day' money aside 'so if we have a bad year, we can still stage next year's event' (Lea Coates, secretary, personal communication 2010). Others continue even despite losses because of perceived external benefits: the Kurri Kurri Nostalgia Festival in 2009 cost $76,000 to stage – assisted by the NSW State Government to the tune of $20,000 and by Cessnock Council for another $5,000. Approximately $10,000 was generated by market stalls, a huge proportion of revenues (stallholders were charged up to $440 per site for the two days of the event), and entry to a show and shine car competition recouped another $4–5,000. The event ran at a loss but this was more than ameliorated by the fact that it injected approximately $4 million into the Kurri Kurri economy through visitor expenditure, with shops and accommodation full in an otherwise economically-depressed town (Jodi Tweed, organiser, personal communication. 2010).

In small places such as Byron Bay, Woodford and Daylesford, a related problem is their small ratepayer base, insufficient to provide necessary funds for adequate infrastructure to handle large influxes of visitors. With small populations they struggle to raise necessary taxes to provide sufficient parks, public toilets, campgrounds, carparks, or to upgrade local roads to cope with traffic peaks, vividly illustrated at the 2010 Splendour in the Grass Festival at Woodford, where local roads were jammed for over six hours and schoolchildren stuck on buses on their way home, to the consternation of local parents. Likewise there may not be enough taxis, or even sufficient capacity in local hospitals.

Particular costs are attached to outdoor location and the use of natural landscapes; rain and wind have disrupted various festivals, discouraged visitors and reduced incomes. The Wangaratta Jazz Festival struggled financially for two years after losing its major sponsor and being hit by weather extremes, so failing to meet projected ticket sales, and was eventually bailed out in 2011 by the City

Table 4.3   Music festival turnover and funding. NSW, Victoria and Tasmania, 2007

	Turnover		Funding support	
$	**Number**	**%**	**Number**	**%**
0–50,000	44	50	76	84
50,000–100,000	21	24	6	7
100,000–250,000	11	12	5	6
250,000–500,000	6	7	2	2
500,000–1 million	3	3	0	0
1 million–5 million	3	3	1	1
Greater than 5 million	1	1	0	0

of Wangaratta Council. Woodford experienced three years of torrential rain in the 2000s which necessitated an expensive capital works outlay to make music viable in difficult conditions. The Parkes Elvis Festival barely survived early years marked by floods and bushfires (Chapter 6). The unpredictably of weather extremes adds to the uncertainties and costs attached to all festivals.

A Panacea for Seasonality?

Festivals are a means to anchor tourism economies in particular seasons. In Darwin, a distinct winter dry season means that festivals are concentrated in only a few months of the year, which is also the tourist high season. Festivals draw crowds that anchor that tourist season and are pivotal dates around which the city's creative workforce (musicians, visual artists, museum curators) organise their yearly activities. Artists, musicians and creative workers take advantage of the city's dry weather to transform public spaces into open-air music venues, exhibition spaces and markets.

In ski-fields music festivals are connected to seasonality in two contrasting ways: essential to the peak tourist seasons, usually structured around winter snowfalls, as a means for competing villages and resorts to market themselves as the fun, party place to stay; and in otherwise quiet off-seasons – deliberately timed to fill otherwise empty chalets. Visitors come not for snow but for cool weather in the summer months, in high alpine locations with snowless but still stunning landscapes, to watch bands, dance and relax. Hotham (Victoria) offers a 'cool summer festival', also billed as 'Australia's highest independent music festival' whereas in NSW the Perisher Snowy Mountains of Music Festival ('Australia's coolest festival') takes place in midwinter. The value of festivals in Parkes and Tamworth to hotels, cafes and restaurants is amplified because they are held in

January, an otherwise quiet time. Music festivals thus become part of pragmatic strategies by regional tourism development promoters to even out trade across the year and reduce the problem of seasonal slumps.

There are nevertheless concerns about oversupply of festivals in the summer holiday period. For the manager of one young Australian band, Defect:

> I think that last year there was a real problem with how common festivals were. The tickets cost $70 or $80, and last year there were about six or seven festivals, and some of the numbers were so down. Springboard [a skate culture festival] was a shocker. I think there were 600 through the gate; last year there were 12,000. There were just too many big festivals. The kids don't have that kind of money, and they go to one or two festivals that summer, but they can't find that $80 or $90 a month or every three weeks. There are just not enough kids who go to festivals, to spend that money. In America, sure, you've got the population base to handle it. But here it's a problem, we need the festivals, we need the bands to get up and play and the kids to hear them, but not at that price and that frequency. (Quoted in Gibson 2007:78)

Conversely, and reflecting the same problem, there can be shortages of big name acts with sufficient pulling power to guarantee viable crowd sizes. Even metropolitan festivals such as Sydney's Big Day Out, V Festival and Good Vibrations have struggled to attract both headline acts and crowds; with costly tickets 'there are simply not enough good bands on festival line-ups' (Davey 2011:30). Big Day Out promoter Ken West describes the situation as a 'perfect storm in effect. The competition levels in Australia went crazy. The bidding wars went crazy. Everything got bidded up' (quoted in fasterlouder.com.au, 12 December 2011). Some enthusiasts disillusioned with mediocre line-ups were instead saving their money to time overseas holidays with festivals, such Fuji Rock in Japan, Roskilde or Coachella in California – where the line-ups are superior.

Festivals need hotels, transport, retail facilities, cafes, bars and restaurants, but not worth building for one festival, or under-utilised without year-round tourism. In Tamworth, Woodford and Gympie, music festivals led to permanent facilities and venues funded by state government and other benefactors. Under constant threat of 'white elephant' status, such facilities have either been designed as multi-purpose, or have been filled by councils staging festivals at other times of the year, such as Tamworth's Hats Off To Country Festival, held in winter as a corollary to the main January event. Even small towns can become 'festival capitals' by diversifying and distributing festivals across seasons: hence Port Fairy (population 2,600) in Victoria – home to a famous folk festival held every March since 1977 – staged a Spring Music Festival in October (an otherwise very quiet tourist period), a Festival of Words every September, and a Winter Weekends Festival, 'actually 3 weekends spread over June to August each year which was established four years ago to boost tourism to the town and surrounding region. The festival aims to showcase Port Fairy as a romantic and dynamic all-year round destination'.

Rural places and smaller towns away from cities, highways and tourist routes are hard-pressed to develop repeated attractions in this way, to attract world famous acts, or to justify investments in permanent infrastructure and facilities. Even so, as the experience of Port Fairy shows, few places are associated with only a single event, and it is certainly possible for small places to develop a strategy that focuses on several modestly-sized events, with minimal fixed infrastructure investment. On the NSW Far South Coast, none of the towns in the region are large enough to warrant investment in festival facilities, and opportunities to sustain cultural tourism and arts businesses year round are rare. But for Jen Hunt, Director of the Southeast Regional Arts Board, 'the advantage of a festival, particularly in our context of small populations, and real seasonality ... is because it's a short burst of activity. It suits our capacity better and suits our infrastructure better to just come in and do something over the course of a weekend or a week and pack it all up, rather than trying to sustain it year-long' (personal communication 2007). Such strategies deliver useful but not enormous visitor expenditure over several weekends, without requiring much infrastructure.

Job Creation

Just as estimating visitor expenditure is fraught with problems, so too is calculating how many jobs are created by festivals (Hughes 1994). From our survey, an average of 4.6 full-time jobs were directly created in the planning stage of festivals, alongside 2.4 part-time jobs – slightly more than for all festival types in terms of full-time work, and less in part-time work. An additional 35.8 full-time jobs and 11.5 part-time jobs were on average created during the festival itself (Table 4.5). Job numbers during festivals were markedly higher for music festivals than other types (nearly three times as much, in the case of full-time work running the festival), probably a function of a small number of very large music festivals skewing the results. Across all music festivals in the three states, 848 jobs were directly created in planning and operations. The most common were event managers/directors/ coordinators (25 per cent of jobs created), administration and accounting positions (24 per cent), ground-keepers, ground staff and facilities managers (12 per cent), public relations and marketing (9 per cent) and artistic services (including artists and musical directors – 8.5 per cent). Other paid positions included retail staff, cleaners, security, catering, stage crew, announcers, and tourism and community development planners. In addition, respondents claimed that another 46 directly related jobs were on average created in the wider community (i.e. not employed by the festival itself). Combining these statistics, music festivals appear to produce around 15,600 jobs in planning and operation and 13,000 jobs in the community, in the rural and regional areas of the three states. Actual conditions and length of employment vary enormously, but in overall terms, music festivals are deceptively effective creators of local jobs – a function of the very diverse range of inputs and specialist skills required.

Table 4.5   Paid employment: music festivals in NSW, Victoria and Tasmania, 2007

Time period	Type of work	Average	Min	Max	Total jobs
Planning the festival	Full-time	4.6	1	26	60
	Part-time	2.4	1	12	59
Running the festival	Full-time	35.8	1	400	465
	Part-time	11.5	1	80	264

Source: authors

Job creation varies with festival format, size, location and type. At Goulburn and Parkes, where events take place in existing buildings or in free public parks, minimal work is required in security, unlike ticketed, single-site commercial concerts such as Splendour in the Grass where the security presence is huge. At even the smallest music festivals there is usually a paid sound engineer to set up and control the PA, while sound and lighting crews at Falls and Splendour are large and costly. The larger regional centres such as Lismore, Tamworth and Cairns have companies that provide PAs, portable toilets, sound engineers, stage builders and roadies, but small towns do not and must import equipment and skills from elsewhere.

For those working in local cafes, restaurants and pubs, there is additional weekend work and overtime payments. A third of local people in Parkes worked some extra hours over the duration of the Elvis Festival. Even the local police force may gain overtime payments, and hospitals put on extra shifts. At the Tamworth Country Music Festival in 2011, for example, there were 1,360 admissions to Tamworth's Emergency Department, up 50 per cent on normal levels: 'we see some lower limb stuff from line dancing – sprained ankles and even broken ankles. I suspect it's because of their heels.' (Nick Ryan, Director; quoted in Olding 2011a:9). Extra medical staff were brought in to deal with injuries and interns began duties a week later to avoid clashing with the expected rush of patients. Even mishaps translate into a peculiar kind of indirect employment impact: 'There's a lot of what we call "diseases of exuberance" … people drinking too much, getting into fights and falling over'.

More difficult to estimate, but certainly pivotal, is volunteer work, but what volunteers do varies enormously. At the Merimbula Jazz Festival literally everything is done on a volunteer basis; at the Goulburn Blues Festival volunteers are given free passes, have to abide by a code of conduct, work morning, afternoon and evening shifts, assist with inquiries, marshal crowds and distribute leaflets. At the Forth Valley Blues Festival:

> Because it is a 13 hour event we have a large roster of approximately 20 volunteers, each accredited to serve in the bar. The local Lions Club (6 people)

> helps with the parking, as do the Dragons Abreast ladies (8–10) who raise money
> for breast cancer support. The local volunteer fire brigade maintains the water
> and paper to the chemical toilets, and the local scouts help with clean-up the day
> after. St John's is our first aid provider. Each of these groups gets at least $500
> for their help. (Lea Coates, personal communication 2010)

Our festivals survey provided insights into the extent of volunteer support. The most common activities were setting up and packing up equipment, cleaning-up, traffic and crowd control, but the full list of volunteer duties was enormous: everything from box office sales to coordinating fashion parades, dealing with red tape to children's face painting. Festival organisers estimated that 16.7 days were spent by the average volunteer assisting their festival during its planning phase, and 4.8 days on average during the actual event. Extrapolating this for the 288 music festivals we identified in the three states (and assuming the average music festival had 5 volunteer workers – a very conservative estimate given that, for instance, the medium-sized Cygnet Folk Festival (Tasmania) uses 200 volunteers), festivals generated the equivalent of over 31,000 days of volunteer labour (equivalent to 85 years) across the three states. Music festivals are thus deeply embedded in local economies and communities through volunteerism.

Musical Work

Festivals have always been a part of the mix of income-earning options for working musicians, and often are linked to the recording industry, so performing an important employment function for record companies and musicians. CD and download sales are likely to be enhanced by festival appearances, and festivals allow emerging artists access to larger audiences than otherwise possible. The careers of many musicians have taken off following captivating festival performances – Jimi Hendrix at Woodstock and Monterey, U2 at Live Aid – while Ben Harper, Jack Johnson and Michael Franti all have popular support well beyond their record sales, due to regular impressive performances at festivals. 'Heritage' performers have thrived through festivals (Chapter 2). Recent Australian experience shows that festivals are increasingly important for the incomes earned by musicians in any given year, and are a more successful outlet for the promotion of new releases where radio airplay is scant (Gibson 2007). In the 1990s bands such as Spiderbait, Regurgitator, Grinspoon and Magic Dirt effectively used the festival circuit to support album releases (which often only received airplay on the publicly-owned, non-commercial station Triple J); conversely bands such as the John Butler Trio, Cat Empire, Frenzal Rhomb, The Waifs and Machine Gun Fellatio became so well known as festival barnstormers that they were headline acts before achieving widespread airplay, hit singles or major label support. As Ninan et al. (2004:16) put it, 'smaller independent bands have learnt to manufacture "instant markets" through the festival touring circuit'. The Meredith Music Festival consciously signs up-and-coming bands otherwise struggling to gain exposure at more commercial events. Likewise the Tablelands Folk Festival in Far North Queensland hires both better-known performers and 'emerging artists from our region'. In most places local performers cost rather less. Specialist festivals matter a great deal: Indigenous Australian groups such as Nokturnl and the Stiff Gins developed loyal support well before releasing CDs; and festivals such as Metalstock in Scone enable bands like Anarchsphere, Enlightened by Darkness, Mythyca and Rake Sodomy to perform to much larger crowds than would ever be possible in pubs in their home towns. When Byron Bay's East Coast Blues Festival became the East Coast Blues and Roots Festival in 1998, the 'broadening of the base was an opportunity to get people like Kasey Chambers, Tiddas and Matt Walker in front of large festival audiences who were unfamiliar with their work' (Elder 2002:21). Following such exposure at Tamworth, where an impression was made on media gatekeepers, Kasey Chambers went on to secure airplay and become a household name in Australia.

A perennial question is how much of the 'cut' is returned to musicians – facts not normally shared by organisers or musicians. In the case of the Merimbula Jazz Festival (NSW), its unusual format stacked the balance firmly in favour of musicians: the festival was entirely organised by volunteers, and all proceeds from tickets, after costs, went directly to musicians. Performers had to pay a $10 registration fee but could also be a part of Jazz Quest where those aged under 25 had an opportunity to win recording time (valued at $800). The High & Dry Festival (St Albans, NSW), whose aim is 'to support, develop and sustain creative culture' through supporting young emerging rock bands, is organised along similar profit-sharing lines – through a non-profit organisation, High & Dry Festival Incorporated. Artists' share of the pay was little in years that just broke even, but much more when ticket sales were strong (Carr 2009). At the 2009 Nanga Music Festival in Dwellingup half of the modest profit of $2,000 was distributed to 'up-and-coming artists in need of the money' (Rob Phillips, personal communication 2010). Other festivals share a similar philosophy, operating outside the sphere of waged labour, firmly non-profit and proudly 'amateur'. The Harrietville Bluegrass Convention (Victoria) features over 30 Australian and American bluegrass bands, none of whom are paid (the entire festival is volunteer-operated, and all volunteers are themselves musicians). The Inverloch Jazz Festival, a non-profit community event, compels big band performers to register and pay a token entry fee for inclusion on the bill, with time slots strictly limited to two x 45 minutes each. Typically around 75 bands register. Musicians are provided drinks tickets to redeem at the bar and guaranteed a place in the Saturday morning street parade. The emphasis is much less on stardom and much more on musical participation and appreciation. At most commercial concerts nothing like this exists, and performers are paid a fee linked to their 'market value': big name acts with established major label reputations might typically receive $10–25,000, with household name headliners $300,000 upwards – even millions in the case of major international acts. For most though the cut is very much smaller, and not guided by originality or technical ability. Hence accomplished and distinguished national performers at the Opera in the Paddock were paid $500 while the best Elvis impersonators at Parkes could earn $10,000 a show.

Frequently involvement is not about money but about other aspects of career development. The Coffs Harbour Buskers and Comedy Festival, which aims 'to provide and develop the concept of street theatre and to provide opportunities for performers', selects 'aspiring artists' and each year over a hundred applications to participate are received, from as far away as Siberia and Uzbekistan. Some have begun a career from there. At the Nanga Music Festival 'a focus of the festival is on encouraging younger and emerging artists into the folk music scene ... we encouraged six emerging acts with short concert slots, as well as providing opportunities for artists who are just finding their feet to perform at scheduled open mike sessions, campfire singalong/jam sessions and the blind date concert' (Rob Phillips, personal communication 2010). Capacity building is perhaps no better exemplified than at the Generations in Jazz Festival in Mount Gambier (SA). With Australian jazz legend James Morrison as its patron (and with a coveted scholarship on offer in his name), it attracts nearly two thousand high school aged jazz musicians who get the opportunity to perform with the nation's best jazz musicians, who act as mentors, and to compete for various prizes and scholarships. Taken seriously by experienced jazz musicians, the theme is investment in the future of jazz in Australia, currently seen as a 'marginal art form, struggling for air' (Wilson 2008:16), by providing a high quality festival opportunity for teenage performers. This and the Wangaratta Jazz Festival, considered the creative pinnacle of Australia's improvised jazz scene, provide crucial lifeblood for musicians otherwise struggling in a genre in danger of becoming a 'permanent underground'. Despite an excess of talent pouring out of jazz courses in state-funded music conservatories, 'times are tough. Musicians are paid less than $200 for each performance and that doesn't cover rehearsals. Most musicians ... need second jobs. New CDs rarely sell more than a few hundred copies' (Wilson 2008:16). Festivals at Wangaratta and Mount Gambier enable jazz to remain viable.

At the Goulburn Blues Festival, as at Wangaratta, the networking opportunities were as important as incomes earned. In the words of Stephen Iorio from blues band The Vagrants, 'we got many opportunities from the gig and earned a lot of respect. It is hard to break into the scene and we all very much appreciate the opportunity'. Likewise, for Matt Ellery from The Sly Tipsters: 'We appreciate the exposure on the notice board, which I think helped the fact that we had good audiences for both spots we played ... We had an absolute ball and made some connections which we are sure will lead to some gigs in the area through the year'.

Another advantage for musicians is that festivals take the major responsibility for marketing, and bear the risk of low attendances, accidents or poor reviews. In pubs, bands have to manage most of the marketing, and are paid either through 'door deals' (where they earn their wage from door takings) or through bar cuts (where a percentage of drink sales are returned to the band as payment) – both methods that place high risks of under-remuneration on performers (Gibson 2003).

Because music festivals usually take place in parks, paddocks, showgrounds and stadia rather than pubs, they attract older audiences sick of rowdy pubs, and they also help underage performers gain exposure, as well as enable other bands to build all-ages audiences. For these reasons, musicians have usually welcomed festivals.

Conversely, festivals can cut into the market for weekly local performances. Live music pubs have struggled in recent years, at the same time that festivals have grown. Yet performers in their early careers may become marginalised in smaller festival side-tents at awkward times, or dwarfed by major acts. As the manager of Defect argued,

> If you go for the festivals, how many small independent bands are clamouring to get on that little local stage, for nothing, and get their twenty minutes? They [Defect] were on the Warped Tour two years ago; they played on the local stage. These guys need to be on the major stage, need to get in the major cities. (Quoted in Gibson 2007:77)

Tensions can be particularly apparent at major festivals with famous headline acts, where local bands struggle to compete. In part external competition is inevitable – music festivals, like art and film festivals, often import metropolitan or international stars, both for local audiences and to tempt tourists away from other regions. Indeed the most commercial festivals usually have few or no slots open to local musicians, as at Splendour in the Grass, and thus the opportunities for genuine exposure are restricted. Hence in contrast to the Goulburn Blues Festival, the East Coast Blues and Roots Festival favours artists that have already secured record deals and established reputations, and even 'heritage' artists from non-blues genres are brought onto the bill to attract nostalgic baby-boomers. Few spots are available to local bands. Our festival survey gave further insight into the extent to which performers are imported: of all the inputs required, musical talent had by far the smallest per centage of local or regional contributions (Table 4.1). For all other types of inputs over three-quarters were sourced locally, but less than half the performers were local. This varied widely: four of the 28 participating festivals had no local bands at all and another nine had fewer than 20 per cent of the slots available for local performers.

'Heritage' performers at commercial winery concerts likewise welcome the opportunity to connect with audiences who cannot see or hear them elsewhere, and make money directly from selling CDs – much more per unit than through record shops or online distribution because the record company and distributors are cut out of the sale price. For over a decade the market for Australian folk recordings on CD has been principally the folk festival circuit (Neuenfeldt 2000). At one winery concert Stephen Cummings sold 500 CDs, making it his best seller in a decade (Zuel 2005).

On the fringes of festivals performers may be even more successful. Many festivals have spaces for buskers and some positively encourage them, notably at Coffs Harbour. At Parkes the buskers on the main street complement the more formal musical presentations on the stage in the park and the indoor venues. Not only do they compete for prizes, but many sell their own CDs. Some – including Black Elvis ('Elvis Parsnip') – did very well from selling their own home produced CDs. In 2010 Crap Elvis, a performer of idiosyncratic talent, sold more than 150 CDs at $10 each, which had cost him about 80 cents each to produce. At Tamworth, buskers have long been a central element, making Peel Street, the town's main street, the most important space for the festival (and for shopping). Part of the attraction of buskers was to evoke democratisation and the Australian value of a 'fair go' – letting everyone have their chance – which in turn enabled the festival to market itself through appeals to nationalistic sentiments. But controversies arose when the festival started to license buskers; some musicians felt this threatened the very values the festival cherished and marketed so heavily. People wanted the truly awful as well as the astonishingly good buskers in preference to a sanitised, authorised selection of street performers.

Meanwhile the Woodford Folk Festival, attempting to walk the same fine line between open arms and quality control allows a huge variety of both professional and amateur performers, but limits acts to performing there to a maximum of three years, to ensure a constant turnover and keep the program fresh: according to General Manager Amanda Jackes, 'Everyone wants to be able to discover someone new at the festival, and that is always an exciting process to go through … The best advertisement is word of mouth. Reputations are established, and enthusiasm for particular acts can lead to them being invited to return the following year' (Soppe 2009:5). Its roster of 2800 acts is unsurpassed elsewhere, fostering a sense of inclusiveness – but some regulation proved necessary for it to remain that way.

Musicians have on the whole embraced the shift from local pub gigs to the festival circuit, often for personal as well as economic reasons. Aboriginal musicians who find it difficult to travel great distances from remote homelands in order to tour, prefer to perform at a smaller number of festivals than at numerous, poorer-paid pub gigs in large cities, where racism can be worse (Dunbar-Hall and Gibson 2004). World music festivals and Aboriginal community celebrations tend to be more inclusive, and have sympathetic directors and management, while festivals with significant tourist audiences – such as Woodford's Festival of the Dreaming – provide opportunities to communicate and educate spectators about Aboriginal culture (Chapter 5). Finally, beyond career development and remuneration, festivals appeal to musicians because there is a thrill involved in being part of big occasions: being remembered by audiences at a great live event that cannot be repeated, the allure of playing to large enthusiastic crowds.

Linkages and Networks

Beyond monetary and employment impacts are the nature and qualities of social and economic linkages catalysed by festivals, illustrating how festivals act as a 'glue' within the regional economy and community, creating dependencies and reciprocities (Mackellar 2007; Moscardo et al. 2009). Networks buttress commercial relationships on the supply-side, assist in learning and maintaining skills, and adapt to changing circumstances. Relationships are generally bi-directional and they rely on mutual trust – between for instance, performers and festival organisers, which in the case of the Wangaratta Jazz Festival has been argued to be absolutely pivotal to its ongoing credibility and audience success (Curtis 2010). Keven Oxford, organiser of the East Coast Blues and Roots Festival, argued that maintaining the reputation of the event among musicians was as important as continuing to please audiences, to ensure a steady stream of quality international acts, since these drawcards would guarantee the festival's viability: 'those [overseas] artists go back and tell other people playing on bills or on tour that they've just been in Australia, played this festival in Byron Bay, had a great time and that the crowds were really receptive' (quoted in Shedden 2000:16). Management structure and expertise is invaluable. At the Australian Festival of Chamber Music in Charters Towers (Queensland), festival organisers used local contacts forged through the board of management to incorporate into the event an Outback Tour, themed dinners and concerts and guest speaker talks: 'The key is the board – we have good board members that have a range of skills and important contacts. This board have their contacts in food, in wine, entertainment, catering. That has really helped us in pulling something like this off. It's a lot of work' (quoted in Moscardo et al. 2009:16). A key ingredient in festival management is 'who you know'.

National and state governments provide financial support for festivals and local councils fund, advertise and support them in other ways. Alice Springs' annual music festival, simply called The Concert, is underwritten by the Northern Territory Government, who directly contribute $100,000 towards costs. Alice Springs Town Council provides the venue, Anzac Oval, at no cost, with the remainder of the approximately $280,000 overall costs recouped through ticket sales (at $60–70 each) (Paul Cattermole, General Manager, personal communication 2010). For the Northern Territory Government it was envisaged as an economic growth stimulant, but also a means of supporting lifestyle and social activities – to simply entertain the community. The Falls Festival in Marion Bay, Tasmania, is reliant on government funding to cover shortfalls: although generating many millions of dollars in economic activity through visitor spending, operating margins are slim and risks high, hence according to promoter Simon Day, 'if we don't get the funding, I think it would be very difficult to stage the Falls Festival' (quoted in fasterlouder.com.au, 3 January 2012).

Governments have also provided cultural grants to stimulate innovation (for example the Festivals Australia program of the Federal Government), while tourism agencies such as Tourism NSW provide some regional festivals with 'flagship' funding (for example the Parkes Elvis Revival Festival, Opera in the Paddock, Kurri Kurri Nostalgia Festival) up to $10,000 for a one-off event, or $20,000 triennially – contingent on the event promoting and creating tourism to host regions. Arguably more effective have been regional arts organisations, boards and programs, financed through a Federal Government regional arts fund, in combination with equivalent state ministries. The Country Arts Support Program of Regional Arts NSW, for instance, provides financial backing for artists to tour country areas, building networks and enabling better quality line-ups than might otherwise be possible. At the 2011 Dorrigo Folk and Bluegrass Festival, such funding enabled Western Australian band Bluegrass Parkway to travel across the country. That festival also received a Festivals Australia grant to run a youth arts project, and was awarded flagship status by Tourism NSW. Other festivals prefer to remain independent of such funding – hence Jen Hunt, from South East Arts, cited the Merimbula Jazz Festival that 'prides themselves on being unfunded. I offered help but no, they don't need it, thank you very much. So that's alright, that's fine'.

Regional Arts Boards broker relationships with other segments of regional arts communities, through regionally-appointed regional arts managers and assisting with activities such as promotion and media relations. As Jen Hunt explains,

> they are all volunteer community initiatives. We will happily include their inserts in any of our mail-outs, put them on the web, make sure they're on the calendar; we will line up interviews with the ABC, give them our general marketing support. We will meet with them and help advise and assist in terms of funding possibilities, program development … could one of our tours help?

Institutional support has also been useful in addressing less obvious problems involved in mounting festivals in remote areas. Festival managers in remote areas are often divorced from the professional and personal networks that might otherwise provide didactic experiences, in turn improving the quality and marketability of festivals (Hede and Rentschler 2007). Regional Arts Victoria accordingly ran a program in the mid-2000s to assist volunteer festival managers to improve festival management and focus artistic direction. Mentoring proved to be one of the more significant forms of institutional support. State and federal arts agencies have increasingly supported audience development (Barlow and Shibli 2007), less formally the task of 'getting bums on seats', now recognised as far from straightforward.

Sponsorship is another ubiquitous form of linkage. While festivals invariably seek sponsorship for financial survival, sponsors also benefit from the relationship. The rural division of NSW State Rail, CountryLink, have sponsored the Parkes Elvis Festival for several years. While the basic economics of running a return train to Parkes, even almost completely full, is only 'good' the train is such a popular feature of all promotion and media coverage of the Festival that it is annually covered on most breakfast television shows and generates a 'positive brand awareness'. Moreover most festivals benefit from local economic activities having some community consciousness in supporting local ventures, such as North Parkes Mine, Regional Express (Rex) airlines and Country Energy (slogan – 'We live here too'). Mining giant Alcoa sponsors the tiny Nanga Festival and provides volunteers in the form of mining workers, who become 'roadies' for the festival (Alcoa Foundation 2010). Telstra and Toyota have sponsored the Tamworth Country Music Festival for many years: the former to generate positive associations in a place that has been otherwise critical of its under-provision of equitable services to rural communities, the latter to 'Australianise' their brand image – especially to the rural market who buy their utes and 4-wheel drive vehicles more than any other brand. Toyota has also sponsored the Gympie Country Music Muster with precisely the same intent (Edwards 2011). Yet for some small festivals, such as Tasmania's Forth Valley Blues Festival, big corporate sponsors are often 'more trouble than it's worth' (Lea Coates, personal communication 2010) given their expectations, legal requirements and demands for logo prominence, and difficulties securing contributions from within large organisations. More commonly, and prosaically, vast numbers of small businesses chip in – in Parkes, typical of most places, the real estate agents, the local newspaper and radio station, the bakery and cafes. Sponsorship is sometimes rather more a performance of civic duty – an expression of belonging to a community – than a commercial benefit or imperative. The Illawarra Folk Festival has no less than thirty-five official sponsors, including local newspapers, television and radio stations, the steelworks (historically Wollongong's chief employer), brewers, regional hotels, bus companies and gyms, the regional branch of the mining and construction union and the local medical centre. Links with charity are often sought for public relations as well as altruistic motivations. Local charities benefit from market stalls and most festivals give priority to local organisations – so that Rotary Clubs, bushfire brigades, schools, churches and football clubs all benefit.

The quality of festival networks is very much shaped by their aims and organisational structure: that the vast majority (75 per cent) of music festivals in our survey were run by non-profit organisations was reflected in their aims being linked to the pastimes, passions or pursuits of the individuals on organising committees, or to socially or culturally oriented ends such as building community, rather than as income-generating ventures (Table 4.6). Indeed, 'to make money' was the second rarest response (recorded by only four festivals), while 'to increase regional income' was only noted by a further seven music festivals. In other words, festivals are interested in developing relationships and community consciousness beyond purely commercial considerations (Wearing et al. 2005).

Some commercial festivals make claims to local connections. The Falls Festival has long seen itself as 'different' from other large commercial music festivals in its willingness to engage with local communities. Hence it established the Falls Music and Arts Festival Community Fund to funnel money back into the Lorne and Marion Bay communities where the festival takes place. Through that scheme one dollar from every ticket sold ($16,000 in each state each year) is donated to projects that are voted on by the local communities. In 2008 they also raised $25,000 to donate to the Boxing Day Tsunami appeal. The entire existence of the Dingo Creek Jazz and Blues Festival was conceived in terms of charity fundraising:

Table 4.6   Aims of Music Festivals. NSW, Victoria and Tasmania, 2007

Aim	Number	%
Promote a place/ theme/ activity	35	39
Foster/encourage	22	25
Entertain	18	20
Celebrate	15	17
Show(case) a place/ theme/ activity	15	17
Build community	15	17
Fundraise	10	11
Increase regional income	7	8
Educate	5	6
Make money	4	4
Compete	2	2

Source: authors

On the day Sunshine Coast winemakers David and Marg Gillespie's first-born daughter Rachael would have turned 21 had she not died from SIDS-related causes, a new regional Queensland event was born. Out of a desire to recognise the 'milestone' in their family's life, the Dingo Creek Jazz and Blues Inc association was founded, the festival has since 2002 borne beautiful fruit, of the musical, emotional and community-spirit varieties. By maintaining an operating-costs only policy, they have already donated more than $73,000 to SIDS and Kids QLD.

At Parkes an art exhibition was mounted on the fringes of the Elvis Festival, to support a local cancer support group. The entry fee ($2) alone generated a significant income, as did Devonshire teas outside. Paintings came from both local people and others in rural NSW, and by the end of the 2009 Festival twelve had been sold, several for more than $100. A handful of local Aboriginal artists were amongst the beneficiaries. Even disasters affecting festival success become a means for stronger links with charity. In 2011 unprecedented floods in Queensland and northern NSW significantly reduced visitor numbers to the Tamworth Country Music Festival. For the first time in memory vacancy signs were lit on Tamworth motels and crowds were estimated to have fallen by ten to forty per cent (Olding 2011a). Despite lost customers, several concerts were quickly reorganised as benefit gigs.

The non-profit sector is both heavily involved in regional festivals, and benefits from them – especially registered community clubs (Weeks and Adams 2006). Such clubs, owned and operated by sporting teams, bowling clubs, returned servicemen's leagues, unions, and women's groups (such as the Country Women's Association) are a ubiquitous and iconic feature of rural Australia, often the largest single entertainment facility in a country town, and a focal point for community programs, recreational pursuits, free shuttle bus services, social programs and activities. They are also a financially vital part of rural Australian life and constitute an important lobby group (Tonts 2005). Frequently they are major festival sponsors, and host events with ready-made live music spaces, PAs, restrooms and even accommodation. In both Parkes and Tamworth, the Leagues Clubs are some of the largest festival venues.

Music clubs and associations are absolutely vital to most regional festivals: local classical music schools, dance clubs, instrument collectors and shops, eisteddfod societies. At Parkes, Wintersun and Kurri Kurri these links extend to rock 'n' roll dance clubs around the state, each of whom send large contingents of dancers to the festival. In the case of the more organised regional music clubs, they have become festival organisers themselves. Thus the Illawarra Folk Club (NSW) organises the annual Illawarra Folk Festival, one of the nation's largest (in January), as well as one-day festivals such as Folk in the Foothills (in October), weekly pub gigs and one-off concerts, bush dances and fundraisers in regional halls and theatres. Such non-profit clubs can become significant players in regional arts economies.

From Commercialism to Community Benefits

Festivals generate income and promote places, though the former is rarely the primary objective. Larger festivals are more likely to be commercial, with outside promoters developing only limited local linkages, but even the most commercial festivals, staged in isolated locations, such as wineries, have some trickledown effects (partly because they attract relatively affluent visitors). Festivals with non-profit committee ownership and/or civic funding typically have less risk and maximise local multipliers compared to concert-format commercial events. Income usually accrues primarily to the organisers, although that depends on the extent to which the whole festival is 'free' or which if any events are ticketed. Again, smaller events are more likely to be free with most expenditure going to local suppliers of food and accommodation, who in every case are key beneficiaries. In most festivals a surprisingly large amount of expenditure trickles down within the community, and around it, even to quite unexpected beneficiaries, such as builders. Employment is generated both directly and indirectly, some of which may be sustained over the course of the year, and most of which is local. But the most marketable performers, who command high fees, and technicians, usually come from the city. Other festivals generate minimal paid employment: whole music festivals are run by volunteers, local music clubs and associations. Without volunteers, such festivals simply would not exist, and they too generate income in other ways and enhance a sense of community.

Many economic impacts are necessarily incalculable and imprecise, but they certainly exist. According to Mary Nolan at Meredith, 'We could see the little towns were going to have greater trouble surviving, particularly the [community] groups in the town. To do the catering, offering it to them, has meant the survival of some of them'. Visitors spend money in various circumstances, and incomes are earned in equally diverse ways. Context matters enormously – from the demography of audiences, the style of music, the size of host community, the location of the festival site in relation to town and village centres, and proximity or otherwise to major metropolitan centres. Some individual music festivals can be big business, but more typically festivals are significant when places have larger numbers of smaller events spread over the calendar and more deeply embedded in local economies through a range of relationships, capacities and reciprocities. Consequently it has been argued that 'the "out of region" tourist who is a festival-goer is primarily just that, someone who is interested in the festival. To extend visits beyond the festival, both temporally and spatially, would appear to be the challenge' (Saleh and Ryan 1993:297). Seeking to retain festival-goers beyond the festival, and even to return outside the festival period, are almost mantras in the festivals and event management business. Yet such aspirations may not always be widely shared. Host communities may be quite glad the festival only lasts for a weekend and that life returns to normal on Monday morning.

Regional and community development impacts extend well beyond the immediate concerns of financial impact (Moscardo 2008). Hence for the Mayor of tiny Winton (a town of less than 1,000 people) in central-west Queensland: 'The benefit of having the Queensland Music Festival here far outweighs the $40,000 we (the council) put in, it far outreaches it in the value to the community. We're a very proud community, and we're known as one of the friendliest towns – this adds to that recognition' (quoted in Sorensen 2007b:8). As Dwyer et al. (2001:167) argue, 'after all, it is community attachment to the festival that gives rise to economic effects in the first place'. Communities may prefer to create an intimate atmosphere and cherish quality over quantity. Hence the Meredith Music Festival sells limited numbers of tickets via a ballot (half of which are reserved for subscribed community members) and all acts perform on a single stage, unlike other rock music festivals of its type, because 'Meredith's philosophy is quality over quantity'. Festival economics are adjusted accordingly. Nanga Music Festival in Dwellingup is limited to 300 people so that 'artists and patrons can mingle, and there are a maximum of two activities on at the same time' (Rob Phillips, personal communication 2010). Audiences at the Blackwood River Chamber Festival are restricted to no more than 140 people (since it is held in a small church), but it survives regardless. With tickets ranging from $190 to $350, it needed a core audience of 100 to remain viable, but otherwise it 'runs smoothly, with low-key administration and nothing to distract from the music. All it needs to be assured of continuing is another 25 - 30 regular concert-goers. The tickets bought at the end of this Festival for next year's Festival, 2012, have ensured that the books can be balanced for this year'. According to its organiser 'the Shire has never contributed financially to the running of the Festival and local sponsors have been hard to find'. Yet even such a tiny festival makes a contribution in a small place (Bridgetown, with a population of 2,000) through healthy bookings in accommodation and relationships forged with local caterers, chefs and winemakers.

Festivals also enable skill development – most obviously of performers, but also of promoters and managers –and perhaps of local entrepreneurs. They may build confidence and provide a role for otherwise diffident and dissident teenagers and minority groups. Income is inevitably unevenly distributed between the people and places that are involved. So too are the environmental impacts. Festivals can promote places, but ironically they can be disruptive and not to everyone's taste. Difference of opinion may lead to disputes over the location and duration, and some degree of conflict –reflecting how different people perceive not just festivals, but wider society and the role and future of their towns. Such antagonisms and complications are discussed in the following chapter.

Chapter 5

Whose Community? Conflict and Identity

Music festivals have an impact on particular places, most obviously economic, as discussed in the previous chapter, but also social, cultural, environmental and ultimately political. Music festivals make noise and, for some, especially in rural settings, alien noise of any kind is an unwelcome intrusion. Likewise they bring visitors, some of whom may themselves be noisy and even disruptive, or simply exhibit values, behaviours or dress-styles that are unusual, so that economic benefits may clash with social disruption. Sometimes there are simply a lot of visitors. How such issues are assessed and balanced, and by whom, may affect the longevity of festivals, their content, their location, their profitability and their role in regional development. Even where festivals are avowedly to promote local interests, such 'local interests' are never homogeneous, may be perceived in quite different ways and can be contested. Festivals can therefore be the instigator and site of political struggles but they can also bring communities together, however temporarily and tentatively, in shaping a common goal of celebrating local place. Indeed most music festivals – other than some of the more commercial – are intricately linked to particular places and intended to promote, internally and externally, a sense of place and community.

Festivals can be controversial, through issues such as the operation and control of events, perceptions of public nuisance and environmental degradation, and apparent incursions of outsiders into quiet communities. They have sometimes engendered strong criticism and opposition from local residents, though music and the presumption of visiting 'hordes' have always triggered moral panic. Acquiescence and recognition of benefits may now be more probable, despite congestion and disruption, while smaller, more obviously community festivals with local participation have fared much better. Opposition to festivals tends to become greater as the festival becomes larger, and as the number of visitors, as in most facets of tourism, grows to the extent that it affects 'community carrying capacity' (Beeton 2006). Local people feel overwhelmed, even if only over a long weekend, as the festival appears beyond local control and ownership, and environmental pressures become evident.

Local Community

Many of the social issues that surround festivals concern local participation. Who runs the festivals? What happens to the profits? Who provides the inputs? Who are the volunteers to marshal the traffic and crowds? Who will run the cake stalls and sell the raffle tickets? Such issues are mundane but crucial, and can become sources of friction if some feel excluded (or wish to be excluded) and others resent being called upon year after year but perceive few real gains. Who then do local festivals belong to and who experiences the costs and benefits? Music festivals, like any festivals, may promote social cohesion and a sense of belonging, but may just as easily alienate local people and discourage their participation. Much depends on the nature of the festival (and even its timing), the organisational structure and goals, and how it is first introduced and organised.

Although seemingly largely homogeneous in ethnic terms, Australian country towns are divided in other ways. Some of this is reflected in divisions between the 'established' residents, said to have their kin in the churchyards, and recent arrivals, but also by personal preferences, whims and foibles – though the extreme divisions that once divided country towns have largely gone. Contemporary divisions nevertheless mean that towns are never homogeneous communities and divisions are obvious in football teams and sports codes, churches, schools, clubs, politics and, of course, in residential divisions by age, class and income. There are different sides of the railway tracks and the main streets.

Only occasionally are such divisions entirely transcended, and community festivals can be one means of doing this. Even so, while it is commonly said that 'festivals are an expression of local identity and reflect the internal life of the community' (Derrett 2009:107), communities are inherently divided, and all kinds of music, like other cultural pursuits, have both adherents and detractors (though the latter may simply be tolerant). Gaining community support may not therefore be easy. Even the most overt and inclusive planning and communication cannot be comprehensive and nor can all decisions be without contention; belonging and emotional connection are not easily created (Schwarz and Tait 2007). Events of various kinds nurture resilience, community and a sense of belonging, where different groups of local people, the media and local organisations combine towards a single goal, though even then integrating diverse groups and objectives sometimes means that such ventures can be short-lived (Connell and McManus 2011). While 'festivals seem to satisfy an instinct for community … and sustain a shared sense of occasion and excitement' (Derrett 2009:107) this may be quite transient. Moreover while a sense of shared community is evident amongst those participating in festivals, whether local residents or visitors, festivals also exclude some people. Not everyone feels the need to support or attend a festival centred on a musical genre that is not to their taste, or that transforms a familiar environment into a mass of noisy, sometimes unruly visitors. In Parkes a quarter of the townsfolk go about their business as they would do any other weekend, ignoring the festival, and others leave town, though actual hostility is slight. Likewise creating formal support for a festival, whether in councils or the private sector, and these overlap, can be challenging.

Festival success usually results in greater local support, as visitors patronise local businesses and income is generated, and local people gradually become more involved. After a decade of growing commercial success Parkes' Elvis Festival eventually drew in many of the local community. Over half the local population participated, some gained additional employment and wages and many were volunteers or engaged in home hosting visitors (Chapter 6). Not only were local people more involved but the 'local' community actually expanded; fully a third of households had friends and relatives coming to stay with them over the festival period, and so caught up with them. Unsurprisingly, following both social and economic benefits, indifference and inertia turned into support. Elsewhere, on the other hand, commercialisation may threaten gains by creating new divisions, so raising questions over participation and ownership.

Organising festivals is demanding, and it is unsurprising that festivals like at Parkes and Tamworth have a full-time council official dealing with management, while others work on related tourism and business issues. Smaller festivals may be run entirely by volunteers, creating a huge burden of work and responsibility. Derrett argues that such volunteers 'choose how they can formally and informally best collaborate with and lead like-minded folk to deliver a festival that authentically represents the best interests of other residents' (2009:107). But that assumes both that such organisers are altruistic, and also that the 'best interests' of others are knowable and wholly shared. In practice organisers are highly likely to be self-interested – it is *their* festival – and to have objectives (such as hiring particular bands or food companies) that satisfy their own needs and, where commerce is involved, may threaten the self-interests of others. Nonetheless, most festivals purport to represent and support their towns and have formalised community goals (Chapter 4).

Festival organisation and management require financial acumen, entrepreneurial ability, advertising flair and, above all, a wealth of connections (in the media, with business, schools, clubs, and with local people). The challenge is to build social networks and balance these effectively without alienating key groups, and so develop a sense of trust between multiple partners. The complexities of organisation demand knowledge of food marketing, insurance and legal requirements, tax provisions and, not least, the structure and operation of the local community. Not all regional festivals have been able to call upon such rare individuals or even committees. Moreover demands and needs change. Staging festivals may provide 'a fresh and constantly renewing experience, an elixir that keeps community relevant and responsive to the needs of the times' (Derrett 2009:109). Yet they may just as easily fall behind the times and stagnate as vested interests refuse to change, new ideas are passed over, power relations worsen, inflexibility dominates and other festivals innovate and change.

Numerous festivals were begun by a small group of people, sometimes just a couple, as in Parkes and Opera in the Paddock, with no official status – supported only by their own enthusiasm and capital, and later by a handful of like-minded enthusiasts. Meredith Music Festival began in 1991 as 'a party out in the bush' for 200 family, 'friends and friends-of-friends' of the Nolan farming family, who held it on their 1100 acre farm, 'just far enough away where everyone could come and stay the night and no one would be tempted to drive home … no one knew what it would evolve into'. In Parkes the early supporters of the Elvis Festival primarily experienced opprobrium and opposition, Bermagui ignored the Four Winds Festival while Inverell Council attached no significance to a night of opera in a paddock fifteen kilometres out of town. Only when they began to become successful, and the towns received obvious economic benefits, did the councils belatedly support them.

It is rare for everyone to be subsumed in common purpose, and even rarer for harmony and unity to survive over the years, as sponsors and committee members come and go, and festivals change size, focus and content. Many festival committee members have local business interests, and while that may lead to sponsorship, it may also lead to conflicts over the location of venues and particular events. Media promotion and sponsorship in cash or kind can be invaluable. Much the largest venue in Parkes is Woolworths' undercover car park in the town centre, where the Sunday morning Elvis gospel service is held, for a crowd of about 2,000 people. Without access to that venue the service would have to be held in a much smaller or more peripheral location.

At their most successful festivals can create and nourish social capital in small towns, loosely a greater sense of cooperation, goodwill, harmony, trust, belonging and reciprocity, that contribute to some greater sense of local connectivity and wellbeing, but that is difficult to demonstrate because it is largely immeasurable (Arcodia and Whitford 2006). Festivals certainly create and renew social networks, sustain and stimulate local entrepreneurs, and engender new skills, all of which may be renewed annually (or more frequently where many festivals occur in a particular town). They can literally provide a stage for local talent and outlets for local goods, and 'create a positive image of the host community, instil community pride, promote clean-ups and fix-ups and make business sponsors happy' (Mayerfield and Crompton 1995: 41). Physical benefits may even be derived from new infrastructure. Over and over again in Parkes local people simply said 'The Festival is a wonderful thing for Parkes' without feeling any need to specify particular social or economic benefits. Their psychological wellbeing was evident, but that too is intangible, just as it is for the participants (e.g. Packer and Ballantyne 2010). Indeed, even when festivals barely make money and local businesses gain little or nothing, local people and businesses still remain supportive due to less tangible benefits, such as creating a positive image for towns, bringing in tourists and 'bringing the community together' (Wood and Thomas 2009: 156). Moreover there is an inherent value in participation, even passively, as an escape from routine.

Over time the leaders, even visionaries, who initiated festivals get older; their commitment, energy and enthusiasm for innovation may flag, and at various festivals, without new volunteers and new ideas, festivals may fade or disappear (e.g. Derrett 2009; Davies 2011; Schwarz and Tait 2007). Alternatively commodification results in the structure of the festivals becoming routine, and a sense of excitement and spontaneity disappears under the dead weight of predictability and homogeneity.

As festivals become established and grow larger there is a possibility that they become normative, repetitious, and ultimately, mundane.

Festivals have occasionally floundered and failed – but it is inevitably hard to know how many and why they failed, without detailed local knowledge, and that local knowledge often disappears alongside the failed festival. Even successful festivals have gone through difficult periods. The Meredith Music Festival was evicted from its original site by government authorities who determined it was contravening crown land covenants – forcing its farming family hosts to quickly find (and invest significant infrastructure in) an alternative location elsewhere on the property. The Parkes Festival would have collapsed after a few years, when drought, bush fires and local indifference threatened it, had not the council and rugby team supported it just in time. Council support gave the festival legitimacy, enabling it to receive more wide-ranging sponsorship and more effective promotion (Chapter 6). Even usually successful festivals have missed years for particular reasons or, as at Bermagui, become biennial to reduce the burdens of organisation for a small group of people. Others have radically changed structure and 'ownership', as the outcome of dissent or debt (as happened at Goulburn).

More obviously commercial festivals may be more likely to cease, when profitability declines. The Offshore Festival at Torquay (Victoria), close to the famous surfing beach, was successful in the late 1990s – selling 20,000 tickets in 2000 – but was opposed by a small group of local residents who campaigned against the festival, and resorted to legal channels when their requests that the music end at midnight were ignored. The festival was consequently unable to gain a liquor licence in 2001 and then closed down. Similarly the York Jazz Festival (WA) ran successfully for many years until 2009 when it became impossible to continue 'due to a hostile and divided local community and a constantly whinging jazz community in WA' (K. Lee, personal communication 2010). Earthcore, a rave dance party in Toolangi Forest north of Melbourne, closed down in 2008 after fifteen years, after its promoter declared 'it's done its cycle. I'm shutting it, and it's the end of an era', as negative media reports, conflict over environmental objectives and the demands of scheduling the event took their toll (Drever 2008). Variants on bloated ego trips, incompetence, thievery, bad booking choices, risky bets, and poor management have posed problems for commercial festivals elsewhere. The Great Southern Blues Festival was run successfully in Narooma (NSW) for many years before new owners, with commercial intent, moved it to larger premises (and a larger town) at Batemans Bay, in the hope of selling more tickets. But fans loyal to the festival and to Narooma dissented, and in 2011 the festival had to be cancelled due to low ticket sales. In contrast, smaller community festivals have fewer costs and more formal organisation, take fewer risks and may be bailed out by local councils if disaster strikes.

Authenticity, Credibility and Meaning

Festivals have powerful symbolic dimensions, which partly explain some local opposition. They represent social practices, constituted within cultural, economic and political actions and networks: 'Festivals are cultural artefacts which are not simply bought and "consumed" but which are also accorded meaning through their active incorporation into people's lives' (Waterman 1998:56). The content of festivals is highly important for the participation of both local people and visitors and for the ability to secure their subsequent involvement, hence the need for the right content and ambience. Contemporary festivals, even in a more commercial era, involve personal experiences, and in smaller towns this is more obviously so. For participants the actual meaning of participation, and the pleasure gained from this, is the most significant dimension of festivals. Although some organisers go to great lengths to improve based on visitor feedback, cultural meaning may count for little to other promoters with more narrow concerns over logistics and profit margins.

Intense experiences linking participants with festivals are argued to have been most prevalent in the 1960s, hence in some part the continued nostalgia for the era that produced Woodstock, Monterey, the Isle of Wight and the emergence of Glastonbury. For current festival-goers who are also baby-boomers, this coincides with the years of their adolescence, first loves, first (sometimes fast) cars, and with the heyday of Elvis Presley. Festivals often stress nostalgia, including Wintersun (Mackellar 2009b), Ararat's Jailhouse Rock Festival (Victoria) and the GarterBelts and Gasoline Nostalgia Festival (Mount Tamborine, Queensland): 'a celebration of the cars, music, art, movies and culture born from the 1940s and 1950s. The weekend will feature the hot rod carnivale, vintage markets and traders, live rockabilly, western swing and roots music, a vintage soap box derby, pin up booth, "kustom kulture art" exhibition, nostalgia movies and much much more'. The Kurri Kurri Nostalgia Festival developed a strong community and volunteer base and thrived, filling the entire town's accommodation out of season. Its website promises: 'We look forward to seeing lots of dancing, polished cars, hot rods, swing skirts, retro fashion and smiling faces. Catch Elvis on the pavement, you'll find Marilyn roaming too. You can also enjoy stilt walkers, rock 'n' roll duos and ukulele fun'. Festival-goers of a certain age dominate, and are highly committed to, such festivals.

Both content and place are important, and music festivals may reflect the changing nature of the places in which they are hosted. Increasing recognition of the importance of social cohesion has seen places like Dubbo (NSW) host an Aboriginal music festival and Woolgoolga in northern NSW stage a festival celebrating Sikh music, food and culture (Sikhs being the largest migrant group in town). In the early twentieth century Barraba, north of Tamworth, was a thriving asbestos mining town; now it is nearly deserted but, with a dose of irony, has hosted two festivals whose titles play on this decline: Australia's Smallest Country Music Festival and Australia's Smallest Jazz and Blues Festival. Centres of alternative culture like Bellingen, with its Global Carnival (Chapter 2), host festivals that celebrate difference, grass-roots politics and environmental themes.

Credibility may also be acquired in unexpected ways, even when no link to place and past ever existed. An Elvis Festival may seem to have no resonance with an Australian country town (especially since Elvis never left the northern hemisphere) yet the acquisition of a large collection of memorabilia in 2008 enabled Parkes to set up a new museum (the 'King's Castle') that gave Elvis a permanent if vicarious home in town and the Festival a year-long presence. At Meredith, it was the presence of an open-minded farming couple who let their son and his friends organise rowdy rock festivals on their land. At Wangaratta in the 1980s, local people sought to establish a festival, and decided upon jazz, because there were then few other jazz festivals in Australia, though the town had no contemporary or past links to jazz performance or performers. Over time clever management brought many of the best Australian and overseas artists to the town, and Wangaratta acquired new status as the definitive jazz festival centre (Curtis 2010). Certainly authenticity and credibility are valued. As one visitor to the Brigadoon Scottish Festival said: 'I'm disappointed that I don't have Scottish heritage … I think because I feel a sense of connection here, but history tells me that I shouldn't feel it' (quoted in Ruting and Li 2011:278). Distinctiveness in any form gave festivals a memorable and usually positive presence.

As festivals become larger, distinctiveness and credibility can disappear, subsumed under a growing veneer and reality of commercialism. For one observer in England, by the end of the twentieth century: 'the gatherings of the nineties are far removed from the laid-back smaller-scale festivals of the late sixties and early seventies. Today's festivals … seem to be more about making money, flogging products and squeezing in punters than peace, love and harmony' (Jones 1998:2). Even in Parkes, where credibility was at best tenuous, both local people and visitors feared the Festival being swamped by commercialism: 'I hope the Festival as originally intended maintains its integrity' and 'I believe that it has lost the plot and is too commercialised now'. Others criticised the trivialisation of Elvis Presley though bad impersonators (Chapter 6). For some, bigger was by no means better. At Brigadoon, some elements of the festival were seen as detrimental to Scottish authenticity, including stalls selling 'ethnic' foods (Chinese and Turkish cuisines) or merely not selling anything Scottish, while sponsorship too was seen as compromising the festival spirit (Ruting and Li 2011:276). But at both these festivals, and others, most visitors were neither concerned with authenticity, or about its diminution, but simply wanted an enjoyable time. Meaning, identity, music and commercialism cohabit uneasily in festival promotion and performance.

Where festivals have become recognised in regional economic planning, they have often gained more media interest, tourist arrivals, commercial sponsorship, professional coordination and investment from government. Local debates emerge about the directions, meanings and impacts of more slickly-run, professional events. Even though some larger, more established festivals continue to be governed by non-profit organisations, and usually retain social and community goals, they now employ expert event managers, and may marginalise – or even simply replace – grass-roots local participation in their management (Davies 2011). As this professionalisation occurs, festivals may struggle to retain a sense of local ownership and belonging. A tension thus characterises festivals: recognition marks their success as a means of alternative economic development, and further promotion may enhance this. But this might only prove welcome if sympathetic to the spontaneity and enthusiasm that inspired local people to stage festivals in the first place, and the social empowerment that followed local involvement and success.

A Place for Local People?

Festivals are rarely established without some opposition – more formally on planning grounds, where the impacts of crowds on public safety, noise and the environment are of concern. Or, scarcely more subtly, there are objections to the kinds of people that festivals might attract – a loose and generalised moral panic. Opposition to festivals has also come from those who saw them as a threat to their notions of what their town should be. Rather later they have been opposed because they have become too large and threaten 'community carrying capacity', or some people's perceptions of that. Festivals necessarily change places as people move in, and the most characteristic opposition to festivals comes from those who resent change, and any disruption to established routines. Weekend festivals clash with shopping, street parades prevent parking close to stores (or other amenities), noise challenges those who prefer peace and quiet. Conservatism is common. Yet most festivals have started small, many have been supported by prominent citizens and have usually been ignored rather than opposed. Indeed, even in many small towns such as Parkes, numerous residents exhibited apathy and disinterest and continued to go about their business as if the festival was invisible. More frequently objections to festivals occur as they grow and impinge on residents' sense of place and sometimes on their actual use of space (Chapter 9). In some contexts festivals have ignored local talent (Chapter 4); in Ireland too, organisers of the Clifden Country Blues Festival attempted to 'package' it for a particular type of overseas tourist: 'There was a deliberate strategy to exclude local bands on the grounds that the quality of musicianship would not be sufficiently high to enhance the event's reputation and to attract audiences to the event' (Quinn 1996:391–92). Festivals are thus not always reflections of local identities and musical expressions, especially as commercial considerations have become dominant.

Despite the many paeans to community and the manner in which festivals bring people together and stimulate togetherness, in practice they can never wholly do that. Invariably some people are excluded, occasionally deliberately, but more often of their own volition; there are other priorities, they dislike that kind (or any kind) of music, noise and crowds, they are old or sick, or they have little in common with those who organise the festival and no sympathy with its objectives. At Parkes, alongside 'traffic congestion' and 'lack of access to shops', others were 'not really bothered by it', 'I don't attend the festival but understand how great it is for the town' and others simply went away. At Bermagui one local resident said

> The Four Winds Festival didn't really hit my radar over the weekend. I was busy with family, and we had plans to go fishing. On Friday afternoon I could hear the drums and stuff, and then we could see from our balcony all these people wandering about over the park. We hadn't a clue what they were doing. No interest in the Four Winds Festival. It's crap. They were all still hanging around the park when we headed off to the pub with friends. (Quoted in Duffy and Waitt 2011:54)

There is after all no reason why any festival should be attractive to the entire heterogeneous population of small town Australia.

In many parts of the world minority groups have been actively excluded from festivals, as they have from other spheres of life, or have felt themselves to be excluded, usually by virtue of ethnicity. Some have developed their own music festivals, where an ethnic or gendered sense of identity has been particularly important, and the creation of a defined and ethnic or gendered space is at least as important as the music (Gibson and Connell 2005:249–51). All Australian towns have an Indigenous Aboriginal and, less frequently, Torres Strait Islander population, sometimes in significant numbers and proportions, but often marginal – economically, socially and spatially – to the functioning of those towns. That marginality is sometimes reflected in their presence, or more frequently absence, from many festivals. Indeed Aboriginal people have commonly established distinctive festivals, to promote their own sense of identity. Many such festivals stand apart from commercial concerns, and most are in relatively remote towns in northern and north-western Australia, or deep in the outback.

State-sponsored festivals like Yeperenye (Alice Springs) unite as many as 14,000 Aboriginal people from across the country, collectively representing 45 language groups. In remote Arnhem Land in northern Australia the Garma festival, held annually at Gulkula since 1999, and established by the famous indigenous band Yothu Yindi, similarly triumphs local Yolngu culture and draws in both Aboriginal and non-Aboriginal visitors, typically about 2,000 people (Gebicki 2003, Phipps 2011). Gulkula is where the ancestor Ganbulabula brought the yidaki (didjeridu) into being, hence it figures prominently, in a festival designed to encourage the practice, preservation and maintenance of traditional dance, song, art and ceremony to ensure local cultural renewal and survival. In several respects education plays a key role, for local Aboriginal people and non-Aboriginal visitors. In every sense such Indigenous festivals are more than merely a weekend social musical event.

Such Indigenous festivals are regarded as essential for preserving, maintaining and celebrating Aboriginal cultures (Neuenfeldt 1995), but also provide a means of expressing the social, economic and political issues that concern Indigenous people. As one participant has pointed out: 'It's about our learning and healing and cultural expressions. In most mainstream festivals the artistic control is done by non-Aboriginal people and we slot in however they see the artistic side' (quoted in Albert 2001:15, cf. Slater 2007, 2010). Furthermore, as one Aboriginal leader has observed: 'Having a festival is a fine thing but where are the structures to help sustain the culture and enable the rest of Australia to have some better insight?' (Patrick Dodson, quoted in Steketee 2001:5). Nonetheless such festivals challenge essentialist presentations and travesties of Aboriginal culture in many commercial shows.

In large parts of more densely settled regional Australia, where Aboriginal populations are small, Indigenous festivals are quite rare. As Anne Marshall from Southeast Regional Arts NSW observed,

> we don't have a lot of Indigenous festivals because there's no money and no interest. This is a red-necked area of the worst kind so … they do have Indigenous festivals like the NAIDOC [National Aboriginal and Islander Day of Commemoration] week celebrations and things like that but there's never been the money or the support and you wouldn't get it out of the community. (personal communication 2007)

Aboriginal people play a marginal role in mainstream festivals, even where they have personal interests in the themes, and most accounts of regional festivals ignore the possibility of an Aboriginal presence. Even the Top Half Folk Festival, at various venues in the Northern Territory, had minimal Aboriginal participation (Duffy 2009). In Tamworth's early days Aboriginal country singers complained of racism from publicans who refused to give them a gig, even though performers such as Jimmy Little were nationally known. In later years Aboriginal people took matters into their own hands and staged Aboriginal-only concerts in community halls under the decentralised management structure of that festival (Chapter 8). Artists such as Troy Cassar-Daley, of Indigenous heritage, became successful at Tamworth in the mainstream arenas but with few patrons aware of his Aboriginality.

At times Indigenous participation may merely be tokenism, and little to do with the local Indigenous population. At the 1997 Opera in the Outback, an Aboriginal choir played a significant part, but some of the audience felt that their inclusion was inappropriate since they were dressed in 'western clothing', and their performance 'did not integrate well with the orchestral music' hence there were calls for more opportunities to see Aboriginal dancing, music and art, a perspective that was probably inconsistent with local Aboriginal traditions (Richard Trembath Research 2007:9, 27). Here and no doubt elsewhere essentialism has sought to confine Aboriginal people to a 'traditional' role. Aboriginal performers themselves struggle with expectations of how they should perform – hence for contemporary Aboriginal rappers from Nowra (NSW) the only opportunities to perform were at wholly-Aboriginal hip-hop festivals; at other mainstream festivals they could only secure paid work performing as 'tribal' dancers and musicians (Warren and Evitt 2010). By contrast (and possibly uniquely) at Bermagui contemporary

Aboriginal music groups and even rap music have been included within a classical festival, and the 2011 Opera in the Paddock included a yidaki (didjeridu) solo 'With acknowledgment to the traditional owners, the Kamilaroi People' (Chapter 7). A growing number of festivals have likewise sought to at least honour the traditional occupants of the places where festivals are staged. The Kurri Kurri Nostalgia Festival thus invites visitors: 'Come and join us for a traditional aboriginal smoking ceremony as we kick off the festival by honouring our heritage and ancestors'. The Waverock Weekender (WA) similarly has a 'welcome to country, encouraging understanding of Nyungar relationship with country'. The High & Dry Festival takes place on land owned by the Metropolitan Aboriginal Land Council, hence its organisers have actively worked to promote Aboriginal employment (Carr 2009). One of the factors accounting for the success of the Woodford Folk Festival has been its consultation with and involvement of the local Aboriginal population (Neuenfeldt 2002); hence Woodford describes itself as Australia's biggest Aboriginal festival. Moreover the largest primarily music festival in closely settled Australia with significant Aboriginal participation is The Dreaming, held at Woodford since 2005, with 'over 200 high profile Indigenous acts from Australia and around the World … complete with ceremony grounds, traditional healing, art galleries, rituals, fire story circles, and workshops … The festival offers an intimate Indigenous experience with an embracing atmosphere described by audiences as awakening, enriching, inspiring and *deadly* [Aboriginal English = awesome]'. In 2008, 13 per cent of the visitors identified as Aboriginal or Torres Strait Islander (and 7 per cent as overseas indigenous, mainly from the Pacific islands and North America), an extraordinarily high proportion in south-eastern Australia. It has been claimed that in 2008 some 140 Aboriginal language groups were involved in the Festival. Such festivals enable encounters between Aboriginal and non-Aboriginal people not possible elsewhere, with some educational benefits.

The Place of Noise

Music festivals produce music that may be perceived as noise, but the form, context (and timing) matter: classical music festivals might have just as detrimental an impact on surrounding noise levels (at least as measured in decibels), and on local parking and traffic congestion, but rarely elicit the same kind of responses as youth rock festivals or techno dance parties. This reflects the wider privileging of, and discrimination against, certain social groups. A politics of 'music as noise' (Attali 1985) is present at festivals; certain genres, particularly those enjoyed by young people, are portrayed as 'not real music' or simply 'noise', unwelcome sounds to ears alienated by the particular style.

Central to negative reactions of local residents are moral panics, where residents fear drugs, alcoholic excess or sexual promiscuity, rather than simply opposing the music. Alien noise is a symbol of alterity and excess. In these cases, residents react to the music, but also to festival-goers as visitors and tourists, in much the same way that other types of tourism elicit resistance, particularly those involving large influxes of people from very different cultural backgrounds to locals. Such perceptions might be based on genuine concerns for local social and environmental issues, previous experience, conservatism towards outsiders and cultural intermixing, implicit racism and belief in generalised representations of young people as 'deviant' and in need of surveillance and control. Indeed not all visitors to festivals are necessarily gentle souls, merely interested in the music. Some are intent on getting drunk or high – clubbing transferred to the country. In 2008 in Parkes both visitors and local people were disturbed by the appearance of a surly and visually aggressive group of Fourth Reich bikies, with swastika adorned leather jackets, out of keeping with the Festival. But in Parkes too, some local youth, resenting outsiders in 'their' pubs and clubs, were aggressive towards them. At the 2011 Yackandandah Folk Festival (Victoria) 'one sour note was a few noisy campers. Turns out they were not even festival-goers and crashed our event. Unfortunately that means that next year we will be paying for security'. Nonetheless these were probably exceptions; panic far outweighs problems and, as at Tasmania's Forth Valley Blues Festival, 'local people not fond of Blues music now choose to vacate on the day, so we have very few complaints about noise' (Lea Coates, personal communication 2010). Elsewhere, as Meredith Music Festival has shown, excessive noise and anti-social behaviour can be managed more effectively with peer pressure than by ramping up the formal security presence – what that festival calls a 'no dickhead policy':

> Essentially this is a self-policing policy whereby 'the dickhead' is not celebrated at the festival. Dickheads or people involved in dickhead behaviour will usually find that a solid citizen will firmly but politely inform them that their dickhead behaviour is not admired or appreciated. The Dickhead will usually realise they are being a dickhead and pull their head in. If not, our Helpers or Staff or even Security might make a discreet intervention. So if you are a Dickhead, this festival isn't for you.

Tensions have arisen especially where the promoters of commercial festivals have sought appropriate locations to stage large events (Chapter 9). The 'original' rave spaces of the late 1980s and early 1990s usually relied on, and transformed, locations associated with purposes other than musical performance. Early raves often took place in rural locations, challenging familiar urban-rural disjunctures, and destabilising 'the perceived axis between urban location and authenticity' (Gilbert and Pearson 1999:23), before later returning to the anonymity of the cities. In Australia the organisers of the Enchanted Forest raves in the 2000s sought beautiful rural locations no more than two hours from Adelaide, but also sought variety by changing these yearly, and specifically sought places where noise would pose no problems. Local residents recorded no disruptions but police often took a more ruthless view of what constituted a noise problem, and moved the raves on. In absolute contrast Lorne, a Victorian town of 1,000 people, was known as a 'trouble spot' due to anti-social behaviour by large crowds that congregated there on New Year's Eve. The arrival of the Falls Festival 'provided young local community members with a safe alternative form of entertainment, leading to a decline in the number of incidents over the New Year's Eve period' while also financially contributing to local community projects (Deloitte Access Economics 2011:46).

Festivals that have emerged from a local community, have rarely generated much antipathy, especially as they have begun from a small base. Opposition has often been around larger, commercial events: a simplistic not-in-my-backyard (NIMBY) response that encourages location in peripheral showgrounds. Opposition has however rarely been focused on noise but either on the wider behaviour of the participants – that centre on rowdiness, drunkenness, debauchery and any number of potential sins – or the environmental impact of the festival, that extends beyond noise pollution.

Environmental Challenges

Festivals bring large numbers of people together in small spaces. Some have been notorious for the environmental damage wrought by crowds living, dancing, performing, toileting and consuming in a tiny area for several days. Yet even the most successful festivals (in terms of environmental management) can never entirely avoid traffic congestion, local frustrations and some degree of tension. How festivals are managed, and local opposition defused, and the specific gains within particular places are crucial to longevity and wider success. Consultation, information provision and discussion are invaluable. This is particularly evident for larger festivals, such as at Byron Bay, although, conversely, environmental impacts may be least where small places support small festivals.

Many of the largest festivals on greenfield sites outside town boundaries have developed explicit environmental policies, posted on their web pages, such as that for Woodford. Indeed, with the number of visitors having grown from 900 at the first Maleny festival in 1987 to 20,000 per day for six days by 2009, the festival had little choice. Even the site, owned by the festival, has been enlarged through adjacent land acquisition and transformed (with more than 80,000 native trees planted) into a 202 hectare park. A $1.1 million waste treatment plant, funded by the Queensland and Federal Governments, was set up on site that would save it $200,000 a year in cartage fees, reduce the event's carbon emissions by 11 per cent and provide 7 mega litres of water a year for irrigation: 'The carbon neutral plant uses a sequence of 14 processes to convert waste into water that will be used to irrigate the land' (Soppe 2009:5; Wright 2009). Capital works programmes at the site have included the upgrading of services including sewerage, potable water, traffic control, parking, camping areas, electricity supply, garbage collection and other amenities. Woodford's formal Environment Policy starts by emphasising that 'The Queensland Folk Federation is committed to environmental sustainability …

our first responsibility is to create a safe and healthy site for the Festival friends. As land managers we believe we have an obligation to conserve and enhance the natural environment. Through this policy we set out to become a leader amongst cultural organisations in environmental matters'. That leadership involves policies on tree planting (including to 'actively pursue the planting of rare and endangered species endemic to the area'), erosion, recycling, sewerage, public transport, education and advocacy.

At many festivals, especially on greenfield sites, festivals have developed improved on-site environmental management practices. At 2009 Splendour in the Grass, patrons paid an extra amount on each beer can as a 'recycling tax', but could return their empty beer cans and receive a ticket redeemable for their next drink. According to Di Stefano and Lee 'The effect of this system was mayhem. Skinflints ran around the festival pilfering through wheelie bins, approaching drinkers and trading in time watching bands for time aluminium scabbing' (2009:12). However, more than 98 per cent of all cans sold were recycled, offsetting more than 630 tonnes of greenhouse emissions. Such schemes are more typical of larger events. In our festival survey, only a third had an environmental management strategy or local environmental plan; one quarter was compelled by local authorities to complete a development application or environmental impact statement and, of those that were not, less than a quarter undertook an environmental impact study voluntarily. 'Green' initiatives remain largely ad hoc, and are often about marketing and being seen to 'do the right thing'.

By contrast some festivals have more exemplary procedures. At Peat's Ridge, where the Festival now calls itself the Peats Ridge Sustainable Arts and Music Festival, these involve composting toilets, biodiesel generators, and organic waste disposal. It claims

> many industry and even world leading initiatives in practice at the Festival. Just a few of these initiatives include 100 percent renewable energy to run our office and onsite through solar and biodiesel generators, reduced flush onsite toilets, grey water management and reuse, a container deposit system, organic waste composting, reclaimed materials for decoration, solar thermal showers, certified organic food at our stalls, biodegradable cutlery, onsite bike couriers, soy based ink printing and natural cleaning products.

The Falls Festival has taken similar initiatives, with a mission statement where the festivals seek to 'create pioneering and dynamic sustainable and responsible festivals that celebrate and facilitate deep social, cultural and environmental engagement and connectedness giving young at heart music lovers a unique and extraordinary experience'. In 2009 the Lorne event (Victoria) alone produced 29 tonnes of recycling, and the flush-free composting toilets were estimated to have saved 91,200 litres of fresh drinking water (Falls Festival 2010). Peat's Ridge also requires food stalls to have a minimum of 50 per cent organic produce, prevents Coke and other brand name juices being sold, and only permits organic soft drinks and wine. The range of innovative developments at both Peat's Ridge and Falls has resulted in both being regarded as global leaders (Jones 2009). On a smaller scale many festivals, such as the Dingo Creek Jazz and Blues Festival, stress 'Please show consideration and remember this is a no BYO alcohol, no glass venue and please don't bring your pets'. The Nannup Music Festival (WA) proudly proclaims itself smoke-free. The Dorrigo Folk and Bluegrass Festival has made performance areas 'smoke, drug and alcohol and dog free'. At Meredith, at the very start of the festival, the crowd will choose a 'clean-up song' (in 2010 it was Missy Elliot's *Get Ur Freak On*) and 'a couple of times each day the song comes on and it's a cue for everyone to pick up the trash around them (cans, bottles, food etc.). It really promotes that community vibe that Meredith is so famous for' (Elyse Stanes, pers. com. 2011). The Bermagui Festival of Four Winds has sought to develop specific environmental policies that would turn it into a carbon positive festival that would feed energy into the grid, and has also sought to make the whole site 'zero landfill' by not selling such things as disposable plastic wine 'glasses' (Chapter 7). The Opera in the Paddock sells nothing and most visitors recycle all their own waste. Even in Parkes, where there are over 10,000 visitors, any visible environmental impact has gone within twenty-four hours (discounting the carbon emissions produced in getting there). Such directions are rather easier for smaller festivals, over shorter time periods, and also perhaps where visitors are organised enough to bring their own wine glasses and similar goods. Nonetheless by far the largest environmental impacts of festivals are not on-site, but rather the carbon emissions required transporting visitors to them – up to 80 per cent of the total ecological footprint in the case of festivals with high levels of car dependency (Gibson and Wong 2011). Some events such as Splendour in the Grass in Byron Bay are aware of this and provide bus services from major cities or offset ticket pricing that incorporates a travel component. At many other events, however, how to reduce the environmental impacts of travel remains an unexamined and unanswered challenge.

Challenges to environmental sustainability come from the remote location of many festivals, the need to travel by car and the ensuing carbon footprint. More than 70 per cent of out-of-town visitors to Parkes travelled by car; some 86 per cent of visitors to Woodford went by car partly because it is otherwise largely inaccessible and partly because it is a 'live-in' festival so tents, clothes and other goods must be carried. Woodford encourages, somewhat forlornly, use of public transport and The Falls has a festival–run public transport system linking the site to local townships. In 2010 it also offset an estimated 125 tonnes of greenhouse gas (up from 90 tonnes in 2009) through investments in wind farms in Gujarat, India (Falls Festival 2010). At similar out-of-town festivals, such as Opera in the Paddock and Peat's Ridge, the only realistic means of access is by road, but organisers have encouraged visitors to car-pool or travel in special buses. Alongside carbon emissions, cars create traffic congestion. When the Splendour in the Grass festival moved from Byron Bay to Woodford in 2010,

> someone forgot to factor in that thousands of cars can't all smoothly enter and exit via the same road … As punters desperate to catch their flights broke down fences and trespassed over property, word had it that organisers had to pay an adjoining farm owner $20,000 to ease traffic through his property onto the highway. (*The Brag* 2010)

Waste management similarly is a perennial concern. At the 2010 Splendour in the Grass festival at Woodford 'the soulless and trash-strewn paddocks most campers found themselves in for the weekend won few fans' (Connellan and Mack 2010:10).

A number of festivals have deliberately chosen idyllic out of town locations where contact with 'nature' is heightened, but pressures to be environmentally conscious are even greater. The Bilyana Festival of Folk Rhythm, whose webpage invites visitors to 'walk in the hills, swim in the creek [and] do not bring any booze and bad attitudes' is one of many festivals in a 'truly amazing natural amphitheatre' with a creek that surrounds the stage and the property, adjoining the Chiltern Mt Pilot National Park, at Eldorado in rural Victoria. The Festival was established at the family farm of Hamish Skermer, described as the 'music world's king of the compost toilet' and who describes himself as 'an un-Kenny' (Shedden 2011b), hence the Bilyana Festival is distinctively environmentally conscious. A handful of festivals have embraced a wholly environmental perspective. The 2010 Ballarat Acoustic Music Festival, that coincided with global Earth Hour, was a festival with no beer, no electricity (hence no PA system) and no roadies, resulting in hundreds of visitors filling previously unknown or seldom-used venues for a 'truly unique live music experience'. A range of musicians and groups, from classical to country, were illuminated with candles and fuel lanterns and 'it just gave out that amazing warm candle-lit glow'.

Outside the few relatively large commercial festivals in regional Australia, most are quite small, with rarely more than 10,000 visitors sometimes spread over several days and over a wide area, hence the kinds of human problems that occur at larger festivals – such as crowd violence and crushing, over-indulgence in drugs or injuries from diving into 'mosh pits' – are almost entirely absent, and the kinds of sophisticated crowd management needed there are unnecessary. Risk management is less crucial. Nonetheless numerous Tamworth visitors also had to visit the hospital (Chapter 4) and in 2009 at Splendour in the Grass (Byron Bay):

> Outside the grounds, young and old jockeyed good drug deals for themselves and their friends. Fluoro boys shelved pills, and that hippie with her basket of homebaked goods still indiscreetly provided a kitchen to tent service. Yet this year the chemical access was much less … there were 89 warnings for cannabis possession and 129 unlucky others who had to face court for pills and powder. One creepy 30 year old was busted with 120 pills on his person'. (Di Stefano and Lee 2009:12)

Such problems partly explain emerging local distaste for the festival (Chapter 9). Otherwise dehydration, drunkenness, rowdiness and sunburn are the usual limits of regional festival problems, and rarely do these cause much reaction. Concern over the social and environmental impacts of festivals is thus usually associated with a small number of very large festivals.

While concerts and festival-goers may usually be thought of as inflicting damage on the environment, in some cases the converse is true. As the *Sydney Morning Herald* recorded of the 2010 Four Winds Festival:

> A light shower crescendoed to a thundering downpour, drowning out the subtleties of ninth-century chants and washing away the road, to leave 1,000 music lovers stranded in a field with little more than music and oysters to keep us going. There are worse fates. (Cunningham 2010)

Festivals run obvious environmental risks of rather different kinds. Overall, as the organiser and founder of the Falls Festival, Simon Daly, has argued: 'The music industry, which is often seen as not being the cleanest living business, has been a bit of a frontrunner in going green' (quoted in Shedden 2007) – especially at festivals, where making efforts towards reducing harm is increasingly important.

Discord and Harmony

In certain contexts, festivals may be divisive. No musical festivals, if they can be so described, are more political than the sectarian religious marches of Northern Ireland, that are a deliberate, dramatic and confrontational invoking of the history, religion and tradition of Protestant settlers. Wagner Festivals in Bayreuth have been controversial for Wagner's associations with German nationalism, and his descendants with national socialism. But such extremes are rare and conflicts over music festivals are more usually about such banal, yet important, issues as noise, congestion, disruption, who profits, and whether staging a festival is worthwhile for economic and social reasons. Moreover most festivals exist without significant conflicts, can easily be avoided if intolerable, and more often demonstrate how a range of people come together to work towards a common goal. Cooperation may extend regionally; on the South Coast of NSW the Merimbula Jazz Festival takes place in June, and the Moruya Jazz Festival in October, choreographed to mesh with each other and with other regional activities.

More subtle issues reflect notions of authenticity, credibility and local identity, as festivals give participants the opportunity to express identity and negotiate themes of belonging, whether to local places or to musical communities. Perhaps, in a few cases, they really do 'permit encounters with authentic expressions of culture' (Derrett 2009:108) but that is debatable in the commercialised festival scene. What they certainly do is create and/or enhance images of particular places, and simply having a festival, which in itself suggests 'an appealing and consolidated sense of community' (Derrett 2009:108), however erroneous that might be, is invaluable. In the vast majority of places people who were once sceptical or uninterested have become participants in and supporters of local festivals. Only the largest commercial festivals have been 'forced' out of town (Chapter 9).

Festivals fail when they become inflexible and predictable - the fate of many agricultural shows (especially in a post-productivist countryside) - and flexibility may not always be easy to achieve, when 'tradition' and 'authenticity', however these may be perceived, are argued to be what sustains many festivals. Flexibility is also improbable when unchanging committees merely relive past glories and reject innovation. Yet the vast majority of festivals have thrived rather than died. The second part of this book examines how some festivals have succeeded and how the range of economic social and environmental issues discussed thus far come together in particular places.

PART II
MUSIC FESTIVALS:
REINVENTING
REGIONAL PLACES

Chapter 6
Parkes: Australia's 'Elvis-town'

> If these things don't happen for these communities they'll die. It's as simple as that. And every place has to have something like this. I guess Parkes is lucky in a way because Parkes has a 'thing' that they can put their own stamp on. Because a lot of cities don't have that … they have festivals but they are only relevant to their own communities – whereas Elvis is relevant to the whole world. (Parkes Festival visitor, 2007)

The growth of the Elvis Festival in Parkes highlights how a remote place with constrained economic prospects has created a valuable tourist resource, and subsequently captured national publicity, through a festival based around commemoration of the birthday of Elvis Presley, a performer who had never visited Australia, and certainly not Parkes, nor had any conceivable links to the town. Indeed, Elvis rarely left the American south. As one festival visitor said: it was 'a random concept in a random place'. Its eventual huge success demonstrates how a festival can emerge, against the odds, and how a new 'tradition' can be constructed in a place. Small places, even in remote areas, can develop economic activities through festivals, and create new identities – albeit often contested.

Parkes is a small NSW country town of 10,000 people 350 kilometres from Sydney (Figure 6.1). Like many other inland country towns, it has higher than average unemployment rates, low levels of participation in the labour force (41 per cent of the total population), incomes that are three quarters the national average, and its population has steadily become dominated by those of retirement age (17 per cent being over 65 in 2006). Between 1996 and 2001 Parkes lost 4 per cent of its population, but that has subsequently stabilised at the expense of smaller surrounding towns and it is regularly present at the annual Country Week Expos in Sydney, trying to stimulate urban-rural migration (Connell and McManus 2011). Parkes is essentially a service centre for a part of Australia's wheat-sheep belt, and was plagued with drought for most of the twenty-first century. Farmers have sought to diversify into other crops such as canola, but the precarious nature of wheat exports still troubles the town. Other than its historic radio telescope ('The Dish'), a vital link in the 1969 Apollo moon landing (which became, in 2000, the subject of a popular Australian feature film of the same name), Parkes has little in the way of visitor attractions.

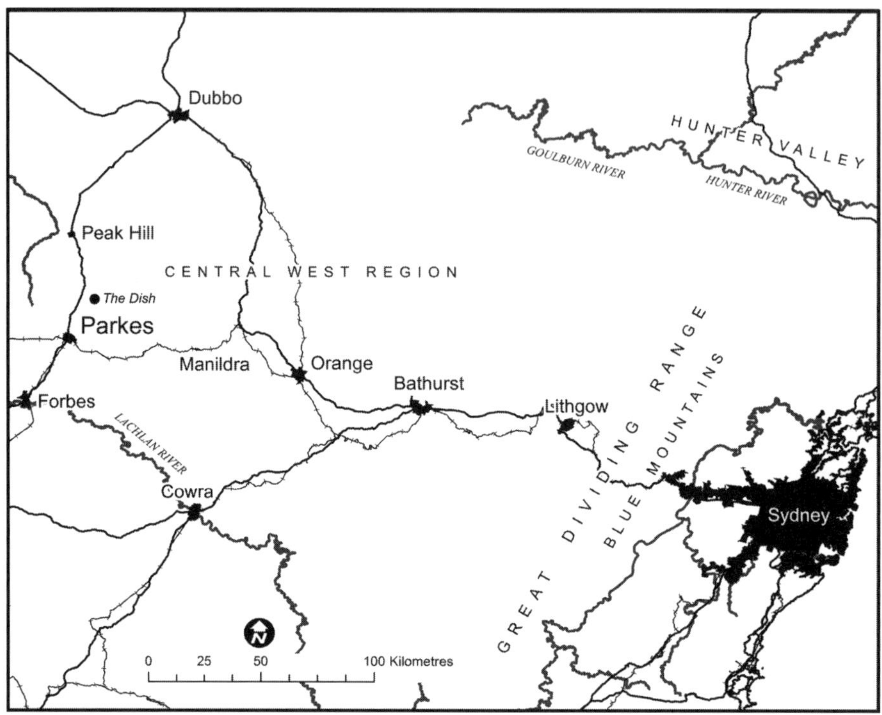

Figure 6.1   Location map, Parkes

Elvis Arrives in Town

The emergence of the Elvis Presley Revival Festival in Parkes was entirely the result of a chance local whim, when a couple of local people, devoted to the memory of Elvis, proposed the idea to local council members, as recalled by one of them, Neville 'Elvis' Lennox:

> It was Bob and Anne Steel up at Gracelands restaurant. They're big Elvis fans and they own the restaurant. They were just having a bit of a talk to the right people at the right time, at one of their functions. They were councillors and they said, "Well there's nothing going on, nothing celebrated that time of year. Elvis's birthday's the eighth. Come along to the next council meeting, we'll put it to the board." It just evolved from there. (personal communication 2004)

Parkes happened to have a club and restaurant called Gracelands, the name (almost) of Elvis' home in Memphis, and a small group of committed fans willing to organise an event. An Elvis Revival committee was formed and, in 1992, what was essentially a very small group of local fans decided to stage Australia's first Elvis festival. The first Elvis Revival Weekend was held in January 1993

(Figure 6.2), coinciding with Elvis' birthday. It began with a dinner organised by Bob Steel, attended by 250 mainly local residents along with one Elvis impersonator. The weekend attracted 500 people from as far as Adelaide, Melbourne and Sydney, and set the theme for those that followed, with Elvis and Priscilla look-alike competitions, a street parade with vintage cars, shop window displays of posters and memorabilia, Elvis movies at the cinema (now closed), and concerts, one of which was at the Gracelands Club.

Figure 6.2   Inaugural Parkes Elvis Revival Festival. Newspaper advertisement, 1993

Source: Brennan-Horley, Connell and Gibson 2007:74

The first festivals were largely ignored by the local media as inappropriate or trivial, despite the dearth of news in midsummer, and that oversight only partially diminished in later years. By contrast, the national media regularly covered the Festival, invariably because of its curiosity value, and as a result of claims by the organising committee that it was keen for Parkes to become the 'Elvis capital' of Australia. For Bob Steel, then chair of the organising committee, the lead-up to the first festival hinted at such national publicity:

> We have been overwhelmed with the attention this festival is receiving. For example, even the *Melbourne Truth* ran an article on the festival, suggesting that we could become the Elvis capital of Australia. Newspapers, television and radio stations have all been giving the festival plenty of coverage and if nothing else, it has certainly given Parkes publicity. (Quoted in the *Parkes Champion Post* 8 January 1993:5)

Ironically this kind of national coverage, and its celebration of tackiness and kitsch, has probably drawn most visitors.

The gradual emergence of Parkes as Australia's Elvis capital played a pivotal role in influencing Neville Lennox to take on the icon's name:

> I prefer Elvis to Neville, me original first name. After the first two years of competition here in the look-alikes – I won that in 93, 94 – and walking up the street or down the street, and you hear people yell out across the street at ya "g'day Elvis" and that. And I said, 'ya know, that would be an idea'. So I put it to me mother, asked her permission to do so and she said "you go ahead and do with it what you want." And I said, "thank you very much", paid 75 dollars and had it legally changed. (personal communication 2004)

An avid collector, Lennox had amassed a formidable amount of Elvis paraphernalia, some of which came from a personal trip to the real Graceland in Memphis in 1997, the same year as his name change:

> I spent four and a half thousand dollars when we were there and had to send half ahead of myself to get back home here. I went over with two suitcases and came home with nine … had to buy an extra set of luggage while I was there. I bought books, pens, watches, bottles of Coca Cola that had Elvis's twentieth anniversary on them – whatever I could get. (personal communication 2004)

His was a catalytic and inspirational influence and both he and his wife, and Bob Steel and his wife, were still serving on the committee eighteen years later.

In its second year, the festival brought visitors from further afield, including Western Australia and Queensland, and added a clambake at Gracelands, with sand and surfboards brought in to transform the car park. The Parkes Tourism

Promotions Officer heralded it a success, and recognised that it had the potential to become an integral part of the annual events calendar:

> The event will provide substantial tourism value for Parkes, in terms of publicity and in cold, hard revenue. The revival could well become a role model for other interest groups keen to promote their festival. A hard core of Elvis stalwarts researched and marketed the concept and banded together to form an effective working team. (*Parkes Champion Post* 5 January 1994:1)

The then Parkes Tourism Manager Kelly Atkinson noted 'The tourism board and council together recognised that January was a very quiet time of year. They were trying to introduce more events onto the calendar having identified tourism as a key market to target' (personal communication 2004). While this suited the pragmatic aim of the local council of the time, namely to improve summer tourism, there was no great local support.

Although interest grew steadily, the organisation of early festivals was a struggle, without local experience of event management and in a less that wholly supportive environment. January in inland Australia is not the obvious time to stage a festival, especially where that involves dressing up and performing outdoors. Maximum daytime temperatures are usually well into the 30s and in 2010 (and other years) even passed 40 degrees Celsius. Residents characteristically took holidays on the coast at that time. Both floods and bushfires prevented access to Parkes in some of the early years. What probably saved the Festival from oblivion was the entry of the local Parkes Rugby Club as enthusiastic supporters and participants. As a player's partner pointed out: 'rugby players like to either get nude or dress up' (SBS 2007), and in this case they chose to dress up as Las Vegas Elvis. Their role in instigating a wave of impersonators proved vital. Aficionados purchased suits in the United States, for upwards – often much upwards – of $500, to the extent that the American manufacturing company eventually became a festival sponsor, but suits could also be hired or purchased locally. By 2010 a Parkes woman was reputed to make more than 40 a year for up to $2,500 each. During the entire period of the Festival the town, and especially the main street and venues, is seemingly awash with Elvis impersonators which creates a colour and atmosphere that for many visitors is the highlight of the Festival. By 2010 there were as many as 500 impersonators at the festival and in 2011 Parkes sought to break the record (646) for the largest number of Elvis impersonators assembled in a single place. Though it failed, by just three, the American Ambassador to Australia, himself a visitor, observed: 'while the best part of the Elvis celebration is the feeling of the people there – it is the only place I've ever been where you feel a little nutty if you are not wearing a sequined jumpsuit' (US Embassy 2010).

A second teething problem was organisation. Typically, festivals in small places lack leadership and other appropriate skills. This hampered professional event management, as explained by the Parkes Tourism Manager, Kelly Atkinson:

> It started off small and started to grow. The word started to get out there and the media coverage started to get out about the festival but I guess the lack of resources and lack of skills among the committee, and lack of support from the community saw numbers start to dwindle and the festival nearly fell over a couple of years ago. That's when the tourism board got back on board again. (personal communication 2004)

As evident in other Australian festivals (Davies 2011) the presence of inspirational leaders can be critical for festival success, but uniqueness was also invaluable.

Eventually the Festival succeeded and attracted growing crowds. At the start of the century there were about 2,500 at the street parade, and one or two hundred at many of the commercial events, with more than 500 estimated to have come from outside the town. In 2006, organisers estimated that over 5,000 people participated in the festival. Media coverage went international in 2002:

> We had Buckwheat noodles, which is a local company that exports its noodles directly to Japan. We had a Japanese TV program come and do filming at the festival, set up a noodle tent down in the park, feeding the Elvises noodles throughout the festival and interviewing them, given Japan's affiliation with Elvis and love for Elvis and crazy things … The next year, 2003, we really hammed it up as far as trying to add more to the program throughout the weekend and also just hamming up the whole media effort. Just trying to get more publicity. (Kelly Atkinson, personal communication 2004)

By the end of the 2000s about 10,000 people were routinely visiting the Festival, especially for the peak Saturday morning parade, and in 2011 numbers were estimated at a record 12,000.

Since 2003 a special train (the Elvis Express) has run from Sydney (Figure 6.3), with the support of NSW Railways (CountryLink), which eventually became the main sponsor of the festival, and the state tourism promotional authority (Figure 6.4). Many of those who travel by train dress as Elvis or Priscilla and CountryLink provides its own Elvis impersonators to perform through the carriages. Its arrival was always greeted by enthusiastic crowds in Parkes, with an Elvis at every door to greet passengers with a lei. By 2010 the Elvis Express had eight carriages and almost 400 passengers: the physical capacity of the engine and the system. Seats for the 2011 Festival train sold out in just 20 minutes. Initially the train ran up on Friday and back on Sunday afternoon, but by 2009 so many more events existed that its return was put back to the Monday morning.

At the Festival

In its early days the Festival was limited in scope and duration. As the advertisement for the first Festival indicated (Figure 6.2) it then largely amounted to two concerts,

Figure 6.3   The town turns out for the arrival of the Elvis Express in Parkes

Figure 6.4   Billboard advertisement for CountryLink Elvis Express

on the Friday and Saturday nights, a street parade and intermittent films. Gaps in the programme could be taken up with greyhound racing in nearby Forbes or a district tour. Over time those gaps were filled, though the duration remained much the same for well over a decade.

The Festival invariably began on the Friday night of the weekend closest to Elvis' birthday (8 January 1935). For years that usually meant dinner and various forms of Elvis entertainment at Gracelands (with all participants encouraged to dress in appropriate annual themes: cowboy, speedway, Hawaiiana – usually linked to Elvis movies). Saturday saw the street parade of vintage cars and motorbikes (and vintage Elvis impersonators), with market stalls (ranging from memorabilia – rarely 'real' – to country handicrafts) in a park on the outskirts of the town centre. The park was the venue for the main sound- alike and look-alike competitions – Elvis, Priscilla, Lisa-Maree and Junior Elvis – and the day concluded with a feature performance by a touring 'professional' Elvis impersonator. Sunday highlights were the well-attended Gospel Church Service, and the unveiling of a new plaque on the Elvis Wall (at the park) to commemorate another 'legend' of Australian rock 'n' roll music (often, in early days, the previous night's top-billing performer). That wall surrounds gates that are a replica of the gates of Presley's Graceland mansion in Memphis. A talent contest with more diverse themes brought the festival to an end as most visitors returned home on Sunday.

By the mid-2000s the duration and number of events had expanded rapidly as the numbers of visitors increased. On some occasions Elvis movies were shown and the local lawn bowling club urged visitors to 'kick off your blue suede shoes' and have a game. An Elvis celebrant could be made available for couples to marry or renew marriage vows during the weekend (Figure 6.5), and this had become a permanent, well publicised and highly popular event by the end of the decade, when thirty to forty couples repeated their marriage vows before the celebrant Andrew 'Elvis' Appleby, and 'serenaded' by one of the more prominent tribute artists. By 2005 the Sunday morning Gospel Service had become much the single largest event with more than 2,000 people: 'a genuine commemoration of Elvis' life, spirituality and music' with tribute artists performing hymns alongside local church choirs. What had begun in the local Baptist church had moved to the giant Woolworths undercover car park, the only 'venue' in town that was capable of holding that many people. Similarly at the start of the decade buskers occupied a few key street corners; by the end of the decade they were on every street corner and intense competition raged between them, with visitors voting for their favourite. The Private Collection of memorabilia of Elvis Lennox – with a pink Cadillac parked in the driveway – was open to visitors, for a $5 entrance fee, but by 2011 that was overshadowed by a newcomer's collection. Parkes' growing Elvis reputation led former Wiggles member Greg Page (the yellow Wiggle in the most popular children's television band in the country) to choose the town to locate his considerable collection of Elvis memorabilia (the fourth largest such collection in the world). It formed the basis of a new permanent museum: the King's Castle, opened in 2009. Parkes is now home to, amongst many other things, *the* gold lamé suit (worn by Elvis on the cover of *50,000,000 Elvis Fans Can't Be Wrong*), as well as Elvis and Priscilla's marriage certificate, and the last Cadillac that Elvis owned.

Figure 6.5   Couples renew wedding vows at the Parkes Elvis Festival, 2007

By 2005 the Festival had outgrown the small Kelly Reserve and, bowing to pressure, the Council moved the venue to Cooke Park in the town centre, so giving the festival much greater visibility and presence, and enabling visitors to more easily patronise the town shops. The main open air stage and markets had moved from a peripheral location to the centre of Parkes. Elvis had come to town. There were many interlocking and overlapping events from breakfasts to evening shows and the festival lasted over three days rather than two. By then many organisations in Parkes were linked in some way. An Elvis Cheeseburger Eating Contest played a brief part in 2008, the same year that the Festival first produced a glossy souvenir programme. Various businesses, particularly restaurants and cafes that provided food, drink and shade, were staying open longer so that earlier concerns of visitors that there was 'nothing to do' on Saturday afternoons, when regional Australian towns characteristically closed down, were no longer true.

At the eighteenth Festival in 2010, which coincided with what would have been Elvis' 75th birthday, there were some 140 distinct events spread over five days (ranging from Bingo with Elvis and Hunka Hunka Breakfast with Elvis, to

It's Now or Never lunches and Elvis trivia quizzes, and dozens of musical events, to rifle shooting and the Elvis Golf Challenge), and involving many hundreds of Elvis impersonators (not all of whom, fortunately, sung). Elvis films ran more or less continuously in the Library, and the Big Hunka bus looped between accommodation and venues. In 2011 the number of events had continued to grow slightly with the first event taking place on the Tuesday before the weekend peak, and the last – a barbeque breakfast – on the Monday morning. Even so, twenty-four hours after it has finished, Cooke Park had returned to normal – with no visible evidence of a local environmental impact – and Parkes had reverted to just another small country town. Elvis had however been revived and 'Revival' had disappeared from the name of the Festival.

The Visitors

Tourist numbers became considerable in the twenty-first century, and are now larger than the population of Parkes. We first surveyed visitors in 2003 (125 respondents), providing data on their demography, expenditure patterns, transport arrangements, accommodation type, motivations to visit and their experiences. Additional surveys were undertaken in every year since, and smaller samples were interviewed in-depth at various Elvis Festivals.

The age of visitors to the festival has always been somewhat older than that at other music festivals, although intriguingly it is almost identical to that at the very different Opera in The Paddock (Chapter 7). The Elvis Festival is dominated by people from the 45–65 year old cohort, who made up over 60 per cent of all visitors in 2003, 2004 and 2006. In 2010 some 84 per cent of survey respondents were aged over 45. This distribution was unsurprising, reflecting the considerable popularity of Elvis with people who experienced their youth when Elvis was alive and an active performer. There was also some 'aging' between 2003 and 2010 partly reflecting return visiting. Younger people were fewer, and many of them saw the event as a fun, kitsch or 'retro' event, and not about nostalgia or reminiscence. Festival visitors came from a range of occupational backgrounds. In 2003 and 2004 the largest group were professionals, a group well known for their propensity to travel and to take in festivals, followed by tradespersons, retirees, and managers and administrators (Brennan-Horley et al. 2007). Professionals and retirees were the two most important groups in 2006. By 2010 the largest group were now retirees, again suggesting return visits, but professionals and tradespeople were well represented.

In 2003 as many as 80 per cent of visitors had not attended an Elvis Revival Festival before, but visitors enthusiastically said that they were likely to return to the festival (as they also did in later years). Of those who had then attended previously, most had visited in several consecutive years – a measure of the presence of 'devotees' at the festival, for whom it was much more than mere entertainment. By 2006 some 62 per cent had not attended before and by 2010 that proportion had fallen to 53 per cent, despite its growing size; return visits had become much more important, as intentions to return had become reality. Of those who had been before, a dozen had been more than ten times. A couple had been to every festival. In 2003 and 2004 word-of-mouth and newspaper advertisements were the most common ways that visitors found out about the festival, and by 2010 word of mouth was again most important but over a third of visitors claimed 'prior knowledge'. The Festival was now well known. Direct advertisement was less crucial.

Much like other festivals (Chapter 3) most visitors came from nearby. Many were from Parkes itself and more than half were from regional NSW, especially the surrounding region. Over time numbers and proportions from distant places steadily grew. Of the 30 per cent who were from further afield most came from Sydney and relatively few from states other than NSW, although both in 2008 and 2010 more than 10 per cent of all visitors came from other states, especially Queensland and Victoria. Most came by car. Whereas non-festival tourists to Parkes were usually from such states as South Australia, Queensland and Victoria, passing through on transcontinental travels, the Festival tapped a new market in eastern NSW. The more distant visitors were more likely to stay several nights, spend substantial sums of money, especially on evening club performances, be 'serious' Elvis enthusiasts (often members of Elvis fan clubs, and rock 'n' roll clubs) and more likely to come repeatedly. By 2010 the Elvis Express had become a reunion of old friends, singing, dancing and reminiscing, and eating Elvis Cupcakes and Love Me Tender Chicken through the journey.

Fun, Fans and Fanatics

Experiencing the 'buzz' of the Festival and soaking up the atmosphere takes multiple forms. For some it is about the music – its lyrics, its stimulus to dancing or its ability to conjure up nostalgia for another era; for others it is about food and drink, even drugs, the stalls of miscellanea, meeting old, and making new, friends, ambling through parks, buying unintended souvenirs, and meeting local people. Festivals may stimulate all the senses, and spontaneously engage a range of emotions, even over a short time period – organised randomness:

> I think the relaxed atmosphere makes it, possibly because it's in a country town but also the fact that you have a lot of older folk here who are just relaxed and there are no youth mucking up or misbehaving …

In many respects people came to the Elvis festival for the same reasons that people went to festivals anywhere else:

> It's a great time for us to get out and have time with our friends … we have meals out together, just relax and dance our socks off. It's just a great interaction with our mates and with people we've met before over the years.

Escaping 'the routine' was important, and the Festival could be an excuse or opportunity for other things. As a 2007 visitor from Sydney said,

> It's so refreshing and it just feels really friendly out here. We went out to the Dish and we've done some shopping, so it's not just the Festival. You know we're out here to support the regional area … it's just such a lovely place, and we'll be telling all our friends to get out here next year.

The Elvis Festival is primarily about music, fun and frivolity, and that offers a wide range of possibilities. For those in home hosting accommodation the main reasons for attending the festival were to 'play and have fun' and for 'the music and entertainment', just as with all visitors. But this group was rather more likely to state that they were Elvis fans.

Most people went to the festival simply for fun, entertainment and relaxation. They had no particular devotion to Elvis but wanted a good week-end out with family and/or friends. Some organised this specifically; for one couple from Newcastle: 'We come each year to meet with family from Canberra and Sydney'. Some visited Parkes for the humorous and the kitsch ('everything was sensational, baby! uhh huh huh!'; 'eating at Gracelands: wow I've been to Gracelands!'). For some a generalised nostalgia was significant, but the actual theme was not necessarily the key to participation. The rationale could vary considerably: 'being with friends', 'It was a birthday present, and it helps Parkes and the economy'. When prompted on their experiences, well over 90 per cent enjoyed the entertainment, 'country hospitality' and music, but the music was background as much as central theme. Between 2003 and 2010 that never changed.

Beyond those who were merely there for an enjoyable day-trip or week-end were those who went beyond passive listening and participation, entering into the spirit of the festival by dressing up, primarily for fun. More recent Festivals have also brought a secondary demographic group who have emerged as an important market: university students and young adults from capital cities seeking the 'kitsch' experience. A festival where anyone can dress up has become the means to considerable fun, frivolity and foolishness. As a man in his mid-20s from Sydney, claiming to be 'the one and only bearded Elvis', said:

> I heard about it on the radio last year and thought it would be a bit of a laugh and a good excuse for a road trip with the boys. We basically came here for a boys weekend and to get on the beers, because hey you've got keep your fluids up in this heat … especially when you're wearing an Elvis jumpsuit … I mean it's a great way to lose some weight, because you sweat like crazy. I think over the past two days I've made it onto every news station, got to dance with more Priscillas than Elvis ever did and have been constantly posing for photos … it's been bloody fantastic. None of us have ever really followed Elvis but coming out here you learn a lot from the fanatics and begin to appreciate more than ever before how good he was.

As one 25-year old stated,

> It's not so much about trying to be Elvis but more about having fun getting dressed up in that era, the 60s and 70s. You learn so much about that period when you get into it. You see the cars in the street that they used to drive … it's great.

A group of Elvis-dressed fans from Sydney

> saw it on the TV last year and we thought 'How good is that? We've got to go'. Because we're Elvis fanatics. In our street we get the stereo out there and there's probably about half a dozen people because we're neighbours. And we got the whole street into this Elvis thing, they're just loving it … we sit out there and sing and drink, it's great! We said we're going to go, just the boys, but then the women wanted to come along. They said 'Parkes it's just all dusty; no way, we're not going to come'; we said 'Just come, you'll be right'. They came out here and they go 'I thought it was all dusty, this is alright; look, they got shops, they got shops like Sydney!' They're having a great time; they're loving it.

Many came in large groups, like 'Beth's group' – thirteen women who had travelled together to celebrate the birthday of one of them and her fascination with Elvis – a trip planned three years earlier (Mackellar 2009a). In 2009 a large group of a dozen, including one man, were from Parents without Partners. Many such groups, invariably women, had matching t-shirts and other outfits, some collectively dressed as 'Brides of Elvis' or Priscilla.

Male impersonators relished the opportunity to kiss strangers (Figure 6.6), use bad Elvis quotes – 'thank you, thank you very much' – with improbable American accents, and have their photos taken by complete strangers (Mackellar 2009a). But 'when they take their wigs off they're just normal people. It really allows them to hide behind the mask and act out'. The festival was carnival – everyday life inverted:

> When you put on an Elvis suit, it changes you. It changes your behaviour, everything changes … it changes the people around you. Everyone that notices you, talks to you and yells out to you. It brings an uninhibited kind of feeling to people that just all comes together. They let loose, they have an excuse.

As another visitor put it: 'the total out of body experience I've received from taking on Elvis's outer body has been amazing'. For another the core of the Festival was: 'Putting on my Elvis jumpsuit, wig and glasses, being on a float in the street parade and making people smile', while

> putting on the Elvis suit lets you be who you want, there's almost no limits to what you can do … well almost … I mean no one knows who you are and I think you forget yourself a bit and just get into the Elvis persona … I've been walking round all weekend doing the 'tilt-in knees' and the 'slow twist' and practising

my 'thank you very much's' … and everybody can't get enough of it, its bloody unreal. I'll have to perfect my moves for next year so I can win the Elvis move-a-like comp because I've got no chance winning the sound-a-like comp.

Many enjoyed the Festival, as much as anything, simply because of its 'laid back atmosphere' and 'all the Elvises in the street' or just 'the music and the spectacle'.

Alongside 'fun', perhaps as important as a general rationale was 'Because I'm an Elvis fan', so that the Festival involved many people who specifically enjoyed Elvis's music. By the late 2000s not only were there frequent return visits to the festival, but half the visitors were there because of the sense of community and the music. The majority of visitors were either fans of Elvis, or were with family and friends who were themselves fans. Many saw it as an opportunity to meet and be with other fans and to let their hair down: 'I put all my Elvis things on this morning. I can't wear it around Warwick [Queensland] because people would think we were a bit queer, but here we can express ourselves'. For others nostalgia dominated: 'It brings back your youth. And it's just the joy you experience now. I play Elvis music every day. Not many days go by that I don't actually sing Elvis music... I spend about five hours a week doing Elvis things'. For such people, some of whom had domestic Elvis shrines, travelling to Parkes was akin to pilgrimage.

Typical responses included 'I always wanted to come', and 'to meet other Elvis fans and celebrate Elvis'. Repeat visitors were even more likely to state that they were Elvis fans, to be returning for the 'Elvis atmosphere', to be enthusiastic about the Festival and to state that they intended to return again: 'Elvis and I were born in the same year', 'My wife shares the same birthday as Elvis', 'It's something different compared to Graceland; we can compare Australian Elvises with US ones', 'He's the best – I have 108 of his LPs and I went to Graceland three years ago' or 'He had the looks and the voice; he was such a spiritual person. I actually joined a church because of him. I was an atheist until I heard him' and simply 'Love for Elvis'. For such people 'being with friends' with similar enthusiasms was important, and for the real fans: 'Getting things for the Elvis collection and seeing people we met last time'. That often involved adulation; 'Elvis' music is timeless', 'There will never be another one of him'.

Elvis fans eagerly anticipated the Festival year after year. As one such participant noted,

> I wanted to come for years but my Dad, whose birthday was the same day as Elvis's, was ill for a number of years, so I did not come. But my dad has passed on and is up with Elvis in heaven singing along. This is my first year and it's been fabulous.

Many, on the verge of retirement, welcomed more spare time and a release from responsibilities to enjoy the festival more. For others nostalgia and reminiscence were key: 'I was brought up with Elvis – he changed our lives as teenagers and he started us doing what you kids do now', 'He was a great singer and a great

Figure 6.6   Elvii

looking man and we [my husband and I] started going together then – he was part of our wedding songs', 'Elvis was my hero and my son was born the day Elvis died so I think of them together'. In every year, the Sunday morning gospel service was invariably described by such fans (and others) as the single most enjoyable experience: a peaceful hour of respect, reflection and devotion.

The Australian Elvis Presley Fan Club always took up one of the stands at the Festival, and offered not merely memorabilia but trips to the United States, from (blue) Hawaii to Las Vegas and Memphis itself, and its stand was a central meeting point for club members. The more expensive concerts were also designed primarily for the keenest fans. The main ticketed concert in 2010, by the acclaimed tribute artist Mark Anthony, was designed to be as far as possible, in content and structure, an authentic replica of a Las Vegas show from the 1970s, incorporating banter with the audience and a number of songs that never became familiar hits. Authenticity was prized. In rather different vein, in 2008 the President of the Fan Club railed against the second prize in the vocalist concert going to a singer (actually a Club committee member) who decided to do a version of Suspicious Minds with didjeridu backing since 'Elvis never had a didgeridoo player backing him' (Australian Elvis Presley Fan Club 2011). Others sought more respect for Elvis. Crap Elvis was denounced: 'If no respect is shown for Elvis, then obviously the Festival will go downhill'. True fans, subscribers to the global Elvis Information Network, even found Parkes unappealing:

> I find the whole Parkes Festival to be distasteful to Elvis' name. There were too many drunken Elvis look-a-likes and B-grade impersonators. These festivals should be a positive reflection on Elvis and not parade a bunch of buffoons and people out for a good time.

> What a big joke the Parkes Festival is. Elvis was the greatest singer the world has ever known and Parkes lets him down badly. They need to be told to talk about his music and his charisma not his hackneyed (thanks to the media) mannerisms. (www.elvisinfonet.com, 2009)

For real fanatics Elvis was not to be trivialised in any way, but they were a minority. A handful of others sought a 'pure' festival, where no music other than Elvis could be heard and only Cadillacs of Elvis' era could be in the street parade.

Many festivals invite some degree of participation beyond mere applause and sense of 'being there', or even dressing up as Elvis. This is particularly evident at Parkes where almost every street corner has an Elvis busker, numerous competitions exist for impersonators of various kinds, karaoke offers chances for the less brave and dressing up is part of the fun: seeing and being seen. Consequently many visitors are there as much to participate, and perhaps win, as to observe, but especially the many tribute artists of various degrees of skill, dedication and enthusiasm. Other than Crap Elvis, who wrote take–offs ('Hunka Hunka Burning Toast') and performed them humorously but badly (on street corners and on the Elvis train), most impersonators preferred to be known as tribute artists. For many tribute artists this is the event of the year. As one from Tasmania observed in 2007:

> [Q. What was your main motivation for coming to the festival?] Well, Elvis. Do you need any other reason than that? This festival means everything because I just reckon Elvis was the King and there will never be another and look what he's created. You only have to look around to see what he's created and around the world. You know, you can't get much bigger than this. [Through impersonating Elvis] you can act out a bit more, you get to meet more people through it, they

seem to come up to you … whereas if you were casually dressed they wouldn't give you a second glance. It gives you a bit of adrenalin; you know … you feel a bit like the King probably would have felt.

For another:

It gives me an opportunity to portray that charismatic feeling back to an audience. Dressing up takes it to a higher level. You're giving an experience that's similar to an Elvis experience … I don't think you become Elvis … but you take people on a musical journey. Women come up and say – they're 50 or 60 years old – "Tonight I was 18 again".

Putting on the costume enabled both fantasy and metamorphosis (Mackellar 2009a). Many fans were frequent visitors. As one returning for the fifth time stated,

We're actually members of Lithgow Workers Rebel Rockers dance club … we're also members of the rockabilly federation and the rock 'n' roll council … It's a great time for us to get out and have time with our friends … so we have meals out together, just relax and dance our socks off and it's just a great interaction with our mates and meet up with people we've met before over the years.

Various other rock 'n' roll clubs, such as the Jailhouse Rockers Club (Bendigo, Victoria), the Footloose Rock and Roll Group (Wollongong), and the Fifties Rock 'n' Roll Club (Newcastle, NSW), also brought substantial numbers.

At least in part to cater for the demand for impersonation, and to secure revenue within Parkes, in 2005 the Festival established its own sales venue, Elvis Central, where wigs, sunglasses, Priscilla eyelashes and various other souvenirs were sold. Fans returning to Sydney on the Elvis train 'displayed their new objects to others [and] openly discussed the shrines they had constructed in their houses' (Mackellar 2009a:16). Acquisition enhanced status. For particularly committed fans, there is no other means of expressing devotion without lengthy and expensive travel to America. However, many wore t-shirts or jewellery that could only be purchased in Memphis, and proudly talked of visiting Graceland and of the 'museums' they had built from memorabilia at home. One had been to Graceland five times (Mackellar 2009a). Many wore carefully and expensively made replica costumes, were members of local Elvis fan clubs and routinely attended the concerts of tribute artists elsewhere, and the Wintersun rock 'n' roll festival in Queensland. Many fans entertained each other – by reminiscences, exchanging and demonstrating knowledge, showing off their mementoes, dress styles, performances and customised classic Cadillac cars – so that the festival was both pleasure and 'serious leisure' – demonstrating a high level of commitment and a detailed knowledge of all things Elvis (Stebbins 1996). For those at the main tribute concerts 'there appeared to be a suspension of disbelief that enabled them to overlook the fact that this was not the real Elvis' (Mackellar 2009a:17).

Such testimonies and behaviour indicate how festivals – even the most seemingly esoteric or incidental – transcend daily life and bring a range of meanings to individual lives.

Parkes Becomes Full

Visitor numbers are substantial given the size of the town, the fact that most stayed for a couple of nights, usually in hotels and motels, and the otherwise relatively small mid-summer tourist market for inland Australia. Parkes has 13 hotels and motels with about 1,000 bed spaces. Until about 2003 it was possible to drive into Parkes on the Saturday morning of the festival, book a motel, watch the parade and enjoy other events and return home on Sunday, as many did. Few then stayed more than one night and local accommodation absorbed the numbers. In 2006 visitors were still averaging only two nights in Parkes, a very slight increase from 2003, but by 2008 were staying an average of three nights and that average was still increasing. By 2005 Parkes had effectively reached the limits of formal local accommodation, and towns like Forbes and Peak Hill, some 35 kilometres away, were also full. Dubbo, even further away, was almost booked out by the end of the decade. In 2008 and 2010 some 69 per cent and 71 per cent of visitors respectively were staying in Parkes. An additional 25 per cent were in Forbes and 6 per cent in Peak Hill in 2008, and in 2010, 18 per cent were in Forbes and others were scattered from Orange to Dubbo. The Festival ran shuttle buses to both Forbes and Peak Hill. The wider region was now benefiting. By the end of each festival signs routinely went up outside all the hotels and motels that Parkes was already fully booked for the following year, a further indication of the strength of return visiting, and some accommodation was booked for two or three years in advance.

In 2004 Parkes established a 'tent city' (Gracelands on the Green) on sports grounds where visitors could hire tents with access to basic facilities, and caravans could also be parked. That was modelled on the experience of the Gympie Muster and the Tamworth Country Music Festival, where similar tent cities had become successful, with the revenue accruing to the operator. It and Parkes' caravan park quickly became full, and by 2010 even Gracelands on the Green was routinely sold out for the following year. In 2006 Parkes decided to establish a home-hosting scheme modelled on similar schemes at events in the larger NSW towns of Gunnedah and Bathurst (Li and Connell 2011). The intention was to meet continually expanding demand, ensure that more revenue from accommodation remained in Parkes and provide a friendly and homely experience.

Parkes residents with spare bedrooms offered their homes as accommodation. In 2010 visitors paid $66 per bed per night, of which $50 went to the host, $10 to the Elvis Festival committee, and the remaining six dollars covered the expenses of the home hosting program coordinator. Hosts provided a continental breakfast and a ride from and to the train station as guests arrived and departed. In 2006, the first year, just four homes and fifteen visitors were involved but the number increased dramatically over time. By 2010, there were 125 homes and 547 guests (and 1,561 bed nights, thus most visitors stayed for three nights), so that home hosting provided a third of the formal beds in Parkes. Motivations for home hosting varied. No hosts claimed to be fans of Elvis, but many had warmed to him over the years, and some dressed as Elvis to welcome their guests. While most hosts were altruistic, did it to support the town, and enjoyed meeting people, the income generated was valuable at a time of economic stagnation. As one host said: 'it's been the saviour of the town with the drought'. Others said: 'the community has helped me and I am putting something back'. Revenue went directly into the hands (and pockets) of local residents, which increased interest in hosting and widened local support for the Festival. Perhaps most convincing of all was the middle aged woman who explained:

> I hated it when it first started. It was ridiculous and stupid and wasn't the image that was at all appropriate to our town. But over the years I watched and could see that it was making money and wasn't so bad. Last year I took in homestays and had six more visitors this year – lovely people – and I made over $600.

Other home-hosts had been similarly doubtful initially but were later swayed by recognition of what the Festival had done for the town, especially during drought.

Most visitors in home-hosting preferred the more extended contact with hosts than was normally possible in hotels and motels and the less obviously commercial context, and had vague notions of meeting local country people. Some had to negotiate different contexts of privacy and shared bathrooms, but invariably enjoyed their experience: 'such good fun', 'they're all so friendly', 'they help us out', 'such nice people' and 'our hosts were very generous with breakfast and running us around'. Beyond human relations: 'the house was so comfortable and such good value for money'. In a wider context other visitors did not choose home-stay, feeling 'uncomfortable at staying in some-one else's home' and feeling that it might be perhaps a hindrance to 'letting one's hair down'. Otherwise the more friendly and outgoing local people were those who were most likely to be involved in home hosting, and the more gregarious visitors were the ones who were most interested in it.

Both hosts and guests were enthusiastic about home-hosting and many returned to the same host in subsequent years. It thus played a part in winning over local people and contributing to the success of the Festival. Unlike Gracelands on the Green the income remained in Parkes. Although not everyone sought to provide home accommodation – or had the space to do so – and not every visitor wanted it, home-hosting reduced the problems of providing festival accommodation, and enabled greater involvement in the Festival from both hosts and guests.

The Economic Impacts of Elvis

Like many small festivals the Elvis Festival made no money in its early years. Local support was subdued or non-existent. But in the 2000s that changed rapidly. By 2004 the economic impact of the festival had already become considerable. Visitors then spent an average of $440 per person over the festival weekend, translating to an injection of over $1.1 million into the local economy. Accommodation (averaging $142 per person), food and drink ($134) and entertainment ($51) were the most common forms of expenditure, with smaller amounts spent on souvenirs ($43) and other services such as fuel ($28). For a town of its size, that expenditure was considerable because there were relatively few services in some categories, while multipliers spread that revenue through the local economy. In 2008 visitors estimated that they spent around $495 in Parkes and a further $240 outside (mainly on accommodation and petrol). In Parkes that expenditure was more or less evenly divided between five categories: festival events, clubs pubs and bars, shopping, accommodation, and food. Entertainment, with the introduction of more professional shows, was now costing rather more. Two years later total visitor expenditure inside and outside Parkes was estimated at around $944, a significant increase from 2008, as people stayed a little longer. Home-hosted visitors spent about twice that of the overall sample of visitors, the outcome of staying locally and staying longer. By 2010 the contribution of the festival to the town was over $5 million. Moreover the impact of the Festival was felt much further away, in towns such as Forbes where people stayed (and consumed), and in campsites, motels and caravan parks in a number of towns nearby or en route, and likewise in petrol stations and cafes far away from Parkes itself. Remarkably by 2011 Cowra, some 100 kilometres away, was advertising home-hosting specifically for the Festival.

Some expenditure went to the local market stalls. In its earliest years there was virtually no commercial presence, and even in 2002 there were merely a dozen stalls doing a desultory business selling local goods. Even Elvis souvenirs were unavailable. By 2008 the number of market stalls had passed a hundred and the main park was so crowded that numbers had to be cut back to 70 in the next two years to allow crowd movement. Stalls sold local rural products – honey, jams, soaps and handicrafts – but the majority of stallholders came from distant towns. Most stalls sold clothing, signs, statues, mats and various foods, from Turkish pizzas to 'exotic filled licorice' and from Chinese massage to the Wagga Wagga Sydney Swans Supporters Club. Not a single stall sold CDs. Only a handful sold Elvis memorabilia. However Elvis Central stocked large quantities of Elvis memorabilia (not all particularly memorable) and in 2010 visitors spent an average of around $82 on Elvis merchandise of different kinds.

Local businesses – the Rotary Club, the Lions Club, schools, churches, the fire brigade and so on – had their own stalls and barbeques that did good business. Indeed most things sold well. As one visitor observed:

> You've got Elvis wine, Elvis beer, Elvis tooth brushes, there's heaps of stuff –
> it's really tacky … the tackier it is the better it is … I mean people are buying 45
> foot Elvis rugs, which is classic behaviour at a festival. People consume all this
> memorabilia because people are in the spirit of it and that's what a festival does,
> it changes your behaviour.

Festival moods can be contagious:

> We are going to renew our wedding vows (after 37 years of marriage) at 12
> o'clock, since we probably won't get to Vegas. I went and bought this shirt
> yesterday in the park to blend in with his colours … Two wigs he bought yesterday
> and he measured up for a suit, so that's another $1300 dollars, so I think we've
> gone through thousands here. They can't tell me they're not making money.

Market stalls were both local – a minority – and from quite distant places, many
from as far as north Queensland on a circuit that took them to festivals all over
the country.

More formally trade increased during the Festival for the majority of Parkes
businesses. A quarter put on extra staff, adding some 30 jobs to the town.
Predictably, restaurants (43 per cent), cafes (33 per cent) and accommodation
facilities (14 per cent) accounted for the bulk of temporary positions created, and
retailing filled the remaining 10 per cent. Restaurants, pubs and cafes on average
at least doubled their business (with the extra trade largely attributable to visitors),
hotels and motels illuminated 'no vacancy' signs (for one of the only times of
the year), and shops (bookshops, record stores, clothes shops, newsagents)
reported substantial increases on normal trading levels. Just one (a retail fabric
store) claimed that business had declined, although many others (including a real
estate agency, a garden centre, a hairdresser and a video store) simply maintained
their usual business (Brennan-Horley et al. 2007). The businesses that initially
mainly benefited were also those with the highest dependency on local suppliers
and labour. The festival improved employment multiplier impacts by generating
extra work in those activities that, in turn, were most closely embedded in the
local economy rather than others that relied on goods and services (such as books
and clothes) imported from state capitals and beyond. Over time the businesses
that benefited most from the influx of visitors stayed open much longer; Saturday
afternoons and even Sundays were much less 'dead' than in earlier years or on
other weekends, and further multiplier effects ensued. Moreover even businesses
like fabric stores that saw no increased trade during the festival, subsequently
benefited when local people sent additional income there. As the festival got larger
more local people became direct and indirect beneficiaries. Elvis had been taken
on board.

Contesting Rural Place Identity: the Dish and the King

Until very recently, Parkes rarely mentioned the Elvis Festival in its standard tourist publications, preferring to advertise itself as the town with 'The Dish', and as a prominent regional commercial centre. Among the local businesses that responded to our 2004 survey, opinions were divided about the appropriateness of the festival as a marker of place identity, as opposed to other options such as 'The Dish'. Only a small percentage did not support the festival (5 per cent) compared with the more general support for it (62 per cent strongly support; 25 per cent mildly support), and more than 70 per cent agreed that the Festival contributed to the town by fostering a greater sense of community. Over 80 per cent strongly agreed that the festival had a positive impact on publicising Parkes as a tourist destination, yet over 65 per cent either mildly or strongly favoured 'The Dish' as a source of more appropriate imagery. Sentiments in favour of the Festival were far from universal (Brennan-Horley et al. 2007). By 2008 businesses were more attuned to Elvis, with 90 per cent now believing the Festival had a positive effect on publicising Parkes, though some 43 per cent still favoured 'The Dish' as the most appropriate marketing image.

Community perceptions were influenced by images displayed by media and popular culture, as was also the case following the cinema release of *The Dish* (2000). This initially provided something of a setback since some saw it as making Parkes look old-fashioned by being based around the first moon landing thirty years earlier (Brennan-Horley et al. 2007). However its commercial success brought new interest and greater enthusiasm:

> Especially since 2000 when *The Dish* was released, people were a little hesitant about the movie because in some respects it made Parkes look a little backward in coming forward. Once they came to understand that that wasn't the message that people were getting, and that the movie was doing positive things for the town, I think that was an education process for tourism in the town. (Kelly Atkinson, personal communication 2004)

In the same way, the growing success of the Elvis Revival Festival changed local perceptions of the event and helped it garner further support and interest from local businesses and the wider community.

Business reaction to the Festival was mirrored in broader community sentiments. As the Festival grew these too became more positive. In 2007 one Parkes respondent observed:

> A lot of the locals don't really like the festival … I mean the fanatical ones that are on the committee and that, they're great and then there's the old folk they don't like everybody coming into town. I think they don't like lining up for their beers at the club!

Some found it bizarre: 'It's almost a cult. These people live and breathe this guy. It's bordering on creepy'; 'we think it hilarious people do this stuff'. However most local people had become supportive, seeing the festival as bringing new faces and excitement to Parkes and providing the impetus for local families to 'do something together' and help their town (Mackellar 2009a:14). A residential survey we conducted immediately after the 2009 Festival found either substantial support, or mere indifference, with little significant hostility. For some it was 'the best thing that has ever happened here'; an 81 year old noted 'it's great for the town and the people'. Another woman argued: 'Those who only think of the Dish live in the past and we have to be more creative now'. Another claimed: 'we all thought it was a mob of hicks at first but it just grew'. While some preferred to stay away from the crowds or Elvis was 'not my thing', just one 61 year old woman was bitterly opposed: 'I hate it; it closes off the main street, there's no access to businesses. Since the first one really rude people came from Sydney. Prices go up. We should promote the Dish and our good restaurants, but we're under the thumb of the council'. More commonly mere apathy discouraged interest. Participation, as in home-hosting, inevitably helped: 'Some people think it's weird until they get involved and then they get sucked in and it's all good'.

In an effort to combine the success of Parkes' two major attractions, the Tourism Office merged the two somewhat opposing figures of Elvis Presley and the Parkes Radio Telescope, so reconciling competing (if not contradictory) images of place:

> I think in the last couple of years Elvis really had nothing to do with the telescope. But we are really trying to tie those together because they have started to become the two best things that Parkes is known for by a general audience. This year for the first time we developed a new image that was used for merchandise that had Elvis singing with the telescope in his hand as a microphone. We're just trying to tie those two together. And so making Elvis unique to Parkes. He's not just any Elvis that could be found anywhere – he's the Parkes Elvis. (Kelly Atkinson, personal communication 2004)

Parkes has welcomed Elvis and given him a new connection to place, while tours to the Dish have become, for many, one part of the Festival. And in 2011 a new festival and theme emerged: Opera at the Dish - a one night performance of opera at the Dish itself. Parkes' identity is no longer just as a sheep or wheat town, nor is it the "crossroads of a nation". It is the place to be consulted about all things Elvis, and to see the Dish.

Winning over the majority of local people was eventually possible. A more detailed survey in 2010 found even more overwhelming support, through recognition of the short-term economic benefits at Festival time and the longer term benefits from tourism, while, significantly, at least 20 per cent stated that their views had changed over the years, and they were now more positive about the Festival. As one said: 'It is such a positive thing for the town and because we are a rural town the place can get very sad after Christmas as the shops get poor, so the Festival boosts the economy and the atmosphere is lovely and happy'. For others the benefits were more low key and personal: 'it gives me a reason to get out of bed for the weekend'. When asked what they thought about the Festival, the first words and phrases that came to mind were usually 'great', or other positive adjectives, and 'lots of fun'. Many had participated (about 60 per cent), a third of those who were ordinarily employed worked extra hours (for extra income) and others were involved as volunteers or additional paid staff. By then there were as many as 200 local volunteers – marshalling traffic and crowds, manning information booths, running stalls and so on – and there was a range of forms of participation from hosting 'Elvis Shoot' events at the local gun club, to being in the church band at the gospel service, making costumes or even just baby-sitting the children of volunteers or participants; there was a role for 'anyone wishing to be part of the "grand theatre" created by a major event such as this' (Jetty Research 2010:26). Two thirds of local residents now loved the festival and hoped it would continue, a third tolerated it and the 'inconveniences associated with it' while less than 1 per cent of the population simply hoped it would disappear.

The majority of local people not only came to terms with festival, but decidedly embraced it. As one homestay host said: 'If it's good for Parkes I'll be in it'. Getting behind the festival became more common. As one 24 year old local man said in 2007:

> I've gone all out, there's no half measures in this town. I've got the wig and suit, the rings and don't forget these awesome sunnies … its tackalicious! I think if we were anywhere else we'd get bashed but around here you just get bought beers, its fucking fantastic. I suppose a lot of us locals have realised how important it is to support an event like this in our own town, because a lot of people are doing it real tough out here with the drought and everything, so by dressing up and getting into the whole spirit of things we can hopefully make it a bigger and better event and get more and more people out here to spend their money.

By the mid-2000s the mayors and councillors routinely dressed up and accompanied the train on the large stage to Parkes, and crowds of several hundred people welcomed the train. The Festival had become part of Parkes life.

Elvis Has Not Left the Town

> If you're going to have an Elvis festival this is a kind of eccentric place to have it, but it's an eccentric thing anyway, so it fits real well. (2007 Visitor)

Parkes has succeeded despite initial scepticism and some opposition, concerned about the image and status of the town. Some preferred the link to The Dish, while others objected to what they saw as a tawdry celebration of popular culture ('Hungover and drunk Elvises in the parade on Saturday morning isn't exactly a great image for the town'). Rowdiness and late night drunkenness were sometimes frowned upon, although many recognised that this was a local response, while some complained 'you can hear it from where we are' – an indication that some found fault wherever they could. But the majority are well aware of the economic benefits and most stores and residents have entered into the Festival spirit. Even a partly divided community has benefited substantially. Parkes has put itself on the map in a lively way, and generated much-needed summer income in a usually stagnant tourist period, cementing it as an important place for tourism especially connected to the affluent baby-boomer and grey nomad markets.

The residents of Parkes have adopted Elvis. He was never their choice as a symbol but in the end they have adjusted and adapted to life with Elvis, just as the wider world has come to see Parkes as the Elvis town. For the first time in 2009 an overseas newspaper, the English *The Independent*, featured Parkes and Elvis in its travel section. Meanwhile at the King's Castle a world-class Elvis museum remains a year-round reminder and tourist attraction, in what was previously a fairly anonymous rural Australian town. Just as importantly the new museum has given Parkes a year-long Elvis presence and, in a place with no other distinct tourist attractions, provides a rationale for visiting and remaining a little longer, remembering the experience and cementing the connection between Parkes and Elvis.

'Two Cars Collide; No-One Injured'

As the front page banner headline from one 2008 edition of the local *Parkes Champion Post* suggests, Parkes is usually a small quiet town where not a great deal happens. The Parkes Elvis Festival demonstrates how a small place can stage a festival in a relatively remote location, and succeed in generating substantial economic benefits, in fostering an unusual sense of community, and in gaining nationwide notoriety and publicity. It has done so without any legitimate local claim to musical heritage, cultural diversity or a remarkably attractive setting. Where other festivals linked to individual musical performers have generated a link to that performer, whether birthplace, death-place, or place of famous recordings (Gibson and Connell 2005), Parkes has wholly invented this association. Indeed, the festival represents about as narrow a rationale for an event as can be imagined: the legendary performer is long dead, and festival visitors arrive to see impersonations or films of the original.

Myth and tradition are not always tied to authenticity and credibility where tourism and festivals are concerned. Like Bundanoon in country NSW, with its Scottish festival (Ruting and Li 2011), Parkes has become the site of an 'invented tradition', where a particular image has been grafted on to a place (Hobsbawm 1983), but here not even linked to a particular imagined historic past. The town has succeeded in spite of itself and created a celebration of kitsch, fantasy and popular culture that is as 'real' as any celebration of Elvis in Australia could be. Its many supporters derive a variety of sensory experiences and pleasures from the Festival, none more so than the serious Elvis fans for whom it is an annual ritual. The town has effectively, if belatedly, deployed what can be seen as 'strategic inauthenticity' (Taylor 1997), placing the town on the tourist map, and creating a form of invented geography. Parkes' identity now resonates nostalgically of an American legend, yet derived from chance – a whim and a struggle by local devotees.

Unlike most other festivals where there is something of a divide between performers and audience, at Parkes the audience are also part of the performance – to be seen and heard, photographed, posed with and greeted – and to be re-encountered from other places and other festivals. 'The diversity of Elvises that walk around town' were for many an ongoing highlight. Others enjoyed the 'freedom of expression to develop the fantasy of Elvis'. Not only visitors but local people, including the mayor, enter into the spirit of performance:

> We dressed up the last couple of days and we had the six matching jackets and we all went in the parade and it was just wonderful… whereas at Tamworth you just sit and listen to everything. At Parkes people can actually get involved and we say hello to the other Elvises. It's much more intimate and personal and it's much funnier. (visitor, 2007)

Parkes provides a vivid sensual experience well beyond passive entertainment.

Both local people and tourists have questioned the longevity and sustainability of the Elvis Festival but it has grown each year and visitors keep returning. In 2004 it was officially supported for the first time by the NSW State government, under the Regional Flagship Events Program. By 2010 the apparent joke had become an institution supported by the local council, the state and the nation. It had also seen off competition – including competition from nearby Forbes which once mounted a jazz festival on the same weekend. In 2001 the small South Australian seaside town of Victor Harbor launched the Festival of the King, this time marking the date of Presley's death; for the first time, Parkes had direct national competition for the 'Elvis market', but that too proved to be short-lived. Both Burra (South Australia) and Maitland (NSW) have also staged Elvis festivals in the present century but without success. Nearby towns also sought to benefit from the Elvis Festival, partly through providing accommodation. Businesses from Manildra, 40 kilometres east of Parkes, advertised in the 2011 programme 'Breakfast in the Vines' with Elvis (and champagne) and a day-long Elvis movie marathon in the cinema. Ten kilometres south of Parkes the Alpaca Country Shop sought visitors ('Yes – even Elvis loves alpacas') and Dubbo Zoo, 50 kilometres north, offered Festival visitors special concessions.

The Elvis Festival has lasted nearly two decades, longer than many festivals. It is by far the biggest event of the year in Parkes, and has become a major source of local revenue and publicity for what was once, but is no longer, a declining town. Success, to the extent that present hotel accommodation is only ever completely full during the Festival, has also encouraged Parkes to stimulate other festival activities at other times. Alongside the Elvis Presley Festival, Parkes has also organised a Country Music Spectacular, the Australian Marbles Championships, a Motorcycle Rally, a Kennel Club Show and Opera at the Dish:

> They've seen what can happen with Elvis. The Country Music festival is really looking to expand and to develop using the Elvis festival as a catalyst. The Country Music festival has to realise that we're never going to be another Tamworth but Elvis can be. It's got that uniqueness and no one else is doing it. (Kelly Atkinson, personal communication 2004)

Somewhat ironically, in 2010, anxious for other festivals at other times of the year, Parkes were contemplating a Tedfest festival for the fictitious Father Ted, the star of the cult comedy television series, simply because there wasn't one in Australia. It did not succeed, though Opera at the Dish may do so, and Parkes has remained primarily true to its Elvis Festival.

Not only has an unlikely festival in an ordinary town overcome adversity and local opposition to become one of the most famous festivals in the country, routinely featured in travel supplements in the national press, but, along with 14 other Australian festivals, mostly metropolitan, it is listed in Frommer's *300 Unmissable Festivals Around the World* (2009) where it is also distinguished as in 2007 setting a new record for the most Elvises (though the plural form is usually referred to in Parkes as Elvii). Parkes had become a global place, and part of a loose network of sites – from six major Elvis festivals in North America to smaller ones in Porthcawl, Bridlington, Benidorm and a range of other towns (Mackellar 2009a; Connelly 2007) – where annual festivals occur. By 2007 Parkes was locked into gentle competition with the many other towns with Elvis festivals, after it was reported in the Guinness Book of Records as having a record 147 Elvis tribute artists simultaneously performing a single song onstage. By 2010 the winner of the Parkes Tribute Artist Competition was representing Australia in the Elvis Tribute Artist World Cup in Wales against competitors from sixteen countries. A handful of overseas visitors took in Parkes as part of a global circuit; as one local resident reported in 2010: 'I home hosted last year and the German girl who stayed said this is the best Elvis festival she has been to of all the ones she's been to overseas'. Success had taken on international dimensions.

Chapter 7
Creating Classical Country

Relatively few music festivals are centred on classical music, however loosely defined (Table 2.2). This may be linked to perceptions that classical music, like jazz, is a metropolitan genre, even though jazz is the cornerstone of innumerable regional festivals. Similarly residual perceptions of classical music as an elite genre, inaccessible to many, have limited or delayed local institutional support for them. It is considered a somewhat elite musical genre, that may attract few visitors to the country, but it is also difficult to stage classical festivals, especially for chamber music, which demand considerable quietness and do not work well outside small, confined spaces. That limits visitor numbers and several festivals, as at Bridgetown and Bangalow, have space for only a few hundred participants. Even the New England Bach Festival, in much larger Armidale, is held in chapels and churches. Reasonably typically, Opera in the Valley (Jamberoo, NSW) attracts around 350 people over two nights. Classical music festivals are usually both small, and in small places. This chapter profiles two such festivals and places in NSW – Opera in the Paddock, near Inverell, and the Four Winds Festival, outside Bermagui.

Remarkably, like the Parkes Elvis Festival, so many classical festivals are accidents of history and geography, products of the hopes of individuals rather than deliberate creations by development organisations. More than in other festival contexts, mobility and personal predilections have been important. The Kowmung Festival in Oberon owes its origin to the visit in 1992 of an Australian violinist and conductor, then resident in the United States, who saw Mozart Street while visiting Oberon. This was said to have brought home to him that composers like Mozart always travelled to the countryside and that is where their music should be heard. He mounted a trial festival in 1996, and the annual festival developed from there (*Sydney Morning Herald* 16 March 2002). It is improbable that Inverell, an unassuming town of 10,000 people, and known, if at all, in a much wider world for agriculture and gem-fossicking opportunities, would ever have decided on an opera festival had it not been for a particular opera singer moving into the neighbourhood. Likewise at Bermagui the motivation of certain individuals was central. At Bridgetown one individual alone was the instigator of the Chamber Music Festival, while the Woodend Winter Arts Festival emerged from an individual's inspiration: 'The late Stuart Stoneman had a vision for his property Duneira. Informed by the great Huntington Collection in California, he sought to create a set of experiences through music, art, books and his glorious garden that would inspire the people in this region and beyond'. The Tyalgum Festival of Classical Music (NSW) began after two violinists moved into the area, and 'has grown from a congenial gathering of colleagues to a fully-fledged festival that stands proud among Australia's finest'. Such festivals started without any aspirations towards elitism, but invariably represented the desire of individuals to hear classical music in local contexts. Both the Opera in the Paddock and the Four Winds Festival began from little more than local wishes to hear good music in a pristine setting.

Opera in the Paddock

The first Opera in the Paddock was held in 2002, with origins that were both artistic and environmental. A professional opera singer, Peta Blyth, married to a farmer, Bill Blyth, discovered that the paddock immediately outside their farmhouse, Mimosa, at Delungra some fifteen kilometres west of Inverell (Figure 7.1), had unusual acoustic qualities. Peta Blyth (who all quotes in this section are from, unless stated) recalled: 'I'd sing here at night and the sound would carry down the valley. I began to think we should really do something with the spot because of the acoustics'. The idea evolved into a one-off concert:

> I have a passion for the art form and love the serenity and beauty of the paddock and the surrounding countryside, and we both wanted to share those things with other people and make a contribution to the community. I started talking about the idea of a concert with some of my opera singer friends. I actually thought we would do it once and would have about a hundred people, and that would be it. Bill had more vision. His idea was to start small and do it well and grow along the way' (New England Focus 2010)

Holding the Opera early in March, towards the end of the Australian summer, took advantage of the best possible climatic conditions and a lull in the farming calendar. Its name was felicitously chosen since it 'felt grounded and non-threatening like Opera sometimes seems to be'. Inverell otherwise hosts the annual Sapphire City Festival, a fairly typical country festival, running over ten days, including a race meeting, concerts, flower and quilt shows, a bowling carnival and gem displays, but supports relatively few other events. A town where utes are as common as cars in the streets, some with the quintessential cattle dogs in the back, was not obviously propitious territory for opera.

The format of Opera in the Paddock is a two part concert on a Saturday evening with a half-hour interval. For its organiser, Peta Blyth, 'the event is a very serious classical concert which attracts people from the city and gives the locals a great lift by inviting their city friends to the country for a concert of equal standard to the city'. For Bill Blyth: 'we try to make it theatrical but not commercial'. Almost all visitors arrive by car or bus, since there are few other possibilities of access to a farmstead some way off a rural highway. Several buses regularly come from Armidale, Glen Innes and elsewhere – an opportunity for consumption to be less constrained. Tickets are checked, programmes sold and

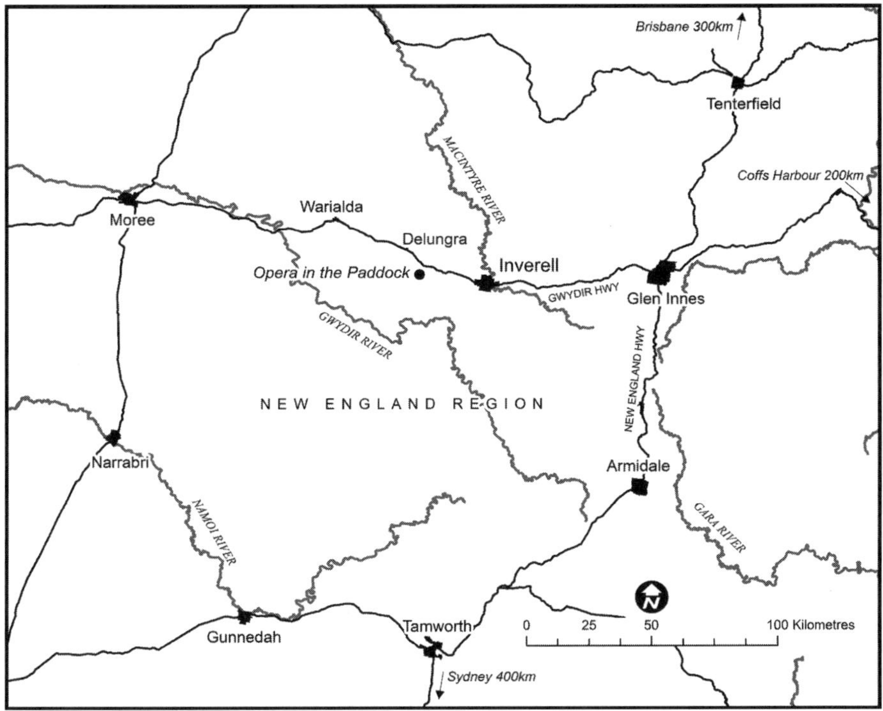

Figure 7.1   Location map, Opera in the Paddock

cars directed to parking spots by formally dressed students, in cocktail dresses, bow ties and iconic Akubra hats.

Various combinations of up to six opera singers, one of whom is Peta Blyth, perform arias from classical Mozart and Verdi operas such as *Don Giovanni* and *Rigoletto,* operetta excerpts from *The Student Prince* and *The Desert Song,* medleys from such composers as Gershwin, Cole Porter and Stephen Sondheim and selections from *The Phantom of the Opera,* with a fourteen piece orchestral background. The audience can sit on the grass, but most bring picnic tables and chairs, and arrive early to eat and drink from their eskies (cooler-boxes) and picnic baskets. All have arrived long before the start, some in bow ties and even dinner jackets, to eat, drink and converse, to see and be seen. The Opera begins at dusk, and distant kookaburras, and other bush noises, from the surrounding river red gums may accompany the singers as twilight descends. Effectively the Opera is scarcely a festival. Performers, audience and repertoire are fixed in place. Visitors could however choose where to place their tables, chairs and picnic hampers – most preferring close to the stage but a handful choosing to isolate themselves from the crowd and blend into distant parts of the paddock. By midnight the paddock is again deserted. A row of portaloos disposed of human waste, visitors invariably took their own rubbish away and twenty-fours later only the base of the stage – the one permanent fixture – gave some indication that this was not just any other paddock.

Since 2008 a lieder concert has been held on the previous Friday night, in conjunction with the Opera, including most of the Opera performers, but in the Inverell Town Hall. It was established 'as a way of giving our audiences a second bite at the cherry'. Lieder, voice accompanied only by piano, a relatively esoteric and unfamiliar contemporary musical form, nevertheless drew an audience of two or three hundred. Some argued that this was because Inverell had little to offer on Friday, or any other, nights; as one local visitor said 'because we don't have much here everybody goes'. In 2010 the lieder concert clashed with a concert by country singer, John Williamson, and numbers fell to 150.

The Blyths set up a non-profit company, Opera North West Ltd, to run the Opera and possibly stage concerts elsewhere. With ticket sales at $50 in 2009 and $55 in 2010 it was not designed to be a commercial operation, and the ticket sales were estimated to represent only 35 per cent of the cost of staging the Opera. The lack of commercialism was reflected in the impossibility of purchasing anything (other than a $10 programme) on site, or indeed within fifteen kilometres of it. By 2010 the Opera was running at a loss despite a large amount of voluntary labour, especially on the day. The need to ensure that it broke even was reflected in discussions of the possibility of bottled water sales, and perhaps other goods (such as t-shirts), and developing sponsorship and a sales arrangement with a local winery. More expensive preferential seating was considered as another option. Even these changes would scarcely influence the non-profit perspective. Sponsorship has belatedly come from Inverell Council, who took five years to support the Opera; some opposition came from the notion that the Blyths were 'affluent people, making money and taking multiple trips abroad'. In 2010 sponsorship amounted to just $5,000. Sponsorship has also come from Country Energy (growing from an initial $250 to $1500 in 2010) and from the German Consulate. Such derisory sums did little to alter balance sheets, and the Opera has considered moving towards some form of community ownership, partly because that might draw in more financial support, but also to relieve the burden on Peta and Bill Blyth. In other words, staging the Opera was a labour of love.

Just as the Opera has largely survived without significant sponsorship, it has also benefited from the enormous goodwill of a number of suppliers, of voluntary labour (for example, to manage parking), and of goods and services. Lighting, critical for an evening performance on a large stage, was provided cheaply by a local retiree. The sound system was much more expensive, so that the whole technical support package cost $7,000.

Marketing is limited. Inverell Council's Tourism Office sells tickets and advertises the Opera with flyers and brochures (Figure 7.2) that are also taken to events where Inverell is promoting itself. Most visitors to the Opera first knew about it from friends and family (about 60 per cent both in 2009 and 2010), followed by direct mailing, which reflected a significant amount of return visiting. The principal other source of information was the regional media, especially newspapers, but that accounted for only 17 per cent of visitors in 2010. Like many festivals Opera in the Paddock had entered into general public consciousness, at least in the broad New England region, and direct advertising by flyers and posters largely only served as a reminder of dates and ticket venues.

Figure 7.2   Opera in the Paddock brochure

The performers come mainly from eastern Australia, with an intended bias to the New England region, but some have come from as far as New Zealand. All were personally known to the organiser, and most returned regularly. Neither wages nor expenses are substantial, but most came because of the pleasure of performing for a large audience in the unusual setting of a paddock, a break from the normal routine and because, for younger musicians, performing in the Paddock was a worthwhile career move. Most enjoyed the Opera as a musical social event where they could keep up contacts and exchange news and information. Younger regional performers especially valued the experience of working with established Australian performers. The conductor was the most expensive. In 2010 the performers were each paid $500 which, with food, accommodation and travel costs, amounted to about $1,000 per head. Staging the Opera was something of a shoestring operation, and keeping costs down has meant that there has always been little time to get orchestra and performers together for rehearsals. Not only are there less than three days for the necessary rehearsals but the limited additional time that singers and orchestra have in the region means that there is even less time to link them into the community, for example by school visits or short town concerts. However QantasLink, the regional arm of Qantas, have sponsored annual workshops in Armidale giving local Armidale singers a chance to perform with and receive feedback from Opera veterans.

The first Opera in 2002 had just four artists. By 2009 it had grown to 22. In 2010 half the fourteen-strong orchestra were from the broad New England region (three from Armidale and the others from Narrabri, Guyra, Tamworth and Stanthorpe, but 'with proper professional background') with other players from Brisbane, Adelaide and elsewhere in Australia. The orchestra composition fluctuates annually to give local performers the opportunity to play with more experienced players from capital cities; orchestra numbers have gradually increased to do that more effectively, so that a couple of newcomers are 'blooded' each year. Similarly at least one of the singers is from the region; 'part of our vision has always been to nurture local talent'. Peta Blyth has argued that the event helps to keep skilled people in the region: 'the ability to perform locally is one more reason for local performers to remain in places like Guyra'.

The audience grew from early small beginnings, with 650 people for the first performance in 2002, rather more than were expected. Numbers reached a peak of around 1,800 in 2007 when 'all the locals came' and has since settled around 1,300. Most visitors came from nearby areas, predominantly from Inverell itself, followed by the large towns of Armidale, Glen Innes and more distant Tamworth. Lower numbers came from smaller nearby towns such as Moree and Warialda. In the four years, 2008–2011, when survey data were collected, Inverell itself never provided less than 25 per cent of the audience. Most of the remainder came from other parts of NSW, including, in 2008, 45 from Sydney, but 72 came from another state (mainly Queensland) and a couple of tickets were purchased in New Zealand. In 2011 one group of 14 people came from New Zealand. The audience at the Opera thus exhibited an almost perfect distance decay relationship: large local numbers tailing off at a distance. The only deviation from this was the consistently, disproportionately larger group from Armidale, a university town and the home of the New England Conservatorium of Music, which suggests a very slight 'elite' bias in attendance. Otherwise visitors came from all parts the region, suggesting that no places were averse to opera but also that the particular, unique ambience had an important role to play.

Visitors were overwhelmingly white, white collar, middle class and more than middle aged. Almost without exception they were Anglo-Celtic. They were significantly older than at most music festivals, with less than a quarter under 45. Indeed the number of participants who were aged over 65 was nearly five times the number aged under 25. Many of these were retired (about 40 per cent in 2009 and 38 per cent in 2011), and some were grey nomads, enjoying the Opera as one of various events on their travels through Australia. (By 2010 the Opera was beginning to target the magazines of grey nomad and caravanning organisations as valuable places for advertisements). In every year, of the participants who were not retired, almost all were white collar workers – with relatively high numbers of teachers, lecturers, accountants and finance officers, doctors, business people and lawyers. A small group of farmers hinted at the rural environment.

Cultural capital might be acquired at the Opera. Local dignitaries, such as the Mayor and Councillors, and the State Member of Parliament, were usually there, as was the German Consul from Sydney, a sponsor of the Opera. Some chose to wear formal garb of bow tie and tails; others were resplendent in different ways. Champagne flowed faster than beer and gourmet cuisine dominated. It was evidently a social event, an important date on the regional calendar, an occasion for conversation and good food and wine, and relaxation in good company. For many the music was important, but as the basis for a distinct ambience as much as for its particular content. Most visitors constantly emphasised 'the ambience, the talent and the company', 'the relaxed atmosphere and location', 'the open air' even simply 'the unique concept'. The 'music' and 'the quality performance' were somewhat less significant than 'socialising'. Above all the musical context, that gave it distinctiveness, and the unusual rural ambience were what drew visitors.

Almost all visitors came in groups. In 2010 a third came as couples; most others came in groups of three or four, and sometimes much larger, with buses from more distant towns. One Narrabri group was 36 strong. Literally no-one came alone; the opera was a social event. More than half in every year were returning; in 2008 and 2009 this proportion was 75 per cent and 83 per cent respectively, a measure of success far beyond that of most festivals but an indication perhaps that there were limits to growth in a relatively isolated rural area. The majority of visitors had been to between one and five Operas in the Paddock and a smaller number had been to almost all of them. Some three quarters of all visitors had experienced opera before, but many only in this particular context.

Half the visitors used no local accommodation; most simply drove to the Opera and back home afterwards. Their economic contribution to Inverell, where many lived, was therefore slight. A quarter stayed with friends and relatives, and the remaining quarter used local accommodation, mainly hotels, motels and guest houses in Inverell. The night of the Opera was one of the few nights in the year when all accommodation in Inverell was booked out (though there were vacancies on adjoining nights). Only the Sapphire Festival resulted in similar 'house full' notices. Smaller numbers of visitors stayed in hotels and motels elsewhere, usually in Glen Innes. Of those from outside the immediate Inverell region, more than half stayed for two nights or more (with some attending both musical events), so that even if those visitors stayed with family or friends there was still a very significant income gain for Inverell accommodation, and for expenditure in other areas. It was not necessarily only those who stayed with friends and relatives who stayed for more than two days; the average stay of those in hotels and motels was 1.6 nights. These patterns, and those on expenditure (below), were consistent over the four years, though visitors to Inverell were gradually staying longer, suggesting that the Opera was making a slowly increasing direct economic contribution to the town.

Although half the Opera visitors, mostly local people, claimed they did nothing else in Inverell, in 2008 almost a third of visitors dined out at least once while they were there and a further third spent some time shopping (and presumably purchasing). By 2011 more than half claimed to do both of these. Most festival visitors, including but not primarily those who had merely driven from Inverell, usually topped up their food supplies or used Inverell as a last stop for cold drinks, before going to the Opera. By midday on the Saturday the largest supermarket in town was struggling to cope – their bread rolls and barbeque chickens were sold out – and cafes and restaurants had equally successful weekends and stayed open longer for the anticipated influx of visitors. The Riverside Cafe claimed its 'busiest day of the year'. The lone bookshop found it 'great for us – lots of people from out of town'. The hardware store offered 'picnic hampers ideal for Opera in the Paddock'. The main dress shop ran successful day-long sales, but many others closed as usual at midday. A country music busker in the middle of the main street, and the record shop with little other than country and western CDs, may perhaps have gained additional revenue. Opera North West have estimated that some $600,000 goes into the town through its direct impact. Since Inverell is not on a major regional highway the Opera provides one particular rationale for people to visit the region. Yet in 2009 at least, neither the weekly *Inverell Times* nor the *Warialda Standard*, from the smaller town west of Delungra, found space to feature the Opera in the edition prior to the event.

The uniqueness of Opera in the Paddock is a particular drawcard accounting for the frequent return of visitors: there is no direct competition whatsoever. Its isolated location and brevity constrain potential growth, beyond what for most visitors is simply one evening's entertainment. It indicates why a several day festival format, even in quite remote places like Deniliquin and Parkes, can attract many more visitors, yet it completely fills Inverell's accommodation. By 2010 therefore the Opera was considering new possibilities – smaller concerts in other regional settings, a more commercial orientation (with hampers and wine for sale) and a 2011 format that included a grand finale with music synchronised with fireworks. From its existing format – largely dependent on the substantial labour inputs of Peta and Bill Blyth – diversification beckoned.

Four Winds Festival

The Four Winds Festival is held biennially near Bermagui, a small town of around 1500 people on the Sapphire Coast, 400 kilometres south of Sydney (Figure 7.3). Bermagui, like many country towns, is remote from metropolitan markets, but with two possible advantages for festivals: its coastal setting and some proximity to the national capital, Canberra, from where it is a location for second homes. Once a significant fishing, agricultural and timber centre it has gradually become a residential, sea-change retirement town, to a significant extent for Victorians moving north, and a small, slowly growing tourist centre.

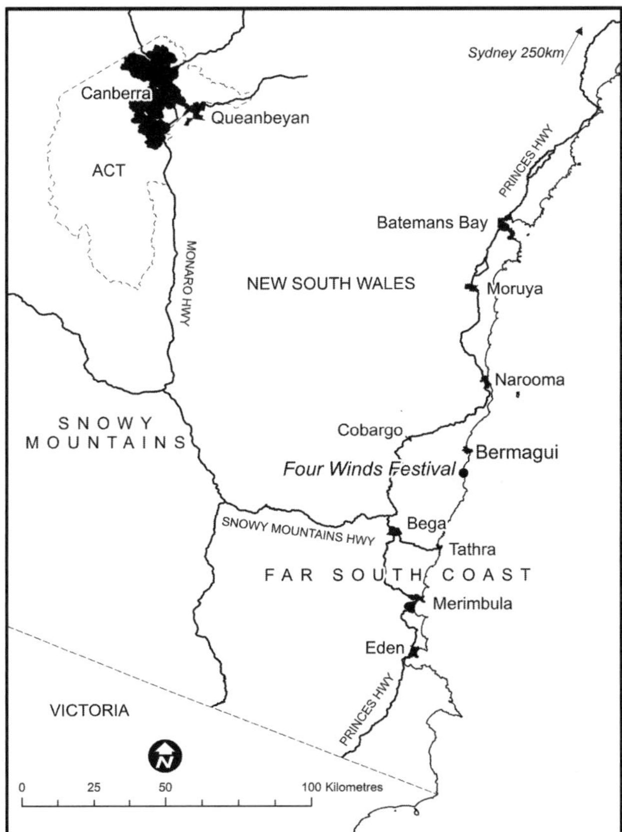

Figure 7.3   Location map, Four Winds Festival

The idea for the Four Winds Festival came from a small group of local people wanting to fill a gap in locally available music. According to Sheila Boughen, Chair of the festival's board (who all quotes in this section are from, unless otherwise stated), 'the community down here seemed to have no or limited access to high quality classic and classical music, so we got together in 1991 to see how we might do something about that. We just don't see why if you live here you shouldn't have access to high quality classical music'. At the same time classical music represented a new niche; 'our gig is the classical gig so we don't step on Merimbula Jazz or Cobargo Folk and anything else'. The Four Winds Festival eventually benefited from some complementarities with other quite different festivals (Chapter 4).

While the initial objective was cultural rather than economic, rather later, recognising socio-economic changes in the area, the Festival committee increasingly felt that since farming, fishing and forestry in the region were in transition a new source of economic development was needed: 'we feel really strongly that culture can be an economic asset for the area and is already an economic asset ... so we definitely see ourselves as part of a new identity for Bermagui and the area'. Recognition of that role by the community was seen as slow to evolve; indeed sixteen years later in 2007 'the community wouldn't even know that. We think that they just think we're a gig at Easter, which is fair enough. But our area is also the start of the Bermagui to Tathra arts trail'. Like many festivals, but especially those with a seemingly elite orientation, the Festival developed few early links with the wider community, where some perceived it as having deliberately chosen an out-of-town site and having made few moves to challenge local notions of elitism.

The Festival began in 1991 and ran annually until 2000 when it became a biennial event since the voluntary board 'got a bit exhausted'. The board had ten unpaid members (more than half from the Bermagui area but some in Canberra and Sydney with local connections) with a paid part-time administrator with high level financial and accounting skills, a similarly part-time paid artistic director, and a part-time production assistant doing most of the logistics, such as booking artists and stage management. Other workers were hired intermittently, especially at festival times when volunteers were also highly involved.

By the end of the 2000s it had developed what it called the four pillars:

1. The place: inspired by and celebrating nature & its beauty, creating a sense of belonging through the program interpreted around the site and our area.
2. People and community: we value relationships by making people feel welcome to our community while increasing our local audience. We are active in developing the role of culture as an asset in our region - local and beyond.
3. Music and performing arts: we focus on fine music of all kinds, with a balance between the new and familiar classical, appropriate to the Festival site and our core audience. We encourage elements of magic and the unexpected which both comfort and challenge.
4. Outreach through arts and education: provide a way of taking great quality music to the schools and community in our region, through an interactive creative process leading to students contributing to the development of the arts. We encourage a love of music and the arts.

A critical element was the Festival's use of an outdoor amphitheatre close to the ocean at Barragga Bay some 10 kilometres south of Bermagui (Figure 7.4). Its existence created the site. The amphitheatre was a privately owned paddock that was initially temporarily terraced, with marquees at the top of the hill for food and wine (and toilets).

Figure 7.4   Four Winds Festival, 2008

The first Festival at Easter 1991 was designed as a test run, by invitation only (a policy that may also have unwittingly shaped notions of elitism). Two hundred people came, but rain came too and the Festival transferred to Bermagui community hall: 'It ended up being a real event and the whole move showed us that it wasn't just the music, it was the community and the place'. The Festival was opened by actress Patricia Kennedy reciting poetry, incidentally accompanied by a flight of ducks descending on the lake behind her, to the applause of an audience of about two hundred, a link with nature that the Festival has constantly stressed.

Like most festivals it has grown steadily over the years, now attracting about 1,000 people on each of the two days. By 2008, about a third were local people, from Bateman's Bay to Merimbula and the hinterland, a third came from Canberra and a further third from elsewhere, mainly Sydney and Melbourne. The goal has been to slowly increase the local audience 'because we feel if we increased overall but it was all outside the local area we wouldn't be fulfilling the reason we exist'. By 2010 it claimed that 45 per cent of audiences were now local people (Frew 2011a). It attracts a largely middle-aged and middle-class audience, wrapped warmly, with many wearing Akubra hats as at Opera in the Paddock. Festival visitors came for several reasons but ambience played a big role:

> We found there were four reasons why people came; they come because when they come and park their cars we open their car doors and greet them and park their cars and that sort of stuff, so they love the welcoming and it's all low key. They love that it isn't full of corporate banners ... and they love the connection to the community like going into town ... everybody wants to be in a little community. Then they love the place and nature; the whole connection to nature is huge because the site is very beautiful. We've done plantings just of native species and it's got a lake behind so you can watch the music and watch the ducks fly in ... and then it's the music ... it's only one of four reasons why people come.

The site was 'carefully managed to confirm the idea of Bermagui as "paradise" and little allowed to disrupt the conventional pleasures of this paradise' so that distracting human sounds, like traffic, were banished to the periphery and the 'power and emotional rewards of the festival were heightened by the combination of sounds of bellbirds, frogs and winds moving through the trees' (Duffy and Waitt 2011:52). The webpage records one visitor remarking 'the frogs started to cycle their rhythm in time with the music ... when the music finished the frogs went on for two bars then went silent'. Later performances in Bermagui were staged in parkland and performers were brought in on, and often performed from the top of, drays. The particularly attractive site and its deliberate isolation from urban life resulted in a very strong connection between visitors and place to the extent that 'the connection to the place is huge and that's why people tolerate music they don't always like'. Indeed 'you can lie down and go to sleep at this thing and no one cares, do a crossword or go up and have a coffee' as opposed to a concert 'where you think "oh bugger it, I've paid 50 bucks for this". Consequently 'people bring their blankets, picnics and chairs and you'll see someone listening to something else on the radio'. Flexibility and atmosphere were invaluable.

Cuisine was an integral part of the Festival, culminating for some in a Saturday night outdoor feast in adjoining woodland. Food and wine were separately organised. As the 2010 Festival web site suggested,

> As we all know Four Winds is a feast of music and art but equally important we want you to experience some of the culinary pleasures of this special region. We have worked hard with local foodies to provide a range of food and wine options which are fairly simple, use local produce where possible and fit in with the feel of Four Winds and the area … Our feast under the stars on Saturday evening will be a more social and informal gathering where the real culinary delights of the area will feature. Look forward to some pleasant surprises. Tickets are limited.

The 2010 programme similarly promised 'the opportunity to sample local wines and delicious homemade foods from our marquee. Plunger coffee, fine teas and local patisserie will be available all day. We will be selling oysters grown in pristine Wapengo Lake and baguettes with gourmet fillings'.

By then a newly arrived Bermagui gelato bar (the Bermagui Gelato Clinic) had deliberately created a 'special Festival gelato': a pecan cinnamon gelato with blackberry sauce, named Passion for Four Winds. The gelato bar was part of a wider transformation of Bermagui, that included the opening of a $5 million retail development including a cafe, wine bar and delicatessen at Bermagui's Fishermen's Wharf, designed by the distinguished architect and local resident Philip Cox, which, as the owner of the gelato bar pointed out, had resulted in social change: 'Traditionally, Bermagui was not somewhere people went out to eat … This summer we've had queues out the door for the first time. We need the region to develop gastro tourism and inspire the locals' (quoted in Baum 2010:5).

Like most festivals marketing budgets have been small and marketing was deliberately informal and personal, being primarily 'relationship marketing', with a quarterly newsletter and two brochures to a database of about 1,500 people, that encourages recipients to 'give one to a friend' with the only overtly commercial marketing being cinema advertisements in Canberra, Narooma and Merimbula. Such marketing therefore assumes a significant amount of return visiting.

From the beginning it was intended that both 'western' and 'eastern music' be performed: a regional attempt to introduce ideas of 'world music', though international artists were necessarily relatively few. The Festival has sought out some of the best national and international performers – the flautist Jane Rutter was the principal performer at the inaugural Festival – and 'we've got a very strong commitment to paying professional fees to musicians so it's seen as a serious gig and we have no trouble getting musicians'. The Festival has introduced avant-garde performers to Australia, such as the American Terry Riley, famous as a leading proponent of minimalism. Achieving the right musical balance has been much debated, and is seen as the main constraint to success and sustainability:

> I think the real risk in people not coming is if we stretch too far into more esoteric music; too much contemporary is definitely a danger ... so we sort of do a risk assessment of the program. There's no doubt you can't annoy your core audience so they like being stretched a bit. But if you turn it into a contemporary music festival it wouldn't work, we'd lose people.

The Festival has also sought to introduce pieces to Australian audiences. In 2010 a new work by Peter Sculthorpe, composed specifically for the Festival, was performed and the Andrea Keller Jazz Quartet also played new works composed for the Festival:

> Andrea visited Bermagui in August to get a feel for the place ... Having immersed herself in the environment, watching the sun rise over the ocean, listening to the birds and feeling the wind on her face Andrea commented: 'I don't want the music to be too descriptive, I would like it to communicate the feeling, space and beauty of this place'.

Part of the Festival's goal was to cherish eclecticism and celebrate all forms of musical expression. On the eve of the 2010 Festival,

> Composers have finished their scores and musicians are rehearsing across the country. Soon they'll be making their journeys to Bermagui, from Europe, Darwin, Melbourne, Sydney, Perth, Tamworth, Bega, Canberra, Byron Bay and Brisbane. Musically, you're in for an incredibly diverse weekend, with everything from Gregorian chant to flamenco, via contemporary Australian jazz, heartland classical music, renaissance treasures, cult 60s film scores, and Indigenous Australian songs in language. Instruments travelling to Bermagui will include a Ron Overs piano, a concert harp, drum kit, viola da gamba, string quartet, guitar, more percussion instruments than you can imagine and I can name, and maybe even a few recorders!

Eclecticism could both challenge and intrigue audiences, and most festival programmes combined new and experimental work with pieces that were likely to be more familiar and accessible. Occasionally the Festival offered ideas and hints on gaining access to the music, when new performers or instruments appeared, such as the rare viola da gamba:

> The quick way to learn real information is to google "viola da gamba." However, to shine at the next barbecue or cocktail party, you should know that the Australian Viola da Gamba Society will be holding their annual workshop in Bermagui over Easter.

Cultural capital was on offer at Bermagui too.

By the late 2000s the Festival was bringing in as many as 35 to 40 musicians for each event, which involved an expenditure of about $150,000, half the total budget. The core of the music

> tends to be familiar, traditional, classical music … string quartets and so on and then we added on, after a few years, a Friday night cabaret gig in town because we realise that Barragga Bay is a bit out of sight and a bit cut off. That gets sold out really quickly as lighter music, more fun and a bit jazzy. Now we've added on also in the last festival a lunchtime forum that Margaret Throsby from the ABC moderates. We call it "Up Close and Personal" and the idea of that is you get a chance to meet people, say living composers and musicians and they talk about how they do their work and give a little demonstration. Next year we've going to have an opening ceremony on the footy oval in town on the Friday afternoon so it's now a three day festival.

Amongst other things the 2008 Up Close and Personal brought composer Peter Sculthorpe and Aboriginal didjeridu player William Barton together to discuss musical composition.

Like most festivals ticket sales contribute only a small part of the revenue – just a third of the income, with further thirds from grants and donations. The Festival has sought corporate support, but 'we haven't had much luck going to companies and getting money from them, because what's in it for them? It's a little country community'. Consequently they developed different kinds of connections, aimed at community philanthropy: 'We had two events last year in Sydney and Melbourne, small intimate events at musicians' houses and raised $45,000 from 60 people from you know, 50 bucks to large money, so we're going to develop the community philanthropy more because it fits in with our philosophy of nurturing and supporting our [low-income] community'. The Festival also established the 'Friends of Four Winds' which sponsored events, brought some performers to Bermagui and gave its members a sense of personal connection. In 2010, $773,000 was raised in a grass-roots campaign, and the Australia Council for the Arts approved a $420,000 grant for the Festival under the Federal Government's *Creative Communities Partnership Initiative.* Local Member of Parliament, Mike Kelly (2010), observed that 'The Four Winds Festival is an institution of the Far South Coast that contributes to the cultural calendar of the whole region and adds many hundreds of thousands of dollars into the local community through the tourism industry'. The grant was intended to broaden the Festival from a focus on professional performances to include greater community participation. By then they had also acquired 250 private donors and pro-bono assistance from the accounting company KPMG and the Sydney Opera House.

Recognition of the need for financial support had coincided with realisation of the value of developing and formalising ties to the local community. The Four Winds Festival was initially criticised for not supporting local people enough but argued that 'we support that and other people do that but our thing was to bring in the highest quality that Australia and now overseas has to offer. So we are doing other things now to nourish and promote local things'. More than a decade later that perspective had shifted. 'Our big push is to connect more and be more visible in the local community regardless of whether you come or not' so that 'we want to put roots down in the culture and in the community'. So much so that by 2011: 'we want to reverse the thinking that classical music is made in cities. Our motto is "Born in Bermagui"' (quoted in Frew 2011a:14). From 2008 the Festival developed an initiative called Barnstorming, 'our community outreach', which involved initially performing at various local schools and establishing public concerts so that 'we get some flow on of people, since we've got a big commitment to local education and to the cultural development of the area'. Thus the 2008 Festival introduced a free opening-day concert in Bermagui itself, with Aboriginal dancers from the local Yuin tribe, as part of an agenda for greater social inclusion. The next Festival two years later was closed by Aboriginal women from The Black Arm Band, who performed a 'celebration of language and cultural survival'. Before the Festival members of the band visited the Wallaga Lake Aboriginal community to share skills, through a series of music workshops, while for the first time a young Aboriginal musician performed rap at the Festival.

Community involvement also extended to work experience and employment: 'In 2006 we invited some local high school students who were doing any sort of arts subjects to come and be, we call them, production assistants so they understood how a festival gets done. They did everything from going to rehearsals and looking after an artist and one of them actually is being offered a part-time job at the festival as a result'. However, even school music teachers have not always been supportive. 'One of them said it was because kids at our school aren't interested in classical music … There's no hostility or anything but I think people see classical music as a bit elitist, out at Barragga Bay and … the more we do things around town the better it'll get, and more young people too, because we have a lot of contemporary music in the festival program and we have world premieres and commission work now. It's quite groundbreaking what we're doing in the music scene'. Nonetheless the Festival went ahead to support a locally based project called *Inspiring*. Prior to the Festival this resulted in a 'world-premiere, one-off performance of students from local schools from Moruya to Eden', with a prestigious Sydney school and a distinguished drummer, David Hewitt. As the Artistic Director of the Festival stated: 'I am committed to generating a lasting creative legacy. There is so much talent within this region that needs to be supported and promoted. Providing opportunities such as this collaboration to young students of the region builds their repertoire and shows them what is possible. Four Winds is so much more than just a Festival'. That too evolved into more local participation in the Festival itself with local dancers, ballerinas and musicians being involved in the 2010 Festival. By 2011 plans were to turn the festival amphitheatre into a permanent cultural hub for the region for new music, master-classes, artist-in-residency programs and local school music teachers. A federal government grant worth over $1.6 million was won towards this, enabling construction of a sewerage system, broadband infrastructure and a new road to access the site. Yet creative frugality was still needed, hence architects Philip Cox and Clinton Murray waived their fees to design a new sound shell and permanent hall for the festival and cultural hub. Somewhat differently a long-term objective has been to keep prices low and accessible, because 'it's a low income area'; in 2008 the tickets were $100 for the two days.

The Festival has sought to develop specific environmental policies that would turn it initially into a carbon–neutral position and subsequently carbon positive and feeding energy into the grid: 'We're doing that in partnership with climatefriendly. com where we offset our artist and production team travel, and we also support local projects, like solar cells on the school'. It also teamed up with Clean Energy for Eternity to help visitors calculate their emissions, and sought to make the whole site 'zero landfill' by not selling such things as disposable plastic wine glasses. The 2008 Four Winds Festival became an accredited carbon-neutral festival, with all the energy use, artists' travel and printing offset with carbon credits. The festival sought to become harmonised with nature musically and atmospherically.

The Role of Place

Both the Opera and Four Winds are relatively small, specialised events that are 'not for everyone', in or near small country towns remote from metropolitan markets, and consequently with constrained potential for growth. Even smaller classical festivals, such as those at Bridgetown and Bangalow, have no real scope for growth without changing the intimate nature of the occasion. For chamber music that is impossible. Nonetheless all have been remarkably successful, although visitor numbers have stabilised or reached their peak, not least in providing an outlet for innovative music. Like other small festivals, both Opera and Four Winds rely on substantial return visiting, with limited resources devoted to formal advertising, and both are conscious of a need to keep the number of visitors relatively small to preserve the spirit of the occasion. However, classical music and opera festivals are rare and different; uniqueness and distinctiveness account for much return visiting. A small, enthusiastic and dedicated group of return visitors also provides the basis for experimentation. The *Sydney Morning Herald* observed of the Four Winds in 2010 that 'it's a tribute to the power of the festival format that a boat fishing village in Australia can host groundbreaking new works played by some of the best musicians and artists on the Pacific rim'. Even small festivals can put small places on large maps, shift images of them and play a part in musical innovation.

Modest festival size and the particular intimacies of small places separated from urban life have enhanced some notions of community. At Bermagui 'The didj[eridu] and energy down my spine, looking across the sea of faces, more familiar people, more people I know, my community'; and for another,

> I look around. I think this is my community you know, I look around and …
> there is the women in the local corner shop and there is the people I know. And
> I just think how lucky we are … And, also this community has drawn this thing
> [together]. (Quoted in Duffy and Waitt 2011:52–53)

Community both stimulates and benefits from the festival. Small festivals in small places, even when focused on specialist music genres, may involve many local people in a range of ways. Moreover both the Opera and the Four Winds devised ways of becoming closer to the town, with 'branches' of the events being staged there and local schoolchildren and regional performers involved, so avoiding perceptions of being 'a bit hidden away and a bit mysterious' and elitist. Likewise the Tyalgum Festival sought to ensure 'that quality performance experiences are offered to regional audiences, particularly young people'. It too 'has expanded to embrace the many aspects of our local creative community, and the extraordinary talent of our youth' by sponsoring and giving prizes for local competitions, developing broader community links, including a Tyalfest for Kids concert 'featuring some of the Tweed's best young classical musicians, in association with the Murwillumbah Festival of Performing Arts and the Tweed Valley Banana Festival: A classical music concert performed BY young people FOR young people!'. But, as at the Four Winds Festival, and no doubt elsewhere, as the local mayor pointed out: 'there will always be a bit of an issue because this type of festival is different from what country people would normally expect to have in their area' (quoted in Frew 2011a:14).

Most classical festivals have also sought links with other arts festivals and communities. Bermagui became part of a local arts trail, known to some as 'the culture corridor'. The Tyalgum Festival collaborated with Caldera Art, which organised a local annual Artfest and whose mission was 'to promote regional biodiversity values and/or raise awareness of a relevant habitat conservation issue'. Part of that collaboration involved having Caldera artists 'in residence' at Tyalgum Hall over the Festival weekend. Visitors could speak with the artists and observe progress of artwork between concerts. The Woodend Winter Arts Festival eventually covered classical music, jazz, literary events and visual arts, with 'a program for young people and children and a series of free community events to ensure that it remains accessible to everyone'. In Inverell a local art exhibition is staged at the same time as the Opera. Over time too most classical festivals have taken on elements of gastronomy, either by providing food and wine within the festival or by involving local restaurants and providores, as at Bermagui. Festivals have thus contributed to a diverse regional revitalisation that has taken some places and regions away from past connections towards a more recreational and cultural landscape where the arts in a broad context – from music and dance to art – have stimulated the local economy.

That sense of place may encourage both new forms of economic growth and migration to some festival places where the ambience has proved particularly attractive. Although the Woodend Winter Arts Festival (100 kilometres north of

Melbourne) had visitors from many places it was 'Melbourne suburbanites (who congregated longingly around local real estate windows)' that typified both the interest of visitors in a possible move, and the pride of local people who had staged the festival there. As the principle organiser of the Four Winds Festivals said in 2007,

> We've had our first people move to the area permanently because of Four Winds … that's a shift that's an indicator of change. They said they were looking to move somewhere and went up and down the NSW coast and they had never been to Four Winds and heard about it and thought "we want to live in a town that does something like that" and when they talk to people they tell people about it.

While that is probably exceptional a successful festival in a pleasant place may stimulate not just return festival visits but return tourism at other times. And good words about places are spread.

Even so a perception remains that classical music is elitist and detached from the interests and preoccupations of small regional towns. In some part that is a function of such festivals being small, many performers being from distant places, and some visitors being unfamiliar with particular styles and formats. Both the Four Winds and the Opera in the Paddock have resisted suggestions either that they become more contemporary and experimental, or that they become more 'popular', with Gilbert and Sullivan. However, as at Bermagui, expansion of festivals is often limited by the size of the venue and, more importantly, the desire 'to keep the intimacy', which depends on small size, lack of parking problems, the ability to meet friends and closeness to the music. Smaller numbers also mean shorter toilet queues, less mass-produced food and fewer environmental problems. Ultimately both the Opera in the Paddock and Four Winds have expanded gently in time and place – taking on new events and moving physically and metaphorically closer to town.

Specialisation, distinctiveness, gastronomic ties, small size and classical music have combined to create and convey cultural capital. Festivals are thus in some ways bound up in class processes and transformations. At these events more than others a sense of acquiring cultural capital is evident, where individuals at the performances seek to acquire social status, simply on the basis of being there, and subsequently retailing the experience. Being part of a particular 'classical' sub-culture, consuming gourmet food, local oysters and fine wine are hallmarks of an emerging bourgeois countryside, fuelled by metropolitan out-migrants.

That has also contributed to a form of marketing, with classical music festivals being used to associate places with 'classy' images and attempts to lure wealthier, older visitors. The symbolic capital associated with classical music, opera – and perhaps also jazz – imbues places with 'class' and sophistication, important images used by tourism promoters to attract exactly the demographic group, older professionals and discerning middle-class tourists with high disposable incomes, that are sought after by many locations as 'ideal' tourists. Ironically many classical festivals were conceived primarily as events to enrich the lives of existing local populations, allowing people living a great distance away from metropolitan opera houses and concert halls to attend high-quality performances that they would not otherwise see. They are partly reflections of the demographic transformations taking place in sea-change and tree-change towns. Yet in creating such festivals they have risked a specialisation that creates a degree of alienation from the local community, who see it as irrelevant to their interests, especially where the Festival is in an 'out-of-town' location. Only gradually, and with much effort from organisers, has that divide been transcended. While visitors to classical festivals are usually relatively well-off, middle class and middle aged, they are not necessarily very different from those at other festivals, and were often there for the same reasons, which also stressed escapism, ambience and togetherness as much as the specific music. Classical music and similar festivals are not at all therefore the antithesis of more 'popular' music festivals. They attract local audiences, have similar social and economic links with local communities and draw on them for support in various ways. Through their specialist orientation, such festivals are more than posh place promotion – they are attempts to stage something high quality, even special, in remote, picturesque locations.

Chapter 8
Tamworth: Australia's Country Music Capital

This chapter explores how an annual country music festival was the catalyst for the remarkable transformation of an Australian town: Tamworth, a major rural centre in northern NSW with a population of 43,000 (Figure 7.1, p. 139). Tamworth has seen extensive transformations in its economy and local identity, linked to country music, as a result of hosting a highly successful annual country music festival. This recent history began with a country music radio show and the growth of a small but dedicated country music 'scene' in Tamworth, made up of instrumentalists and singers, sound engineers, venue owners and event promoters. Through a major festival and related tourism, Tamworth eventually became known as *the* place for country music – the self-appointed 'capital' of country music in Australia (a tag which would, it hoped, eventually stick in the national imagination). By world standards Tamworth's local country music scene is actually quite small. Tamworth promotes itself as Australia's answer to Nashville, Tennessee (a city to which Tamworth has sent festival managers, to learn 'how it's done'), but with a fraction of that city's population, music industry infrastructure and activity. How Tamworth has come to be Australia's 'country music capital' from a modest base is a story of place promotion and overt attempts to harness a festival for regional development gains. It is a status deliberately created as an outcome of strategic place marketing, undertaken by tourism authorities, promotional companies and local government. Since the 1970s, and particularly after exponential growth in the 1980s and 1990s, country music has come to define Tamworth, gaining it unprecedented media attention and creating an intangible, but invaluable stock of meanings able to be deployed in tourism promotions. How that festival, its organisational structure, the music and its related myths (of rural and national identities and 'the country') have transformed place, is the central theme of this chapter.

The rural setting is particularly important: key actors in Tamworth, as well as national and international media and other commercial organisations have invested in the idea that Tamworth, its festival and country music are quintessentially rural. Rurality – a sense of the rural – is central to country music, to promotional images of town and to efforts to re-position Tamworth within a national, Australian geographical imagination. The country music festival put Tamworth on the map of national media attention, but the rurality in country music itself became synonymous with Australian values and ideologies – stimulating a far more ambitious promotional goal to encapsulate nationalist sentiments and become an event symbolic of the whole nation. This chapter traces Tamworth's story: how it grew to become Australia's largest single music festival (and the world's second largest country music festival); how it leveraged off the international growth in the market for country music, as well as harness associations with rurality inherent to that musical genre; and how place images for Tamworth were produced by a particular network of institutional actors alongside the music industry, and by musicians and audiences themselves.

This chapter also discusses how residents have reacted to Tamworth's country music festival and associated place marketing. Antagonisms emerge especially when festivals become large, but in Tamworth are associated with a genre of music that has enormous cultural and symbolic baggage. Country music evokes a rich imagery of rural life, which can be effective in marketing, but is prone to be caricatured as 'hick' or 'redneck': a problem both for festival organisers who want to project a sophisticated image and attract city residents as visitors, and for local residents who don't wish to be associated with 'backward' stereotypes. An analysis of resident surveys reveals how the festival, country music and the tourist transformation of the town have been variously contested and celebrated.

Visits were made to Tamworth between 1997 and 2002, and again in 2005, 2008 and 2009. Over that time, Tamworth's reputation as country music capital continued to be subject to debate – surrounding the festival's 'hick' associations, marginalisation of Aboriginal performers, and its perceived shift to the 'mainstream', for instance through booking rock and roll bands and seemingly drifting from its 'country roots'. Such controversies are not merely a matter of taste, but emphasise how the cultural content and credibility of festivals have implications for viability, and thus regional development. Tamworth organisers have attempted to negotiate these tensions and expectations – that they stay true to their 'roots', that they remain inclusive, but not be too 'redneck' – through shifting strategies for place marketing and promotion. Place marketing is moreover part of a much broader attempt to reposition the town economically, and within a national cultural and geographical imagination, but central to all this is the music itself – *country* music.

The 'Country', and 'Country Music'

Tamworth sought to become 'country music capital' by staging its annual festival and encouraging related tourism. Its claim to such status is simultaneously a pitch for a musical genre, and a claim, by association, for 'country': a more general Australian descriptor for rural places and lifestyles. This slippage, between a musical style imported from North America, and 'country', signifying rural Australia, is a crucial one. It is at the heart of Tamworth's media image. Mythologies within country music – linked to its appeal to roots, the importance of 'directness' and 'honesty' in lyrics – have become features of marketing Tamworth as 'country' in a more generic way (as hospitable, friendly, down-to-earth). The 'country' is antonymic to the cosmopolitanism and sophistication of urban places and their marketing. Tamworth's place marketing campaigns, associated with country music, entail a different sort of cultural politics, hence there are questions about how use of unsophisticated rural imagery (rather than appeals to an elite) catalyses reactions from local populations; and the extent to which, through the festival itself, local populations and tourists participate in the transformation of Tamworth's identity. When Tamworth then claims through its festival to be 'Australia's country music capital', it is actually claiming two things: to be the place at the heart of an iconic music style, and to be the nation's central iconic 'country' place.

The Country Music Festival has been crucial because, with media coverage every year, it has repositioned the entire town in the national imagination, not just attracting tourists, but also shifting reputations for Tamworth in ways that counter headlines of rural decline, replacing tales of decay with 'good news' stories. Tamworth has been arguably the most successful festival in this regard in Australia, so that the fate of the entire town has been altered because of it. Building on the success of its annual country music festival has solidified the reputation of the town in the music industry, given the regional tourism industry a focus and a 'hook' into nationwide awareness, and created more permanent markers of place connected to a musical style.

Country music, as its name suggests, is perceived as the music of rural areas. Notions of an innate link to rural landscapes have become normalised in country music – as if the style of music is 'country' because of its origins in rural areas. Country music is closely linked to American national identity, as a 'native art [whose] inspiration springs from the heart of a nation' (Peterson 1997:199), but has become an iconic genre of rural people and culture globally. It celebrated rural space, though not without doubt and uncertainty; the imagined place of country music was a 'landscape of nostalgic rural salvation and refuge from the cold impersonal nature of the modern cityscape' (Lewis 1997:167). Country music portrayed a 'nostalgia for a rural paradise, symbolised by a yearning for a simpler way of life, a looking back to an uncomplicated place' (Kong 1995:187), and a place where an older social order remained valid, compared with the city.

Country music came to Australia in the early twentieth century, when it was known as 'hillbilly' or 'folk', through radio broadcasts, gramophone discs, at rodeos and vaudeville shows, in sheet music (household playing and singing on piano and ukulele was still popular at the time), at square dances and through cinema, where 'singing cowboy' films, such as those starring Gene Autry, were set against a backdrop of iconic visual imagery: desert landscapes, wagon trails, tough men, hats, holsters, horses and guns. There were parallels in the frontier narratives of the United States (Whiteoak 2003). Further growth in Australian country music was heavily influenced by American TV shows such as *Bonanza* and *On the Range*, which accompanied country music's 'golden age' in the 1950s and 1960s, when Australian performers such as Slim Dusty and Smokey Dawson rose to fame. This era of heightened popularity for country music occurred when rural-urban migration peaked in Australia. Manufacturing jobs in cities provided better opportunities for casual workforces that had previously toured the country in fruit-picking, shearing and other agricultural work, and country musicians such as Dusty and Dawson also moved to the city, in part to be closer to major record companies. Country music found favour with audiences at the very time that the 'country' lifestyle it seemingly represented was being rapidly replaced by suburban life. Much later, in the 1990s, with the advent of cable television, country music's second boom period in the United States (led by Garth Brooks and Alan Jackson, among others), was paralleled in Australia by a new set of country music stars such as Gina Jeffreys, Troy Cassar-Daley and Lee Kernighan.

Across these eras, country music added to and entrenched conservative values – of home, heterosexuality, family, and masculine taming of nature – and reflected rural hardship. Songs were as likely to depict sinners as wholesome rural folk, to tell both prison stories and celebrate idyllic rural landscapes. Country music became popular too among Indigenous Australians, largely via radio exposure and tours to remote communities by artists such as Slim Dusty and Ted Egan. In time Aboriginal performers such as Jimmy Little and Vic Simms appropriated country music's love of the land within an Aboriginal oeuvre (Dunbar-Hall and Gibson 2004). Meanwhile an Australian folk tradition, with links to the history of the Australian union movement, emerged and became more strongly associated with activism and socialist nationalism than with rural values. Subsequently at festivals such as Tamworth, folk and country fused and overlapped. Celtic folk roots and American popular culture were both antecedents to the Australian country music scene: a simple, heartfelt music about a colonial landscape, but in another hemisphere, one populated by heroic men (and long-suffering women). Music, radio, film and television combined to provide rich sources of imagery that could be mined and adapted for Australian audiences – nowhere more so than at Tamworth.

Creating 'Country', Promoting Tamworth

From the 1970s Tamworth became widely known through its annual Country Music Festival. Before then, Tamworth had a country music radio show and local venues to capture touring artists – like many other rural towns on the inland highway circuit. A local radio station, 2TM, was the main output of country music, but by the mid-1960s radio had suffered major blows to its audience numbers, with the introduction of television. Consequently 2TM started to run a series of special interest programs during the evening. 'Hoedown', first broadcast in 1965, featuring the latest Australian and American country records and occasional live performances, became widely listened to, eventually dominating 2TM's evening timeslots. Few other radio stations were then playing country music, largely due to the arrival of rock 'n' roll, while the radio station's unusually clear broadcast signal, which could be heard across eastern Australia and some parts of the Pacific from

Tamworth's high plateau location, linked an audience to the town substantially above and beyond its own population.

2TM executives were impressed with the potential to influence a large rural population, and in 1969 for the first time used the tag 'country music capital' for Tamworth, mainly to advertise country music merchandise. The establishment of recording studios around this time also solidified the presence of the country music industry in Tamworth. The Hadley country music studios were opened in 1970; other recording studios, including Opal, Selection and Enrec, followed soon after (Allen 1988:6). The Modern Country Music Association (later the Capital Country Music Association, CCMA) established a local branch in Tamworth, which started a talent show in 1965 and a Jamboree the following year: events scheduled for the Australia Day holiday weekend in January.

In 1973, those events were consolidated, and the Tamworth Country Music Festival became an official event on the country music calendar, with 2TM announcing the winners of the inaugural Australasian Country Music Awards. The Australia Day weekend was ideal because it was normally a quieter time for business and for 2TM: summer holiday-makers hit the highways, heading to the coast *en masse*, and the media were short of news, thus the mere staging of a festival was likely to generate national coverage – in essence free publicity. The already existing CCMA talent quest and Jamboree ran on this weekend and could be expanded into a festival. Though from its beginnings, the Tamworth Country Music Festival was commercially orientated, it was not until later that it was perceived as a serious boost to the local economy, and brought into the broad orbit of regional economic development strategies. Early festivals paid little regard to commerce or nationalist sentiment and were instead much like other contemporary specialist music festivals – focused on participation and musical appreciation, socialising and bringing together scattered musical clubs and societies.

The festival grew and incorporated many separate events; the idea was to produce a program that was so 'busy' visitors would have to return the following year, having not sampled everything on offer in just one visit. The 1980s were its peak growth period, with increased promotion to fill larger venues for the Australian country music 'Golden Guitar' awards night. 2TM established a promotional arm, BAL Marketing, who were responsible for the promotion and success of the festival and the 'country music capital' tag. The festival itself had no formal coordination until 1993 when the Tamworth City Council took up the role, mainly because of the increasing pressure on infrastructure and promotional needs, and the withdrawal of BAL due to lack of profits. The festival's management structure was re-organised accordingly. Rather than the Council running the entire event through professional event management staff, it managed key logistical problems such as traffic and waste management, and allowed everything else to be run by local non-profit organizations and private businesses. There is no single ticketed 'venue', but a constellation of separate venues and spaces, including 23 local pubs. This qualitative, structural decision has been widely regarded as the key to Tamworth's success. The decentralised organisation of the festival resulted in low barriers to entry and events within the festival proliferated. Organisers could claim that they provide an opportunity for anyone who wants to perform at the festival (for instance in free public venues, busking etc.), although as the festival grew there was a need for some umbrella coordination. In terms of available music, the festival is surprisingly diverse. Performances of varying levels of professionalism take place across the town, 'from mind-numbingly awful to staggeringly brilliant', as journalist Iain Shedden (2010:14) put it, including spaces for buskers, line-dancers (Figure 8.1), alternative and Aboriginal country artists. Such inclusiveness has not in itself eradicated wage exploitation (McIntyre 2003), racial politics or social exclusion (Dunbar-Hall and Gibson 2004), but power is extraordinarily decentralised.

Figure 8.1   Visitors attempt to break the line-dancing world record, Tamworth Country Music Festival, 2005

By 2011, the festival had a 10-day program, 2,400 events, 116 venues and nearly 1,000 artists with around 60,000 daily visitors. Easily exceeding the capacity of local hotels and motels, visitors stay up to a hundred kilometres away in other regional towns, and 5,000 stay in residents' spare bedrooms in the largest homestay program of any festival in Australia (Olding 2011b). According to June Smyth, the festival manager, the festival is 'sophisticated, comfortable with itself and provides a wonderful platform for people to celebrate being Aussie' (personal communication 2001). It covers a wide range of 'country' music from country rock to bluegrass, folk, mainstream country music, bush poetry, line and western swing dancing, reflecting the diversity of country music as it fragments and increasingly 'crosses over' with other genres. Performances take place in a range of venues, from informal buskers and singers in a 'tent city' that is constructed by the river to accommodate extra visitors, through to the pub circuit and larger, formal venues such as the Longyard Hotel, the Tamworth Town Hall, and large open air concerts at Bicentennial Park. The festival culminates in a cavalcade down the main street and the presentation of the Golden Guitar awards in a nationally-televised gala event at a purpose-built regional entertainment centre. With its musical diversity it has widened its appeal, simultaneously pitched as a family event, as a destination for budding musicians to 'be discovered', and as a musical festival for 'serious' enthusiasts of country-related genres.

Tamworth Country Music Festival is without doubt a tourist promotion, and tends to attract an older audience – in a 2007 visitor survey of 1,336 visitors (Tourism Tamworth 2007), nine out of every ten participants were outsiders visiting Tamworth for the festival, and 59 per cent were older than 55. Fully 80 per cent were older than 45, a proportion slowly increasing in the following years, with ageing and high levels of repeat visiting (Pegg and Patterson 2010). These are the age groups who were alive at the time of country music's heyday in the 1950s and 1960s, perhaps watching *Bonanza* on TV or listening to Hoedown – and who now with high disposable incomes and time to travel have become lucrative mainstays of other festivals too, from rock 'n' roll to Elvis, classical to jazz. Although Tamworth is a festival of national significance, 40 per cent came from elsewhere in non-metropolitan NSW and a further 23 per cent from proximate Queensland. Only 14 per cent were from Sydney, 13 per cent from Victoria and a tiny 2 per cent from overseas (a couple from Canada and a person each from Argentina, Ireland and the United States). A third of visitors had friends that lived in Tamworth.

A 2008 survey suggested that over half were primarily motivated to be there because of a 'love for country music', but as at Parkes, Bermagui and elsewhere, 'atmosphere' was the most important overall aspect of the festival, followed by the desire to connect socially with 'the friendly and helpful people of Tamworth' (Pegg and Patterson 2010:96). A feature that sets Tamworth apart from most other festivals is the degree of financial and time commitments from participants – such is the festival's scale and scope for endless diversions. In 2007 a substantial 40 per cent of visitors stayed for ten or more days and barely 6 per cent stayed for only one or two days. Hence, average visitor spending was much higher than at other festivals, at $1,500 per person (Tourism Tamworth 2007). Accommodation and food expenditures were inevitably higher with longer average stays, but with a wide variety of souvenirs, western wear clothing, music and food stalls, per capita discretionary spending was also much higher than at other shorter and smaller festivals. Beyond a certain point very large festivals of this type become major investments for visitors, not a casual visit but a holiday in itself (with budgets set accordingly): perhaps no wonder that one in five surveyed in 2007 also said the festival had become too expensive, and a similar proportion felt it had become too commercial.

Reflecting the unusual management structure, half of the surveyed festival visitors in 2007 bought concert tickets over the counter at the event. Only 25 per cent booked in advance over the internet. Unlike other festivals with single concert line-ups, Tamworth's decentred management structure has helped foster a particular culture of festival attendance, which revolves around booking accommodation well in advance, turning up and deciding what to attend then, rather than beforehand. Only the highest profile artists sell a majority of available tickets in advance. Hence much more than at most other festivals the official programs are pivotal: at over 250 pages long by 2011, and claimed as 'one of the world's biggest festival publications', it drives attendance patterns. Not surprisingly, it also features hundreds of advertisements, for corporate sponsors, pubs and special concerts at the festival, for new albums by festival headliners, but also instrument-makers, local colleges, cafes and butchers (who offer special services for tour buses), organised music tours of North America and even other country music festivals in Mildura, Parkes, Tailem Bend (SA), Wandong and Whittlesea (Victoria), Katherine (NT) and Gore (NZ). Additionally, the festival serves as an umbrella for a range of clubs, associations and speciality groups – from bush balladeers to campdrafters and harmonica players – for whom the Jamboree origins, size and timing of the festival (around Australia Day) provide good reason to schedule their own national awards, talent quests and championships within the festival.

A Place Marketer's Dream?

The notion of Tamworth as 'country music capital' was created initially by 2TM and managed by BAL Marketing, and is used by many more individuals and institutions (Figure 8.2). Various interests have a stake in maintaining Tamworth as country music capital, and warding off rival towns such as Gympie, in Queensland, and Mildura in Victoria, who stage competing 'national' country music festivals (Edwards 2011). Tamworth as 'country music capital' is heavily invested in by commercial interests, and is a tag thoroughly mobilised in national broadcasting and local tourism promotion.

Each year at the festival a national media centre is organised by Tamworth promoters to feed press releases and visual images to print and broadcast media. Coverage of the festival generally consists of 'feel good' stories at the conclusion of national nightly news broadcasts, and lighter, catchier stories in early sections of the major city newspapers. Discussing national media publicity, Tamworth's (then) mayor has said that 'no matter how you feel about the music, it has given Tamworth a recognition factor that corporations would describe as a marketer's dream' (Treloar 1996:2). Official press releases and imagery are usually uncritically absorbed by television and print news reporters, so that the place marketing effort of Tamworth as country music capital has resulted in a

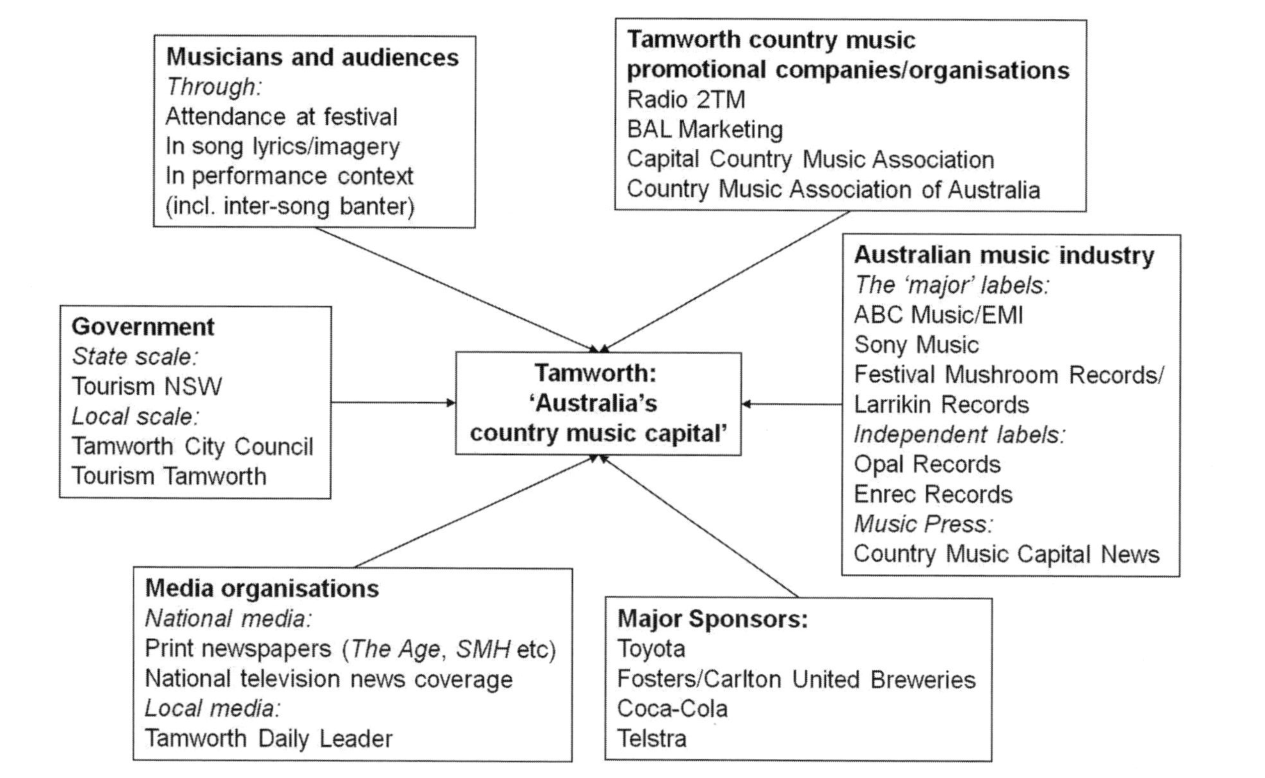

Figure 8.2   **The actor-network that sustains Tamworth as 'country music capital'**

prevailing, sanctioned image becoming the norm, despite the diversity actually apparent in festival performance. In parallel to what Little (1999:439) has argued in the English context,

> a specific view of how 'real' country people think and behave … has become dominant. Values and beliefs of 'rural folk' are being constructed (from inside and outside) as distinct and different – a failure to recognize and share such beliefs casts people as 'other' to authentic country people and ways.

In this case, the Tamworth Country Music Festival has been woven into the fabric of dominant, nationalist mythologies of 'country'. Themes of Australian nationalism, and of 'the rural' within this, are amplified in relation to Tamworth given the timing of its country music festival around the Australia Day holiday, and very much celebrated as a nationalistic event. Tamworth has relied on Australian nationalism and iconic colonial frontier ideas about rurality, and placed itself at the centre of these. In its submission for the 1997 NSW Tourism Awards for Excellence, the Council responded to the question 'How does your event integrate with the natural and/or cultural environment?' with the following statement: 'Tamworth – it's Australia'. Further on in the same application the festival is described as 'a celebration of the Australian Identity … to showcase the sum and substance of being Australian'. Throughout other promotional documents Tamworth and the Country Music Festival are variously described as: 'a celebration of the Australian entity'; 'that feeling of warmth when two strangers on a street actually bid each other nothing more than a simple "g-day"'; with 'happenings [that] classically illustrate the Australian character'. Clichéd versions of Australian identity are mobilised, thus it is claimed that participants can 'fulfil the unique Aussie spirit of 'having a go', enjoy a 'juicy piece of prime beef prepared in an establishment that could have that day taken the beast from the back paddock and placed it onto the char grill', and experience the 'spirit of the Anzacs and images of the Kokoda track' through assertions of 'mateship' (Tamworth City Council files 1997). Organisers claim that 'country music conjures up images of all things rural', a sentiment that can be brought back from the festival in paintings of rural landscapes captured on anything from a beer bottle to a garden spade. In this tourist/media construction Tamworth is depicted as the site of quintessential rural experiences, and this in turn is taken as central to Australian national identity, leading organisers to the following conclusion: 'Tamworth would challenge that nowhere else in Australia … can the culture of our country be personified so accurately in spirit or style… It's where country is' (Tamworth City Council files 1997).

Such sentiments have enabled festival organisers to secure support from several large sponsors who seek to benefit from associated images. Toyota have been major sponsors for nearly two decades, and see the festival as an important component in its strategy to 'Australianise' its brand image, alongside television advertisements set in rural locales. Festival billboards, brochures and advertisements celebrate the 'Toyota Country' brand (Figure 8.3), and promote the company's sponsorship of the awards. Advertisements in the 'Stars, Guitars and Toyota Cars' campaign thus claimed: 'The Toyota Country Music Awards represent the pinnacle of achievement for country musicians and performers in Australia. Toyota are very proud to sponsor this event, because we believe that, in country music, Australia finds its true voice'. Toyota even runs its own festival news radio service: Toyota Festival FM 90.5. Although Toyota's marketing director, Scott Grant, has suggested that the company 'is certainly not into Australiana cheap tricks' (quoted in McKay 2004:1), there is no doubt that the Japanese company seeks to appeal to patriotic Australian sentiments. The company now enjoys the largest share of the Australian car market, and dominates sales of 4-wheel-drive vehicles in rural areas.

In the early 1990s Telstra, Australia's largest telecommunications company, also became a major sponsor. It too, gains from an association with 'country'. After being part-privatised, Telstra faced repeated criticisms for a perceived decline in services to rural communities compared with metropolitan areas. Telstra's festival sponsorship, and its 'Country Wide' advertising campaign, are essentially public relations exercises to counteract negative discourses of 'ignoring the bush', by aligning the company with 'country' imagery via sponsorship of the festival. The 2007 survey suggested that this had had some success: 92 per cent were aware of Telstra's sponsorship of the festival, and 4 out of every 5 were aware of Telstra's 'Country Wide' brand for regional telecommunications service delivery. Indeed, 'country' is now firmly established within the advertising industry as an immensely useful slogan for marketing products and framing tourism promotion (Gilbert and Tung 1990). A 1990s conference organised by the Country Music Associations of America and Australia, entitled *Australia: Sold on Country,* explored the growing importance of using country images to sell products, at which George Elliot, CEO of George Patterson Bates marketing company argued that brands are 'trusted friends' and that nothing is more trusted than the heritage of 'country'. Country was described as 'credible', 'decent', 'honest' and 'consistent'. In times of change it represents 'a place of security and safety'. By positioning itself as 'country music capital', Tamworth seeks association with the generic signifier 'country', such that it can also claim to be the 'capital of *country* Australia'.

However, particular social groups are absent from what has come to be understood as 'country', amplifying marginalisation and exclusion. The Australian heritage presented at Tamworth, and which companies like Toyota and Telstra seek to invoke in sponsorship, is invariably masculine and white, and often informed by American 'cowboy' imagery, marginalising Aboriginality, even though country music is also an important part of Indigenous cultural expressions (Dunbar-Hall and Gibson 2004). In brochures and advertisements, white Anglo-Saxon Australians dominate over other groups; Indigenous Australians are absent, hence tourist expectations of experiencing Aboriginal culture are low, contributing to the poor visibility and lack of appreciation of Aboriginal musicians in the festival.

Figure 8.3   'Toyota Country'

Source: Gibson and Davidson 2004:395

Capturing Music in Tamworth's Built Environment

Tamworth tourism promoters and the local council were very much aware of
the precedent set by Nashville (America's 'home of country music' and a major
recording industry centre) in turning country music into a redevelopment agenda.
As in Nashville, attempts to encourage year-round visitation to Tamworth have
included building a number of permanent reminders of country music in the town's
landscape. Branding and purpose-built attractions are key components. Landscape

re-packaging is an important corollary to place marketing and is more important in Tamworth because music is inherently invisible and so is often made concrete in the built environment to create reminders for the tourist 'gaze' (Gibson and Connell 2005). Hence,

> Very early country music became an excellent marketing tool for Tamworth. The initiation of these items (easily identifiable with country music) became the catalyst for other 'country music landmarks' to be established thus reinforcing the city's image as Country Music Capital throughout the year. Nowadays there are many items that say the city is country music capital and which form an inventory of country music icons. (Tamworth City Council files 1997)

Local entrepreneurs made the first plans for a country music complex in 1979. Country music venues, museums, special walks, parks and memorials built since then all seek to reassure the visitor of Tamworth's status as the 'country music capital'. In 1988, the Golden Guitar, a 12-metre high replica of the trophy presented to the winners of the annual Australasian Country Music Awards, was constructed at the southern entrance to the town on the New England Highway (Figure 8.4). It is the most photographed landmark in Tamworth. The $2.2 million Tamworth Tourist Information Centre was built in the shape of a double neck guitar. Original plans were to build a tourist information centre in the style of a colonial house, not dissimilar to those in countless other Australian country towns. This was rejected in favour of a guitar design after the chairman of Tourism Tamworth sought a design that reflected the town's image and perceived cultural identity. Tamworth is also now branded in a much more formal way through music; the 'country music capital' logo is visible throughout town and displayed on taxis and buses. Tamworth City Council has adopted a guitar and country music logo, displayed on street signs, council vehicles and buildings.

Museums include the Country Music Wax Museum, the Australian Country Music Federation 'Hall of Legends', and the 'Walk a Country Mile' interpretive centre. Each provides information on the history of country music both in Australia and Tamworth and promotes country music artists, focusing especially on the 'pioneers' such as Slim Dusty, Buddy Williams and Tex Morton. A number of memorials in the landscape include 'The Hands of Fame', and its spoof, the 'Noses of Fame' (on a local pub wall), the 'Roll of Renown', a Tamworth Songwriters Association memorial and the 'Winner's walkway'.

In large part, all this seems to have worked. In the 2007 visitor survey, 60 per cent said that they had been to Tamworth in non-festival seasons. The town's roster of hotels and motels has steadily grown, as Tamworth is the obvious place to stop overnight on the long inland highway journey between Sydney and Brisbane (Tamworth is luckily roughly halfway). A festival generated fame for the town, which in turn created reasons to build tourist attractions, venues, restaurants and bars, all of which consolidated the town's reputation as an interesting place for passers-through to stop on their way north or south.

Figure 8.4   The Big Golden Guitar

The Contradictions of 'Country'

By 1989, an article in the *Australian Financial Review* commented that 'Tamworth is now probably the best known town in rural NSW' (Frew 1989:30), attributing this to the festival in January and the establishment of the Longyard Hotel complex (the site of the wax museum and Golden Guitar, a hotel and large live music venue). Though Tamworth had successfully established itself as the 'country music capital', it was faced with a conundrum. Coverage given to Tamworth in metropolitan newspapers focused on 'country' identities, but the town, its residents and tourists, were variously caricatured as 'redneck' (Stevenson 2001:5), 'country hicks' (Stevenson 2001:5), 'dopes with big hats and hayseed behind the ears' (Fyfe

2001:6), 'small minded' (Fyfe 2001:6) and 'chewing on straw, [wearing an] old Stetson hat, 'yee-ha-ing' (Thomas 1994:134).

Tourism agencies and festival promoters in Tamworth have had to negotiate the 'hick' connotation, seeking to simultaneously celebrate a simplistic, 'rural' nationalist version of 'country', away from backward stereotypes. The late 1990s resurgence of country music, led by corporate 'stars' such as Garth Brooks in the United States, and Gina Jeffreys in Australia, saw a concerted move away from associated images of guitars, hats (both the Australian Akubra and the American Stetson), rodeo scenes, hay bales, rhinestone suits, and horses. Artists no longer dressed up in rhinestone suits, ornate western shirts, belts and hats, but appeared in similar garb to their pop, urban 'alternative' and rock music counterparts. Sexualisation of American attractive female 'crossover' performers, such as Shania Twain, had equivalents in Australia, and at Tamworth, such as Tori Darke and Aleyce Simmonds.

By the late 1990s Tamworth was increasingly presented as a more sophisticated experience, one with musical diversity and professional performances. Its website suggested that, 'no longer stamped with a hillbilly image, the music itself has significantly slipped into mainstream' (Tamworth City Council 2004), and in 2001 a 'Welcome to Cosmopolitan Country' campaign was launched. Yet its national media image has little altered: to most urban folk Tamworth is still a place to find national identity, get in touch with the past, and immerse oneself in the 'country'. Attempts at cosmopolitanism in turn garnered criticisms from within. By 2003 'some regulars complain that the festival has become over-sophisticated and is being over-taken by the chardonnay set: yuppies from city centres'. Festival regulars, such as former Australasian harmonica champion Doc Harber, were quoted saying that 'it's become too commercialised now … I can't believe you have to have a permit to busk in the main street. It's not like you can just put out your case and play. And the pubs have become more respectable. The town's changed. New shops, more people' (quoted in Cox 2003:43).

By the late 2000s the commercial success of corporate country had waned (in America and in Australia) and instead a new trend was towards 'roots' identities and images: Troy Cassar-Daley wore reissue vintage western shirts in the style of 1930s and 1940s singing cowboys (but without the rhinestones) and urban subculture/country music crossover niches such as rockabilly and cowboy punk found a place. The folk scene stayed throughout, firmly ensconced in a stance that was anti-commercial and diffident: folk performers were always more likely to wear simple jeans, rural working clothes and plain boots rather than cowboy attire. Kasey Chambers, the most popular female country performer in Australia, challenged the sexualised bimbo persona by appealing to urban pop music fans and by presenting an 'alternative' image.

The most recent brand from Tourism Tamworth is 'city heart, country soul'(Figure 8.5) – a campaign flushed with musical references, images of 'rootsy' cowboy clothes and boots, young female 'alternative' singers, as well as the cosmopolitan comforts of city life (cafes, fine dining, spa stays, luxury accommodation). But lingering concerns about an ageing visitor structure and few young people led organisers to hire Peer Group Media, a Sydney events marketing company in 2009, to help promote the festival and attract corporate sponsors. Subsequently in 2010 and 2011 the festival booked musical acts outside the 'country' music umbrella such as former Australian Idol winner Guy Sebastian, hard rock band The Screaming Jets and synth-pop band The Potbelleez. According to Tamworth Mayor James Treloar, 'country music has changed enormously ... fanatical followers of the genre feel that if you're not playing a guitar and harmonica, you should be banned – but that's not the case. It's a family event – it has a strong emphasis on country music, rather than a sole emphasis on country music' (quoted in Melourney and Moran 2010:3). Others sought to differ. Max Ellis, founder of the 1973 festival, blamed the Sydney consultants for convincing organisers to invite non-country artists. He was quoted as saying 'we have a long and very successful history and I feel that if the country music foundations were jeopardised it would be the end of the festival ... there's certainly a feeling among stakeholders that council is trying to change it from a country music festival to a music festival' (quoted in Melourney and Moran 2010:3). Others such as writer and photographer John Elliott argued that a sense of history and respect for earlier musical influences was the key: 'without that respect it becomes very bad pop music ... and it has to have more a connection to the country than wearing a hat, having a twangy guitar and getting your clip played on the Country Music Channel' (quoted in Shedden 2010:14). Such debates are not merely insular artistic or aesthetic ones, but affect the viability of the festival, whether it becomes stale or alienates loyal audiences, or even remains the natural home for the Golden Guitar awards ceremony, since there has been talk about moving to a 'more TV-friendly' location' (Shedden 2010:14). In country music, credibility is everything – an issue central to on-going management of the festival.

Resident Reactions

Resident reactions to the festival and place marketing are inseparable from images of country music. When Nashville first gained its reputation as the country music centre of the United States, many of its residents were opposed to it due to negative 'hillbilly' connotations. It was not until residents saw how much business country music brought into the city that they began to accept it (Hemphill 1970). Tamworth, like Parkes, followed a similar trajectory. Until 1976, three years after the Tamworth festival began, there was little reaction from residents; the festival was small, and most local residents were not directly involved (Max Ellis, personal communication 2001). However, as Tamworth gained a stronger reputation as the 'country music capital', some expressed a concern about the image country music presented to people outside Tamworth; in the local paper one resident argued, 'We'll be the laughing stock of Australia' (*Northern Daily Leader* 1976:7). This was further amplified by bad press from

Figure 8.5   Tamworth: 'city heart, country soul'

Source: Tourism Tamworth

city newspapers that presented Tamworth as redneck. At this point, the question became, 'Is this really the image we want for a country music capital?' (*Northern Daily Leader* 1977:11). Ironically, earlier twentieth century Tamworth had sought national publicity as a modern centre with metropolitan aspirations, the 'city of light' that was the first to use electric street lighting.

As the festival grew, particularly in the late 1970s to early 1980s, resident reactions shifted. As the visitor to guest ratio increased, residents could not easily avoid the festival, and their reactions became more antagonistic. The festival was described as an 'invasion' (*Northern Daily Leader* 1978:1) and many saw it as the ideal time to leave town to avoid the onslaught of enthusiastic country music fans and urban tourists adopting 'country' identities by dressing up in cowboy hats and moleskins (*Northern Daily Leader* 1980:5). Letters to the editor criticised the festival and country music. 'I hate country music' t-shirts went on sale to locals in 1979 (*Northern Daily Leader* 1979:2). At this time, there was little support for the country music festival from local business and residents. Shops were permitted to open later, but failed to do so, leaving visitors unable to find places to eat (*Northern Daily Leader* 1979:2). To address this, festival organisers, BAL Marketing, and the Tamworth Chamber of Commerce encouraged resident and business support and participation. In 1980 they fed Tamworth's newspaper positive articles outlining economic benefits, such as 'Country music tag pays off' (*Northern Daily Leader* 1980:5) and organised the Cavalcade (a street parade of local businesses), as well as a window dressing competition during the festival.

Over time, resistance to the festival among local residents has waned though not entirely disappeared. The overall results of a 2002 survey of 200 residents (Gibson and Davidson 2004) showed a positive reaction from residents to Tamworth's status as country music capital, and to the festival more specifically, even when Tamworth might run the risk of being represented as 'redneck' or 'hick'. Where once residents sought to leave Tamworth to escape the festival and the inconveniences it brought, by 2002 this had changed: 81 per cent stayed in Tamworth during the festival. The same proportion said they enjoyed the festival, somewhat more than those (60 per cent) who indicated that they had always enjoyed the festival. According to John Sharkey, who runs Tamworth Home Hospitality, the homestay program: 'There are always a few who say that the garbage doesn't get picked up for weeks and all the roads are closed but they don't knock back the money when it comes in' (Olding 2011b:3). Yet in our survey, the potential for individuals to make money had minimal impact on changed perceptions (Gibson and Davidson 2004). Less than 5 per cent of residents cited this. Other reasons for a more positive attitude towards the festival included: that the festival was more 'family orientated' (24 per cent); the increased professionalism of the festival (15 per cent); and the presence of a larger variety of styles of music on offer (15 per cent). A much higher percentage of residents in Tamworth (84 per cent) enjoyed listening to country music than the national average of 32 per cent (CMAA 2000). Some 60 per cent said they appreciated country music more than in the past. Some residents went further than begrudging acceptance and began to join in; like urban tourists they dressed-up in 'country' attire for the festival and even line-danced. For one local resident, 'I'm definitely more likely to wear country gear at this time of year. It's the country music festival so you want to fit in with everyone else' (quoted in Stevenson 2001:5). Tamworth's country music identity is not just a construct of marketing executives and sponsors: various ruralities are performed and materialised by locals and visitors. Attendance at the festival is a means to 'ruralise' identities in personal ways, at least temporarily.

Other benefits included interesting people to meet, the improved appearance of Tamworth and an increase in entertainment facilities. In addition, 61 per cent said the country music festival positively affected quality of life. Two-thirds said that tourism provided an opportunity to meet new people, corroborating stories told by homestay hosts about the benefits – beyond money – of opening their homes to visitors for the festival. According to John Sharkey, 'it's just a friendly place and they'll go out of their way to help people. They'll pick them up from the train station or drive them to a show' (quoted in Olding 2011b:3). One host, Olive Austin, has been quoted as saying 'It started as just having friends stay when they came up. It's never any trouble at all and you usually remain friends with the people too' (quoted in Olding 2011b:3). Festivals catalyse genuine connections between outsiders and residents, as they have done in Parkes, in ways that buttress the 'down-home' and friendly marketing of Tamworth as 'country'.

By 2002 Tamworth residents perceived the festival as essential to the local economy and identity (79 per cent). One local resident put it rather bluntly: 'it's good for the reputation of Tamworth because we haven't got much else here'. There was also support for an increase in the year round promotion of country music (57 per cent). Three-quarters agreed that country music was the main source of tourism and 90 per cent believed that the country music image had benefited Tamworth. On the whole, respondents did not see promotion and marketing activities as distracting from other more pressing City Council needs. Though respondents did not feel that they participated in decision-making regarding the promotion of Tamworth, this was not perceived as a problem, reflecting the extent to which residents were increasingly comfortable with the representations of the town and its associations with country music.

When asked whether country music had a 'hick' image that needed to be avoided, residents were divided. People in white-collar occupations showed more sensitivity toward representations of Tamworth as 'hick', as did those who had lived in Tamworth for more than 35 years (and hence knew Tamworth before it became the 'country music capital'). For one resident: 'it's very hard to shove off the stereotypical image of country people – that you've got to be a redneck, like country music, and be able to line-dance'. This suggests a class dimension to representations of rurality in Tamworth: those residents that were employed in white-collar occupations found it harder to accept the place marketing of Tamworth as the 'country music capital' and its associated rurality. Tamworth's normative 'country' is one that is simple and working-class rather than the more elite or genteel images usually associated with place promotion.

The Trials of Transformation

With an unusually decentralised management structure and an increasingly loose understanding of what 'country music' might be, Tamworth country music festival has grown from roots in a local music club to become the nation's largest music festival. Festival-goers stay longer, and spend more at Tamworth than at just about any other festival. Beyond the music, Tamworth has harnessed the symbolic and cultural appeal of everything 'country', to claim a national significance for the town, to promote year-round tourism and ultimately maximise commercial returns.

Commercialisation of rural culture and 'country' motifs such as cowboy hats, western wear and the music itself has been crucial to Tamworth's success. Images of rural Australian identity, and more specifically constructions of 'country', have spilt over from the genre of country music to become associated with the place itself. Tamworth now actively markets itself as a place of 'honest' country values, hospitality and Australian national identity, all themes familiar within country music. The commodification and transformation of Tamworth has been variously celebrated, negotiated and resisted by different actors within the town and throughout Australia's country music fraternity. For organisers, 'country' is simple and effective, invoking a range of positive connotations that the town as a whole could use in tourism promotions. But 'country' also invited stereotypically negative reactions – of Tamworth as 'hick' or 'redneck', which triggered dissent, while for many musicians, 'country' no longer represented the diversity of styles and themes performed at the festival. Nevertheless, Tamworth has long been a successful example of place marketing, albeit contested, and rural transformation, indicative of the potential of festivals for regional development.

Tamworth's experiences are important because they illustrate how commercially constructed place marketing images have over time been interpreted as sympathetic to local populations, and to working class culture more generally (in contrast to urban and luxury tourist place marketing), but also carry oppressive and racist subtleties: country music, and Tamworth by inference, is a space for white, heterosexual, 'honest' rural Australians, a place of rugged male stockmen and 'down to earth' folk, without an Indigenous or multicultural presence. Place marketing through country music has over time not so much alienated local residents as gradually seeped into their consciousness. Rather than appeal to an elite, Tamworth's place promotion appeals to rural, Anglo-Saxon working class culture. White-collar residents cringe, but most others have embraced Tamworth's images and feel included in its transformation to 'country music capital'. There is both a sense of inclusiveness engendered by the festival's 'family atmosphere' and celebration of Australian rural values, offset by its continued entrenchment of nostalgic (and problematic) images of place that exclude Aboriginal people. Such marketing is not uncontested. Concerns over 'hick' reputation have forced Tamworth's promoters to reconsider the 'country' image and appeal to more sophisticated images (hence even a feature advertising campaign for the festival in

Vogue magazine in Australia in the late 1990s) while performers and performances continue to diversify.

Tamworth faces on-going challenges, despite being the largest country music festival in Australia, demonstrating how no festival can simply rest on its laurels or remain unchanged. According to Rebel Thompson, the managing director of Tourism Tamworth, the festival is 'looking to reach out to a younger demographic as well as to families and backpackers' (quoted in Buchanan 2009:5). Shifts to booking non-country music acts for a youth audience showed a willingness on the part of the festival organisers to try different things to remain relevant and avoid stagnation, at risk of alienating festival stalwarts. The factions and differences of opinion on this alone emphasise how managing a highly successful festival brings trials and tribulations: the pressure to deliver ever-increasing results or even just maintain momentum. Competitor festivals too eat away at Tamworth's market and reputation: in Gympie, another enormous festival in the country music heartland of Queensland, and at Mildura, which has cleverly staged for fifteen years the Australian Independent Country Music Awards, accepting Tamworth's commercial dominance but cornering the market instead on 'credible' alternative country. Indeed no Australian state is without a major country music festival. For sheer size and economic impact however, Tamworth remains unsurpassed, but with the complex mixture of achievements and anxieties that this entails.

Chapter 9

Byron Bay: From Alternative Origins to Festival Overkill?

In many ways, the themes discussed throughout this book – the development, social and environmental impacts of festivals – come together and culminate in one town, Byron Bay, where festivals have been particularly large and conspicuous. Festivals have been one means through which Byron Bay's identity as cultural mecca and 'alternative' tourist destination in Australia has been created, yet it has paradoxically brought intense commercial pressures to bear on the town (Derrett 2003). It shows what is possible through festival-led development and related tourism spillover effects, but also the limits to what is considered acceptable. This is a story of the economic, cultural and symbolic transformation of a once insignificant whaling and abattoir town located on the Far North Coast of NSW (Figure 9.1) into a counterculture mecca, tourism hotspot, festival capital and ultimately site of intense community conflicts over the direction and impacts of development. Byron Bay cultivated a reputation as a weird freaky place where diversity and tolerance ruled, and festivals found a natural home: a town where festivals anchored the development of a nascent tourism industry, focused on surfing, backpackers, dance parties and beaches – a parallel to Goa in India and Koh Samui in Thailand. Bigger and bigger festivals emerged as the town moved from freakland to the mainstream. Economic benefits ensued; pressures of commercialism, property price rises and influxes of visitors afflicted local residents, and festivals became the flashpoints of conflict. This chapter concerns not just the impact of specific events, but the wider transition of a town from alternative haven to a fashionable place where people now worry about house prices and newcomers.

Far North Coast NSW – the Rise of the Rainbow Region

The Far North Coast of NSW is a coastal region that has undergone significant demographic, cultural and economic change since the 1970s, increasingly perceived as a 'lifestyle' or 'creative' region, rather than a somewhat conservative agricultural and fishing region (as it once had been viewed). This was in part a legacy of countercultural traditions dating back to the establishment of the Aquarius Festival in Nimbin in 1973, the first major 'hippie' festival in Australia, which attracted musicians, artists and students to the area. The region has seen some of the highest rates of population growth in Australia since then, attracting retirees,

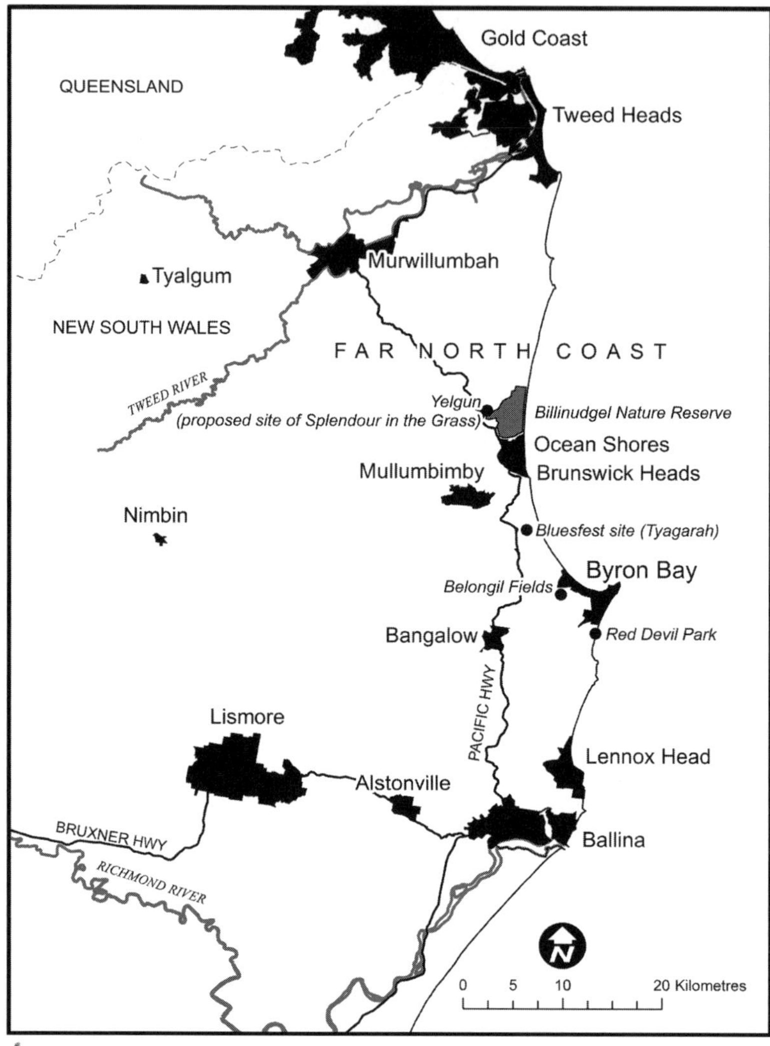

Figure 9.1   Location map, Byron Bay

students, the unemployed and travellers to its natural and cultural environment. Counter-urban migration in this long-established sea-change region has had a major impact, placing significant pressures on infrastructure and especially on the fragile coastal zone (Essex and Brown 1997). The town has a strong 'alternative' discourse of economy and identity; it is seen by others, and increasingly positions itself, as different from metropolitan areas in style of economic development, although this is certainly being augmented by new forms of consumerism (architecturally designed beach houses, homewares shops, 'trendy' cafes). Music festivals contribute to this discourse of 'alternative economy' in Byron Bay, in addition to informal sector activities (regular market stalls, arts and crafts, drug trade), community opposition to large-scale resort and property developments, local economic trading schemes, artistic and organic food cooperatives, and the communes still scattered in the hinterland (Gibson and Connell 2003).

The same features that have drawn migrants to the area since the 1970s – environmental quality, 'alternative' cultural activities and creative industries – have also attracted increased numbers of tourists, especially from metropolitan centres where it has a reputation as a 'special' place, of idyllic beaches, warm weather and a distinct alternative cultural ambience. By 2010 the Far North Coast was receiving 1.8 million domestic visitors, 235,000 international tourists and 3.4 million day trippers annually (Tourism NSW 2010), making it the second most popular destination in the state behind Sydney. Byron Bay especially attracts backpackers, being in the same network metaphorically and physically as Goa, Ibiza, Bali and Koh Samui. Over 55,000 backpackers visit Byron Bay annually, contributing approximately $7 million annually to the town's economy (Gibson and Connell 2003), and intensifying the sense of global convergence present in the town. Byron Bay is now the third most popular backpacker destination in Australia, behind Sydney and Cairns. With expenditure in the region totalling more than $1.3 billion annually (Tourism NSW 2010), tourism has become the single most important industry.

During the 1990s and 2000s Byron Bay's alternative reputation, nightlife and gorgeous beaches increasingly put it on the hipster map. Gwyneth Paltrow, Mick Jagger, Elle McPherson, Paris Hilton and Jennifer Anniston were all spotted in its cafes; television producers, movie directors and writers purchased exclusive first or second homes to get away from urban noise and paparazzi, and companies producing everything from ice cream to coffee, cookies and shampoo began putting 'Byron Bay' in their brand name to win new metropolitan customers already familiar with the town's alternative reputation. Musicians saw the town as a convenient location to break up busy touring schedules, with well-known national and international bands and artists (including Paul Kelly, Bob Dylan and Ben Harper) choosing to perform there and take time out mid-tour (Harper eventually bought property in the hinterland as a second home). Those who purchased property early or paid exorbitant real estate prices later became increasingly defensive about the town's character, 'spirit' and purpose, galvanised around campaigns to stop McDonalds, Club Med and other multinational corporations moving into town. The local council shifted from being a typical National Party, conservative agricultural stronghold to be dominated by the Greens and independents, exceptional in regional Australia. That was reflected in increasingly tighter development controls and even the introduction through land use planning laws of a population cap to prevent suburban sprawl and further growth. Fame brought money, notoriety, popularity, but also perennial pressures on the town to accept ever more in-migrants and tourists. Drastic measures such as literally blocking roads into town other than for locals on major events and dates such as New Year's Eve were contemplated and enacted – what Derrett (2009:113) described as 'active de-marketing of the town' – and increasingly the community and council adopted a critical stance (if not outright obstruction) to tourism and further urban development. Byron Bay still retains some of its alternative character, and many of the original countercultural pioneers remain in the town or in the hills around, but arguably by the late 2000s the limits to tourism had been reached. The town was becoming a victim of its own success.

A Festival-Led Transition?

It would be an exaggeration to suggest Byron Bay's transformation was a direct result of festivals (unlike that of Tamworth). Nonetheless, festivals have played their part in the town's transformation, and in turn, have become sites of community conflict and debate. Festivals began prominently with the decision of the National Union of Students to host the 1973 Aquarius Festival, a major 'alternative lifestyles' event, at nearby Nimbin. Because of its spectacular surrounding landscapes and old physical structures such as butteries, left over from the dairy industry, Nimbin became a haven for city-dwellers seeking rural refuge. The Aquarius Festival drew attention to the region's sublime subtropical rainforests (subsequently world heritage listed), while vacated dairy farms provided space not just for the festival but for many Aquarius participants to establish communes, influencing the economic and cultural life of the region (Hannan 2003). The trend toward 'dropping out' from large cities was catalysed by the festival, which had music as its central core. In time the region's countercultural reputation brought people in search of 'alternative' lifestyles more permanently: permaculture enthusiasts, surfing subcultures, artists, musicians and itinerants. Alternative settlers took advantage of cheap urban and rural property prices and moved in, some to establish communes, others to live off unemployment benefits and attempt to build creative arts careers. Festivals and more regular musical nights (such as full moon parties held in dance halls) were early features of the countercultural transformation.

The establishment of new rock festivals in the 1980s solidified Byron Bay's reputation as a place to experience music outside the mainstream, particularly as part of a tourist experience. Two major holiday periods – the January summer break and Easter long weekend – featured major new festivals that set Byron Bay apart from the numerous family-orientated holiday destinations along Australia's east coast. The first, organised by Keven Oxford, who later ran the East Coast Blues and Roots Festival (see below), was Sunrock 78, held over the Australia Day weekend in January 1978 with headliners Billy Thorpe and the Aztecs plus a line-up of mostly punk bands from Brisbane and Sydney. Over the next couple of decades, better highways and more adventurous and financially independent students car-pooled en masse to Byron Bay festivals, especially from Sydney and Melbourne, with camping gear in tow. Byron Bay quickly became the most important coastal destination for students from capital cities, offering good beaches and reliable surf breaks for daytime activities, and numerous pubs, clubs and parties at night. Festivals were the lure: the East Coast Blues and Roots Festival (or simply 'Bluesfest') and Homebake (for alternative Australian rock) quickly acquired legendary status on 1990s university campuses, bragged about by those lucky enough to secure tickets and to have successfully made the pilgrimage. Byron Bay festivals came to define a generation – now called Generation X – marking them and the bands they listened to as different from their baby-boomer parents, as defiantly, distinctly, 'alternative' (this was also the time of the rise of 'grunge', 'indie rock' and 'alternative rock'). Young parents took their children for beachside holidays at Coffs Harbour or Ballina; baby-boomers paid high prices to holiday in chi-chi resorts such as Noosa and Port Douglas; retirees visited sleepy towns such as Yamba, while surfers, backpackers, musicians and students headed instead to Byron Bay to camp cheaply at festivals, drink, take drugs, maybe have a romantic encounter and recover on the beach the day afterwards.

The East Coast Blues and Roots Festival in particular has become an internationally-renowned event every Easter. Established in 1990, it now attracts 60,000 visitors and generates tens of millions in tourist revenue (Gibson and Connell 2005). After 20 years of promoting various acts in the United States and Australia, including the ground-breaking Ourimbah Pop Festival in 1970, and later for the company Live Coverage Promotions (responsible for international tours to the North Coast by BB King, Blondie, Fairport Convention and Osibisa), Keven Oxford saw an opportunity to establish a festival in Byron Bay pitched at a rock-lovers audience, and that drew in the sort of acts he was already promoting:

> I was sitting on a grassy hill overlooking San Francisco … listening to act after act perform at the San Francisco Blues Festival. I was suddenly struck by this overpowering urge to stage a similar event in Australia. Everybody seemed to be having a great time, and there was an unmistakable vibe. I was convinced this would work in Australia, especially in Byron Bay. (personal communication 1999)

Oxford recalled early festivals that lost money, but thrilled crowds, and in time decided to stage the festival in the Byron Bay Arts Factory, a converted abattoir, which he and a partner would manage (The Arts Factory also became a legendary stopover for touring bands outside the festival period): 'There are a million coming of age stories out there from fans who spent one of the best nights of their life crammed with 1,500 other crazed rock 'n' roll maniacs in a converted pig slaughterhouse' (personal communication 1999). In 1993 the festival moved to larger premises at Belongil Fields, on the western edge of town; and in 1997 moved again to Red Devil Park, the local rugby league club's grounds. It moved again to even larger premises in 2010 (see below). Early on the festival was simply known as a blues festival, with acts such as Charlie Musselwhite and The Dutch Tilders, and later it became a 'blues and roots' festival enabling folk, country, Aboriginal, zydeco, funk, jazz, punk and reggae acts onto the bill (Elder 2002). Typically the line-up combines half a dozen big name international acts (including over the years Ben Harper, Spearhead, Angelique Kidjo, Luka Bloom, Buddy Guy, Taj Mahal, Emmylou Harris, Joan Armatrading, Robert Cray) and a longer line-up of Australian singer-songwriters (Renee Geyer, Paul Kelly, Kasey Chambers) and rock bands (Midnight Oil, John Butler Trio, the Saints) as well as blues/folk stalwarts (Backsliders, Chris Wilson). A very high proportion of festival-goers (70 per cent) are from out of town. The East Coast Blues and Roots Festival capitalises on the town's reputation and 'alternative' ethos, positioning itself as 'earthy', in contrast to mass commercialised pop and rock festivals held in big cities. Successive years in which heavy Easter rains turned the festival into a mud-bath only heightened its reputation as down-to-earth, rustic and free from metropolitan pretensions.

Splendour in the Grass is an annual rock music festival held in winter, generally marketed toward a younger demographic group (and suitably sponsored by ABC Triple J radio – Australia's publicly-funded national youth broadcasting station). It is a commercial enterprise, Splendour in the Grass Pty Ltd, majority owned by Jessica Ducrou (who a decade earlier founded the Homebake Festival) and Paul Piticco, both entrepreneurs, and a quarter owned by Australian band Powderfinger, who Piticco once managed (Murphy 2010, Whyte and Connellan 2010). Even by 2003, its third consecutive year, Splendour in the Grass had grown to a 12,500 strong audience, and it quickly earned a national reputation through Triple J on-air broadcasts, with headline international acts such as Coldplay, Placebo, The Pixies, The Strokes and PJ Harvey, as well as Australian bands such as Powderfinger (no surprise there), Temper Trap and Frenzal Rhomb. The festival, staged over a weekend in winter in Belongil Fields – a flexible open space on the edge of town that could host major stage and PAs, market stalls, campgrounds and facilities – was initially supported by local businesses as an important event for the local tourism industry, given its timing in the off-season.

Expenditure in the Grass?

Before examining how festivals would come to be embroiled in conflicts over the pace and direction of development in Byron Bay, it is necessary to trace how they transformed the local economy. Byron Bay provides a useful instance where it is possible to observe exactly how the commercial benefits of festivals are distributed. With a small population, but a large tourism industry, and festivals throughout the year attracting different crowds, close analysis of business impact becomes possible. In 2003, during the Splendour in the Grass festival, a small-scale survey of 80 local businesses was undertaken (Table 9.1) to gain a better understanding of the exact way in which such large commercial, concert-format events contributed to the local economy.

Splendour in the Grass attracted a younger clientele than those normally frequenting local businesses in non-festival trading periods. Under normal trading circumstances, under-35 year olds made up about half the customer base of the

Table 9.1   Types of businesses in Byron Bay responding to the survey, 2003

Type of Business	Number	%
Retail	27	33.8
Food outlets/ restaurants/ cafes/ bakeries	16	20
Services	8	10
Supermarket/ Bottle shop/ Chemists/ Butchers	8	10
Tourist operators/ Travel agencies	7	8.8
Clothing	5	6.25
Accommodation	4	5
Real Estate	3	3.75
Music	2	2.5
Total	80	100

Source: Gibson et al. 2004

businesses surveyed, but that increased to 90 per cent while the festival took place. This has broader implications for the local economy, and flow-on multiplier effects, because younger patrons attending the festival generally had a lower disposable income and were more likely to choose lower cost accommodation and food outlets. Customer numbers for the majority of businesses increased during the festival period. A third said there had been a 'major increase', however 9 per cent experienced no change in business, while 13 per cent had decreased customer numbers (Figure 9.2).

In terms of turnover, about the same proportion of participating businesses recorded a substantial profit increase (greater than 20 per cent of normal trading) as those that experienced a decline, no impact, or slight positive impacts (between 0–20 per cent of normal trading; Figure 9.3). Of the retail businesses surveyed, over three-quarters reported that turnover increase was below 20 per cent, with half of these again recording no or negative change (Table 9.2). In contrast, three-quarters of food outlets experienced an increase in turnover above 40 per cent. All four clothing businesses surveyed received a turnover increase of between 81–100 per cent; the one music business that responded to the question surprisingly recorded no turnover increase during the festival. Services and general goods businesses (supermarkets, electrical goods, butchers etc.) experienced lower turnover increases, with over two-thirds in each category recording less than 20 per cent or no/negative change. Similarly, five of the seven tourist operators involved in the study recorded an increase in turnover below 20 per cent. Accommodation had an average increase between 41–60 per cent while the two real estate agents recorded increases of between 20 and 40 per cent.

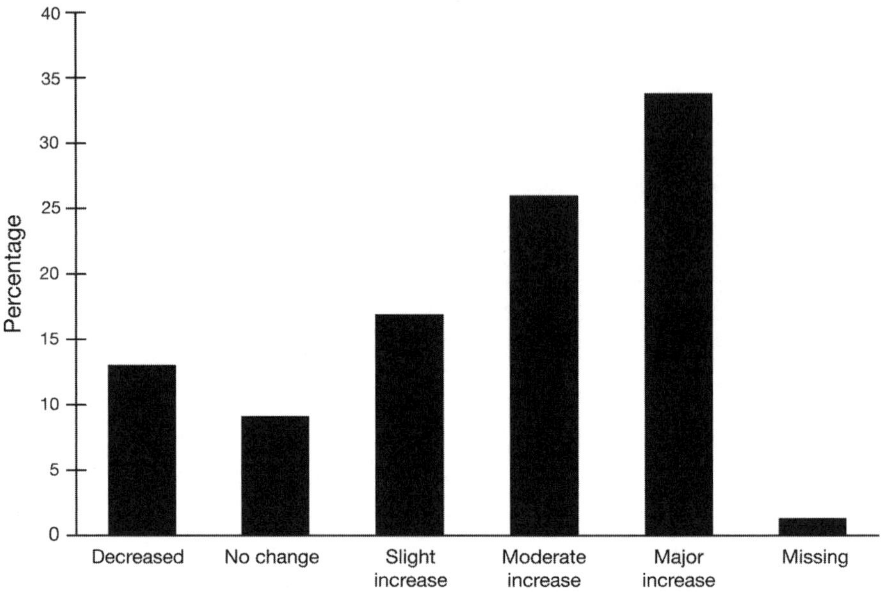

Figure 9.2   Change in the number of customers during Splendour in the Grass 2003

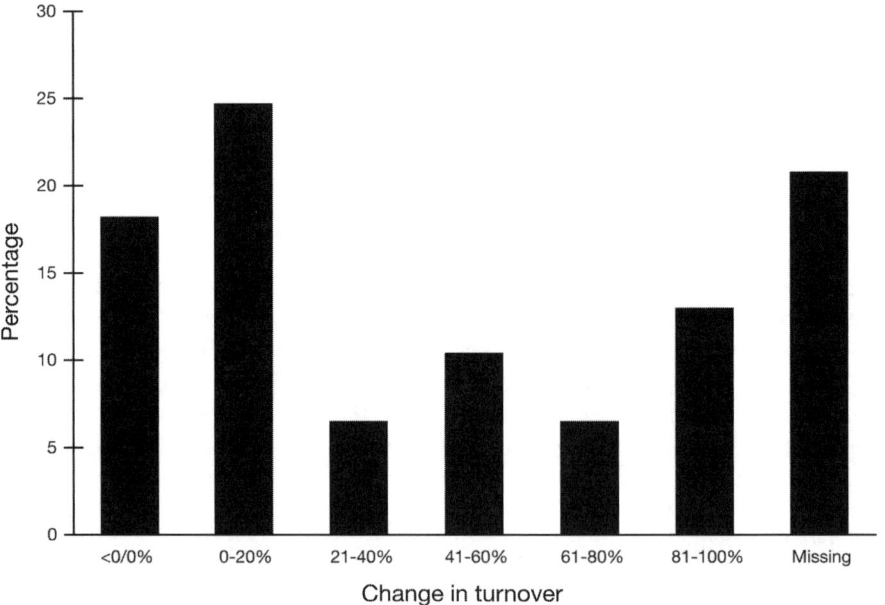

Figure 9.3   Change in turnover during Splendour in the Grass 2003

Table 9.2　　Turnover Increase During Splendour in the Grass 2003

Type of Business	Turnover increase (number and percentage (in brackets))						
	<0/0	0–21	21–40	41–60	61–80	81–100	Total
Retail	7 (38.9)	7 (38.9)	1 (5.5)		1 (5.5)	2 (11.1)	18 (100)
Food Outlets/ Cafes/ Restaurants	2 (16.7)		1 (8.3)	3 (25)	3 (25)	3 (25)	12 (100)
Tourist Operators/ Travel Agencies	1 (14.3)	4 (57.1)		1 (14.3)	1 (14.3)		7 (100)
Clothing						4 (100)	4 (100)
Services	3 (33.3)	3 (33.3)	2 (22.2)	1 (11.1)			9 (100)
Supermarket/ Butchers/ Chemist	1 (20)	3 (60)		1 (20)			5 (100)
Accommodation				2 (100)			2 (100)
Real Estate		1 (50)	1 (50)				2 (100)
Music	1 (100)						1 (100)

Source: Gibson et al. 2004

The detail and diversity of outcomes is important: exactly how crowds move through the town on their way to and from the festival, what they are likely to buy en route, and whether they in turn repel regular local customers who change their shopping habits to evade the festival. Hence for one survey respondent, a publican,

I'm sure there is a percentage of local customers that are turned off by the larger crowd. Having said that, in terms of affecting our business it's really only the Friday where it makes a really big difference. Friday night there's x amount of people in Byron Bay, there's nothing much on at the festival so they want to go into town, and even the campers want to go into town; they don't want to drink out there, they want to come and be in Byron Bay. That certainly resulted in a large increase in trade, but having said that over the weekend it's not a great jump from what we usually do. I'm sure some of the food venues, cafes and restaurants into

> town would see a great increase in the lunch trade before people go to the festival
> but for us it's really only the Friday where there's a massive increase.

For that publican, who was also the licensee who held the exclusive rights to serve alcohol at the festival itself, even the particular bands on at certain stages of the bill impacted on revenue:

> On the Saturday, I think there was more movement around the site by people which was good. Powderfinger and the Living End were on the Saturday night, they were the big draw cards there, so people stayed in the tent and didn't drink as much. But during the day a lot of people were checking out everything, the stalls, the food, the drink, the markets, you know every little bit of it. Whereas the Sunday, the weekend ticket holders had seen everything and now it was time for the music. Sundays are always a quieter trade day from our point of view because someone has to drive first thing the next morning to get to wherever they came from, so people party hard Saturday, and then Sunday they just take it steady and check out the acts.

Conversely for petrol stations their busiest period only came at the end of the festival, when festival-goers were on their way back home.

Many Byron Bay businesses were directly involved with the staging of the Splendour in the Grass Festival, including selling tickets, catering and operating stalls. Of those businesses with direct involvement in the festival, there was general consensus that the festival was profitable. One of these respondents described it as a 'good revenue stream'. Another involved in catering said the festival was extremely beneficial: 'successful … very successful'.

More questionable is whether the festival created any extra employment in the town. Most of the businesses surveyed were very small – two-thirds employed three or less people during regular trading periods. Only one local business, a pub, substantially increased employment ('Employed 120 staff for the 2 days') to cater for their exclusively operated alcohol-sale outlet at the festival site. All other local businesses employed the same number of people during the festival period or slightly increased it. This is linked to a high latent capacity to absorb extra demand, without needing to find extra help, which was typical of smaller retail businesses that usually had one or two staff rostered no matter what the normal level of trade. In the words of one retailer: 'we just used our existing staff and our family. I did employ some other people to do some poster displays, basically we managed to do it ourselves because we weren't taking heaps of money; we managed to do it with our family and our staff for the weekend'. For a backpacker hostel: 'no, we don't employ more people, we just work a bit harder. We just do the same hours as normal, we're just busier while you're doing them. This particular business runs OK with one person behind here'. And likewise for a local pub: 'because it is a quiet time of the year we've got enough staff to cover the increased number of patrons. There's not a lot of difference in having 200 people in the pub or if we have 400 people in the pub, you don't really need a lot more staff, you can work through the extra 200 people with the same amount of staff'. Further analysis revealed a relationship between employment and change in turnover for local businesses. Those that reported a low or even respectable turnover increase (up to 60 per cent) during Splendour in the Grass 2003 tended not to employ extra staff. In contrast, and predictably, half the local businesses with high turnover increases employed extra people during the festival.

Festivals such as Splendour in the Grass – large commercial affairs on the edge of town but with variable links to local interests – thus bring money into town without generating extra jobs directly. Pubs do well, especially when they get the exclusive contract to run the bar at the festival, as do kebab shops, takeaways, camp sites and cheap motels. For a surf clothing shop the 'younger crowd for Splendour was more suited to our business'. Expensive restaurants and homeware shops, catering to an older population, conversely saw very limited direct benefits, but experienced extra trade indirectly as cash circulated through Byron Bay over subsequent weeks. Splendour in the Grass contributed to the overall wealth of Byron Bay, and unlike Parkes, Tamworth, Bermagui or Inverell, that level of wealth was already considerable. As one music retailer described:

> I'd say that Splendour is definitely beneficial; I think probably particularly the liquor outlets and the food outlets, the clothing shops and the music stores. Bear in mind the age group of the people going there, they don't have a lot of money to throw around and I think by the time they pay for their transport here, their accommodation, and their ticket, food and alcohol, I don't think they have a lot of money left over. It's pretty short and sweet.

For a backpacker hostel, the benefits were simply to bring economic activity of any type at an otherwise quiet time of year: 'this place has been full so it's been a good thing. Normally at this time we're not full so it's extra money for us, its extra money for the local council and all the rest of it, it goes down the line'. A local hotelier agreed: 'Yes definitely, it brings a lot of people into Byron Bay during what is traditionally a quiet time of the year. July, August is the lowest part of the tourist season, so it brings a lot of people in'. Visitors to Splendour in the Grass purchase food, alcohol and accommodation, but don't buy many retail goods; they are in Byron Bay primarily for the festival, and do not undertake unrelated experiences.

Businesses were also asked to compare the impacts of Splendour in the Grass with the East Coast Blues and Roots Festival. Splendour in the Grass is both shorter and smaller than Bluesfest, and brings a younger crowd with more limited budgets who prioritise alcohol and food. As journalist Andrew Fraser (2006:16) put it: 'the Bluesfest is for the over-40s if not 50s, with grey ponytails for both sexes. At Splendour the average age is 25 or younger'. This basic difference alters economic impacts. Surveyed businesses reported that the Easter Blues and Roots Festival's longer format and older, wealthier crowd were more lucrative.

In the words of a cafe owner, 'Blues Festival's older crowd spends at restaurants, Splendour crowd just spends on alcohol'. For a restaurateur: 'the people that come for the Blues Festival get out about town and spend their money; the Splendour people do not'. For a fashion shop, Splendour meant 'younger customers, cheaper purchases'. But the detailed situation is more complex. As one accommodation provider suggested, perceived commercial benefits are also a function of time of year, the levels of 'background' trade already occurring at that time, and whether or not putting on extra staff is necessary:

> Yeah, for sure we make more money during the Blues festival, but we're still only at the tail-end of our summer then, so we're still busier at that time of the year. For sure they stay longer during Blues and Roots, people take two, three weeks off and come here for the whole lot. The campsite is generally full for two or three weeks, whereas for Splendour they're only full for two or three nights. But we never employ more people even during Bluesfest. Like at the minute, it's really quiet. That means we don't work that hard, but when it's busy, we work really hard, but that's it, that's how the business is really. We work hard in the summer, and in the winter we really cruise along a bit. We're still really busy with overseas visitors during the Blues and Roots anyway.

A homewares store said that the 'Blues Festival tends to attract a broader range of ages', but 'tends to be busier for us the week prior to and after the festival', when older visitors with the time, luxury and incomes to support an extended stay remain in town, spend time shopping and make a holiday of the experience. The festival itself mattered less than the form of extended tourism it catalysed. Meanwhile for a local hotelier,

> It's the worst time of the year to have the Bluesfest for Byron Bay, simply because it's at Easter and it's in the middle of the Easter holidays. Byron Bay is busy without the Blues Festival, and then the Blues Festival brings in an extra 30,000 people. It really overloads the town for 4–5 days impact, whereas Splendour perhaps only overloads the town for 2 days impact. The Blues Festival is fantastic for the town and I'd hate for it to move. A lot of people plan their holidays and what not around it, there's fantastic acts every year, it's a great festival for the town too, it's just the time they have it, in comparison to Splendour. Splendour is held in a quiet time of the year whereas the Blues Festival is held in a busy time of the year.

Significance, then, is relative to what kind of economic activity would otherwise take place at that time of year.

Festival Development and Environmental Conflicts

Beyond boosts to the local economy, major influxes of festival tourists into a shire of only 30,000 full-time residents (and the town itself with a permanent population of less than 5,000) place intense pressure on urban infrastructure, including road congestion (with squabbles over introduction of parking meters) and human waste, which during the 1990s occasionally overflowed when festivals coincided with rainy spells, pouring raw sewage through residents' backyards (Gibson and Connell 2005). By 2003 the Blues and Roots Festival required 160 portaloos alongside several permanent toilets. Intense debates followed over how to manage peak tourist periods, when the town's population was effectively magnified six-fold. This complex problem is not solely related to festivals, but caught up in a wider debate about the nature of urban and coastal development, and clashes between Byron Bay's increasing popularity and visions of a reclusive 'alternative' retreat. The small urban population, which residents defend as crucial to the intimate, 'special' nature of the locality, has made it difficult for Byron Shire Council to raise adequate taxation revenue to upgrade infrastructure to cope with tourism and especially festivals. Through festivals and tourism Byron Bay has experienced complex tensions between idyllic images of 'alternative' lifestyles, rurality, property values and distance from the excesses of urban capitalism, and its own popularity. In 2002, Byron Shire's then mayor, Tom Wilson, explained:

> We have a population of 30,000 people and 12,000 rateable properties are paying to maintain the shire and the effect of the 1.65 million visitors. There is no direct or indirect cash flow from tourism back to council, which has to deliver the infrastructure and services … Tourism is an extractive industry. Everyone thinks it is a benign, beautiful delivery from heaven. Visitors fly in from around the world, they enjoy our lifestyle, they spend their money and they go home. But when you cease to be a community and become a commodity, small towns like Byron Bay lose their essence. We don't want that to happen. (Quoted in Gregory 2002:47)

During the Splendour in the Grass survey of business owners (that is, of those with direct commercial gains from festivals) there was still a measure of dissent: negative aspects were acknowledged, from 'youth deviance' to placing unnecessary strain upon existing infrastructure ('Byron's too small to handle the large number of people … and infrastructure is not good'). Some argued that economic benefits outweighed other issues ('I think the negatives involved with the festivals are outweighed by the positives … they bring work for the locals, improves publicity for the town'); others felt the festival had reached its capacity point, and were unsupportive of further attendance increases ('great event, however social impacts on residents should be considered if Splendour was to get larger').

Attempts by festivals to mitigate social and environmental impacts have ensued: performances were rescheduled to finish earlier to reduce noise complaints, and after community questioning of what festival organisers were doing to become more sustainable, the Blues and Roots Festival began clarifying its environmental measures and waste management procedures. According to co-organiser Peter Noble,

> doing the right thing is what should be done anyway and I have up till now not publicised our ongoing commitment to social and environmental responsibility. However, I see the importance of increasing public awareness of all the environmental issues and to lead by demonstration ... We have been recycling and using corn starch plates, plantation timber cutlery and delivery of green compost to local organic gardens for a decade. (Quoted in *Byron Shire Echo* 3 April 2007).

In 2010 the Blues and Roots Festival moved to a new 120 hectare site, on a tea tree farm, 11 kilometres outside Byron Bay, with increased camping capacity and the ability to provide comprehensive on-site environmental management: 'When we do move, it will be to a green site. We will be installing wind and solar power, we will have bio-diesel, we will strive to be the best and we will have the same motives through the whole festival' (Peter Noble, quoted in *Byron Shire Echo* 3 April 2007). By 2011 the festival had banned dogs, and during the festival an ecologist and Friends of the Koala volunteers were on site to 'provide assistance [to the koalas] in the event of a koala encounter': the outcome of the site being so close to a rare koala habitat. Taking the festival out of Byron Bay township reduced congestion and noise pollution impacts, easing community criticism while also delivering more control to festival organisers about how the site was managed. However, the out-of-town site risked disturbance to koala habitat and heightened car dependency among participants getting to and from the site, increasing the festival's ecological footprint.

Ecological footprint analysis revealed that car transport used by festival-goers was by far the most significant contributor to the environmental balance sheet of the Splendour in the Grass festival (Gibson and Wong 2011). Its organisers subsequently introduced buses for students from Melbourne and Sydney, as well as improving recycling initiatives and seeking to neutralise greenhouse emissions by purchasing Green Power and carbon offsets. The festival also introduced a new form of carbon offset ticketing:

> Did you know that getting to and from a festival represents the single largest carbon emitting component of any music event. In fact punter travel emissions can outweigh a festival's internal emissions (lighting, freight, generators, etc.) by more than 10:1. Splendour in the Grass is once again offering the incredibly popular Carbon Offset Ticket to audience members. By purchasing a Carbon Offset Ticket you can offset your travel emissions up to 350km (based on a 2.0 litre family sedan). The vast majority of our audience travel within this distance meaning that your travel to and from the festival will be completely offset.

As with the Blues and Roots Festival, heightened criticism of noise pollution, audience behaviour, congestion and the load on local sewerage infrastructure led organisers of Splendour in the Grass to seek a new, larger site beyond the town limits. By 2006 the site's existing capacity was stretched (Figure 9.4). In 2007 the festival proposed to relocate to a dedicated new 256 hectare site purchased by the festival at Yelgun, 20 kilometres north of Byron Bay township, and adjacent to the Billinudgel Nature Reserve. As with the Blues and Roots Festival the new site offered the potential for more comprehensive on-site environmental management and subsequent reduction in noise and congestion in town, but the proposal became highly controversial for its location within a well-recognised and state-protected wildlife corridor, and plans to hold more regular festivals there. Over thirty threatened animal species were known to exist in the area, including koalas (the neighbouring nature reserve is protected under a specific state environmental protection code because of its significance for koalas), masked owls, bats and flying-foxes. The festival and its relocation plans became the subject of an intense local environment/development battle. According to the NSW Nature Conservation Council, in its submission to the Development Application for the 2008 Splendour in the Grass festival site, which they opposed on environmental grounds,

> Establishing a festival on Jones Road, which adjoins the nature reserve could cause many implications for the 34 threatened fauna species adjoining the Billinudgel Nature Reserve, and especially the 26 species living directly within the wildlife corridor, where the festival will be located … The plans incorporate an Emergency Helipad located close to Koala Habitat, causing fragmentation, destruction to Core Koala Habitat, and possibly eventual mortality due to human impact and infrastructure development … The impact of tens of thousands of people traversing through the wildlife corridor will more than likely lead to further fragmentation of the vegetation, which provides a vital path for fauna responding to climatic changes and impact the migration and breeding patterns for threatened fauna in the corridor … The implementation of 40 light towers is proposed throughout the park area, yet there is no assessment of the impacts of these Light Towers on fauna or residents included in the DA … While the Festival appears to minimise its ecological footprint in some respects, this event brings in high numbers of people, causes noise emissions, and the infrastructure requirements are absolutely inappropriate for this site. The close proximity of the festival to threatened fauna should require an alternative site be used. (NCCNSW 2008)

The insertion of a major festival into 'wild' nature thus raised concerns that overpowered the perceived social and environmental gains of moving the festival to a dedicated, out-of-town site. Local opposition contradicted the possibility that such a setting might actually improve environmental awareness among visitors. Metaphors of 'invasion' were frequently invoked by opponents to describe the influx of uncaring festival tourists into an otherwise tranquil location, hence according to Ri Fraser of the local resident action group CONOS (Conservation of North Ocean Shores): 'We're a quiet little community yet we get the full brunt of the noise, the behaviour, the rubbish found in the streets. People camp illegally, leaving mess, peeing and crapping on our gardens' (quoted in Di Stefano and Lee 2009:13). Festivals, it seemed, did not belong in town, because problems of noise, congestion and tourism influxes were seen to outweigh the commercial benefits, but moving a festival to a new 'natural' setting out of town did not necessarily work either.

Figure 9.4   Splendour in the Grass, Byron Bay, 2006

Some saw community complaints as little more than NIMBYism, and not representative of the views of all interests. According to one accommodation provider,

> I'm sure all the businesses would love Splendour in the Grass to be on every weekend, because they're going to sell more tofu burgers or they're going to get more people at the cinema or whatever. The only problem is the infrastructure of the town has trouble dealing with it. A lot of locals don't like it, in fact the locals that live here don't like any concerts going on in the town, they don't like it when it's busy at Christmas and New Year. From their point of view they've bought a nice house in a lovely peaceful town and then all of a sudden it gets bombarded. Well as far as I'm concerned they should have thought of that before, and they've just got to deal with it, but a lot of them don't like it.

One restaurateur who had lived in Byron Bay for over 40 years said 'I have no problem with everyone invading Byron for a couple of days, cause it is good for business, especially on the Friday night. But I am a bit of an exception that way. "Old Byron" hate the festival and everything it brings with it' (quoted in Di Stefano and Lee 2009:12). One newer resident thought that multiple new festivals every year 'would brighten the place up and make this area a worldwide cultural window' (quoted in Di Stefano and Lee 2009:13).

Others pointed out that Splendour's application for a new site was more about profit-maximisation, enabling a tripling of capacity, alongside plans to stage at least two other festivals of comparable size on the new site (Murphy 2010). According to Kali Wendorf from the Tyagarah Sustainable Community Alliance, 'These big events aren't right for the shire. We love small events that are a bit alternative and that are right for Byron, not these big corporate events where overseas acts crowd out the local musicians' (quoted in Fraser 2005:24). Splendour's application for the new festival site was rejected by Byron Shire Council who grew increasingly critical of large festivals. They developed a new Shire events strategy that 'will make it difficult for large events to call Byron Bay home' (Olding 2010a:5), permitting only two festivals per year with audience crowd sizes above 6,000, effectively approving only the East Coast Blues and Roots Festival and the Byron Writers Festival (which attracts approximately 15,000 people) while preventing Splendour from operating in its then format. The Mayor, Jan Barham, was quoted as saying that Generation Y visitors had been ruining the town, 'lifestyles are being impinged upon, people are being kept up all night by partying in the street, by people defecating on lawns ... The idea of more of the same made us wary of being characterised as just a party town or attracting one demographic' (quoted in Olding 2010a:5). But, according to Ed Ahern, president of the local Chamber of Commerce, the town's 'free-thinking spirit has morphed into saying no to everything':

> A small group of vocal, anti-anything residents have literally taken about $25 million out of our community economically, not to mention the youth jobs, community involvement, cultural vibrancy and world class entertainment ... we should be leading the world in green outcomes but instead we just say no to everything and it's all that negative energy from people who are stuck in the 70s. (Quoted in Olding 2010a:5)

Peter Noble from Bluesfest argued: 'Why would you have a policy to stop outside events when they have been so successful and popular? There is no incentive to get involved and do something new because if you get to 6,000 they say "we're going to put the cap on you"' (quoted in Barrett 2011:5). Splendour in the Grass organisers attempted to run a trial event at the new site to test its environmental impacts, but were stopped by a challenge in the state Land and Environment Court. They subsequently decided to abandon Byron Bay altogether: in 2010 moving 200 kilometres north to Woodford, in Queensland, using the established site of the Woodford Folk Festival, where environmental management procedures were already established (see Chapter 5). In the words of Splendour promoter Jessica Ducrou,

> The reason we are leaving is that if this policy is implemented then there is no future for us in Byron Shire. It's a policy which is negative, it's restrictive, it's onerous, it limits the events that can be held in the shire and it really increases the level of compliance they expect. I can't imagine any other council in Australia that would pass up all the jobs and the economic opportunity that comes with Splendour. (Quoted in Fraser 2009:9)

A major, nationally-regarded festival in an iconic 'alternative' town was no longer welcome and moved elsewhere.

Both the Queensland government and Woodford's civic leaders were delighted, welcoming Splendour in the Grass 'with open arms' (Olding 2010a:5). Some 30,000 people bought tickets for the 2010 Woodford Splendour in the Grass Festival (Figure 9.5), double the figure when the event was staged in Byron Bay and generating an estimated $30 million in visitor expenditure, with ticket sales alone providing organisers of the 2010 festival with $13 million (Whyte and Connellan 2010). In the words of Sue Spooner, a take-away shop owner in Woodford: 'my word it's good for business. I just love it when the festival's on and people come into town; you welcome them here and they appreciate you being so friendly. The Folk Festival has given tourism a boost, but hopefully Splendour will keep on coming back ... I think it's going to be terrific for the town' (quoted in White 2010). Others were not so sure – exemplified in online comments to a *Courier Mail* news article about Splendour in the Grass causing immense traffic problems: 'The roads around Woodford are just not designed to cope with so many people arriving at once'; 'You'd think they'd know how to organise the traffic, after all how long has that other stupid festival been held on that site?'; 'It is a ridiculous mess!! Whoever organised this event needs to seriously reconsider their vocation'; and 'All the smiling Moreton Bay Regional Council and State Government politicians should be apologising to the Woodford community, because this will not be back after its 2 year contract due to this slipshod set up'. At Woodford too some local people complained, with echoes of those at Byron Bay:

> As one of this site's unfortunate neighbours I can assure you that this is a disaster – there was a 10 kilometre car park at 3pm and it got much worse ... So much for the organisers' assurances that everything was under control ... At the upcoming election just remember who foisted this event on the locals with no consultation, no regard for adequate infrastructure, and no care for the impact on the people who actually live here. Those who move in for the events treat the area like 'party central' – for those of us who live here it is our home, and used to be our sanctuary. (Linda Ward, 30 July 2010)

Unless carefully managed, mass arrivals of outsiders for festivals anywhere generate resentment – not just, after all, in Byron Bay.

Figure 9.5   Splendour in the Grass, Woodford, 2010

Clashing over a sense of place

'Byron would not be Byron without festivals like this.' (Real estate agent, 2003)

Places can become too popular through festivals. In Daylesford, Victoria, festivals held almost every weekend have bred resentment among residents who simply want to park and do their Saturday shopping without battling city-like traffic jams (Gorman-Murray et al. 2008). In Byron Bay the situation became even more extreme, fostering an anti-tourism, anti-festival attitude in some parts of the community. In the words of its Mayor Jan Barham, it is not just about festivals, but about 'development and business and we need to look at the rest of our community and what impact an overriding identity can have for the rest of our community' (quoted in Barrett 2011:5). Byron was seeking to 'remain special so that 1.5 million visitors can enjoy what we have' (quoted in Olding 2010a:5). Generosity may have waned as distinctiveness was threatened. Concern is perhaps as much about nostalgia for a countercultural, surf hideaway dream now long gone, as about the specific impacts of events or visitor influxes. There are limits to growth, and festivals of all types must negotiate a range of social changes, environmental dangers and development pressures, finding a way to relate to the community and to the surrounding natural world.

It is pure speculation whether the situation facing festivals in Byron Bay would be any different if the nature of the festivals was different – perhaps visual arts, rather than music (certainly there is less controversy surrounding the annual, but very large writers festival with its quite different participants), or if the major music festivals staged there were community-generated, non-profit events arising organically from within the place (as at Parkes, Dorrigo and Meredith), rather than large, commercial affairs brought to the town by entrepreneurial outsiders. There is certainly a qualitative difference between large commercial and 'grass-roots' music festivals. More tensions are generated by large commercial festivals, with concert line-ups (and few or no local bands), souvenirs made in capital cities rather than locally, enclosed arenas that 'trap' expenditure and that generate profits through ticket sales that do not filter back through charities or local non-profit committees. The East Coast Blues and Roots Festival, as large as it is and run by a private company rather than a charity or non-profit foundation, has kept a measure of support in the town, although not without dissent, perhaps because it started as a small affair in a venue that productively reused an abandoned abattoir space, or because Keven Oxford, the director, still lives in town after thirty years. Splendour in the Grass was, by contrast, a large rock concert festival from the start perceived as having been foisted on the town. In the words of one local resident in a letter to the editor of the *Sydney Morning Herald*, 'We'll go on protecting our beautiful environment from wanton destruction and support community aspirations despite the ambitions of shameless profiteers' (Michele Grant, 26 July 2010). But Splendour also brought young people whose behaviour, drugs, dancing and hair – just about everything – offended older generations, even those same people who once led the countercultural revolution themselves. Hence, in the same letter to the editor, Splendour was characterised by its 'mindless violence and stupidity of cashed-up, out-of-it young people dumped en masse into our community' (cf. Davey 2011). For Mac Nicolson, from the lobby group The Coalition for Festival Sanity (representing 30 community and environmental groups) Splendour in the Grass was: 'a permanent nightmare of partying, binge-drinking and drug-taking … an age group which sleep in cars, on beaches' (quoted in Murphy 2010:9). In contrast the East Coast Blues and Roots Festival was, in the words of one journalist: 'Australia's biggest festival of 'real' music. It is not overrun by sweaty, shirtless youths fired up on alcohol or various stimulants, there is a genuine appreciation for the sounds being made on stage and the mosh pit is more likely to be the name of a vegie cafe than a place for aggressive, macho body slamming' (Thomas 2002:10). Generational differences in taste, and an underlying ageism and elitism, matter greatly in explaining the emergence of a hostile local community.

Yet such festivals do in a sense still belong in a place like Byron Bay, depending on what vision of Byron Bay is embraced. For decades now Byron Bay has been known as a countercultural capital, a party town, a backpacker hotspot, an iconic destination. The early countercultural pioneers have become established, now control the local council, and have moved on from their youth. But the town still means the same for younger generations as it did thirty years ago: an alternative mecca where 'mainstream' (conservative) values do not automatically apply. When Splendour in the Grass moved from Byron Bay it was not without disquiet and disappointment from some local people, from businesses, from those in the community who were comfortable with a bit of noise and dirt in the name of fun, and especially among music fans and musicians themselves. For Declan Melia, frontman of rock group British India: 'Byron is a spiritual homeland of music. Woodford I've never heard of before' (quoted in Andersen and White 2010). For one Sydney visitor to Splendour 2010, 'I'd love it back in Byron to be honest. The nights leading up to the festival you can go out, it's good fun and the beach culture is great. It's just too good a place'.

Despite moving in 2010 amidst community conflicts, Splendour in the Grass promoter Jessica Ducrou still planned to lodge an application with the NSW Government to return again to Byron Bay in 2012, even while Byron Council and 33 community and environment groups opposed them. Meanwhile Woodford's Mayor, Allan Sutherland, had 'all but begged them to stay' (Olding 2010b) – even starting a 'save Splendour' campaign. For the chair of the Far North Coast's regional tourism board, Cameron Arnold, 'Splendour is based and always has been based in Byron … it is just a matter of time before a positive announcement is made on that [Yelgun] site and plans can get underway for bringing Splendour back home' (quoted in ABC News 2010). The commercial, symbolic and iconic value of Byron Bay – the place – was too high to resist. Keven Oxford, from the Bluesfest, never wavered in considering Byron Bay the only realistic place to hold his festival:

I've often contemplated whether or not I would have this same kind of success if I was doing this in Wollongong. I don't know that it would work. It may work in the capital cities, but I don't know that I'd even want to risk doing that. Byron Bay is a big part of the equation. (quoted in Shedden 2000:16)

Amidst competing and conflicting visions of place and identity, festivals continue to be a big part of the equation that make Byron Bay Australia's preeminent coastal cultural tourism destination. But, simply because they are such big parts, festivals stoke up controversy.

Chapter 10

Conclusion: Music Festivals and Pathways to Regional Development

We have sought to show in this book how music festivals – seemingly trivial and ephemeral, perhaps even exotic and exclusive, or merely a source of pleasure and entertainment – can have a significant influence within small communities and can play a valuable, although sometimes contested, role in contributing to regional development. The role of festivals is symbolic of the 'post-productivist' countryside, where wheat and sheep are no longer so important, gradually being replaced by the creative arts, gastronomy and tourism. The contributions that festivals make can come through injections of cash into the local economy in ways that stimulate further economic activity – the classic multiplier effect – but they also come in a range of other forms, from place promotion, as in Tamworth, to developing the volunteer economy, as in Goulburn, Woodford and Forth Valley, to simply putting otherwise remote places on the map. In so doing festivals may transform the identity of particular places, not always in ways that are always welcome – sometimes initially, sometimes belatedly.

Perhaps most important of all, festivals play a crucial social role for local communities, most evident in Girgarre, where this book began. Festivals have held small towns like Girgarre together through droughts and recessions, stimulated and maintained identity and community, encouraged the return of former residents, and provided a degree of fun and even a respectable income. Several festivals have deliberately begun with such objectives, and even relatively commercial festivals such as The Falls have been deliberately located in regional areas to provide economic and cultural benefits.

Even improbable locations have created memorable festivals that have boosted regional confidence, generated income and warded of depression and recession. In some cases regional music festivals have embedded themselves in national culture and folklore. The Goulburn Blues Festival and the Tamworth Country Music Festival have become so preeminent in the Australian blues and country music communities, that they have participated in an archiving project by the National Film and Sound Archive to preserve music by Australian artists within the cultural heritage of the nation. Even without pretensions to future heritage significance, and with delightful incongruities of their own, festivals and the places that host them – from Elvis in Parkes to jazz in Wangaratta – encapsulate the diversity and constant evolution of Australian regional life and culture. Many promote innovation and improvisation, and thus play an influential role in developing musical skills and careers. Festivals are increasingly important to maintaining Australian musical diversity.

Although some festivals can be economically lucrative (particularly large commercial festivals, such as those in Byron Bay), most are small-scale, modest affairs centred around the potential for a group of people to express, celebrate and promote their love of a particular activity, place, past or event. They are a means to productivity in community relations beyond the market growth dynamic. However, there is a real distinction between large commercial festivals, where a few days costs several hundred dollars in entrance fees alone, and community festivals where visitors have no necessity to spend anything (though they usually spend more than they anticipated). Reflecting this seeming amateurism, music festivals are very rarely incorporated into formal regional economic development planning. Indeed Events Australia only 'come onboard' to support festivals when they have become reasonably successful. Yet even with limited profits, music festivals – usually modest and mostly not commercial – have a significant cumulative impact, especially in small places (such as Meredith) or in places where there are lots of them (as in Bellingen, Port Fairy and Mildura) and a definite, if sometimes subtle, link to economic development. Festivals are rarely engines for regional development, but where they proliferate in even modest forms are a sign of regional social and economic vitality.

Since most festivals are small, temporary, and with little evident commercial significance, they are often ignored by local planners, regional economic development policy-makers and also academics (Whitford 2004). Only tentatively at best has regional development policy broadened its horizons from what were traditionally considered 'proper' export market-orientated industries like agriculture, or 'sober' themes like infrastructure provision, to ask questions of endogenous growth, social capital, the volunteer sector and the role of cultural activities in development. Yet festivals clearly create substantial employment (although scattered and often impermanent), catalyse community activities, and buttress tourism and place promotion campaigns. Parkes and Tamworth have both acquired a degree of fame, perhaps even notoriety, from their festivals, which have placed them more firmly 'on the map'. Some, such as Goulburn (blues), Lismore (swing dancing) or Wangaratta (jazz) – and even tiny Bridgetown (chamber music, and also a blues festival) – may not be household names but within specialist communities are meccas. A handful of places, like Maitland, have strategically designed and developed music (and other) festivals not just to put themselves on the map but to change the perception of their town, and transform it towards a 'tourist town'. Festivals also develop local skills in leadership, organisation, management and musicianship. Bringing people together who have something in common is a resource in itself, and doing so qualitatively improves local economies and encourages cooperation. In short festivals create social capital. While individual festivals may not produce enormous incomes for particular regional centres, there are considerable cumulative benefits, widely diffused within particular places and across Australia.

In time some festivals have become linked in to local tourism strategies, as at Parkes and Tamworth, evident in their promotion and the way tickets are purchased

– through travel agents and tourist information centres, rather than at record stores or from festival organisers – and are incorporated into tour packages inseparable from other basic elements of tourism such as accommodation and transport. But here and elsewhere, from Byron Bay to Woodford and Port Fairy, this has been a slow process, sometimes taking more than a decade from risky beginnings to being embraced by regional tourism promotional agencies and incorporated into tourist business linkages. Formal incorporation usually trails behind festivals having become embedded in local social networks and relationships of reciprocity between charities, clubs, associations and interest groups in the community. That this is so is ironic, because festivals staged and managed by local organisations generate more regional income, goodwill and social capital, than enormous commercial festivals such as those at Byron Bay, where profit is the defining motive for the festival, and much of that profit leaves the region (or never arrives in the first place). Again, there are important distinctions between overtly commercial festivals, advertised nationally with tickets sold through national agencies, and wholly local events where any advertising is a luxury, and indeed who struggle to get information on their festival to a wider audience beyond the local newspaper and regional radio station. While visitors to the largest festivals spend substantial amounts of money in the area, on food and accommodation (despite the profusion of tents), they may be cordoned off and their substantial ticket costs syphoned elsewhere. Festivals operate most effectively when they have significant community support behind them, which in turn contributes to maximising economic rewards. While boy scout hot dog stalls may not generate thousands of dollars the money that is generated stays and supports local social activities.

As Inverell's Opera in the Paddock demonstrates, organisational skills are not always or even usually directed to maximising profits, but to being creatively frugal – keeping ticket prices reasonably affordable, marshalling voluntary resources, calling on favours, perfecting the art of quid-pro-quo and drawing on credibility and respect from audiences, musicians and technical crew to contribute in altruistic ways (when lucrative returns are not possible). Large commercial concert-format festivals excel at excess – and commensurately generate high profits for promoters. But it is grass roots music festivals that most accurately reflect rural Australia's enduring resourcefulness and community spirit. Where festivals appear detached from local life there can be strong reaction to their environmental and social impacts and the eventual migration to more remote greenfield sites – even crossing state borders, as in Splendour in the Grass. Conversely festivals that have worked hard to more fully incorporate communities – from Bermagui to Dorrigo and Parkes – have grown, gained local trust and found a source of people and ideas for renewal.

What is remarkable about many of the festivals highlighted here is that they began on a whim or by chance, through fortunate moments when a few people or even a lone individual had an idea that could be turned into an event: random concepts in sometimes random places. The High & Dry Festival was 'organised in just 10 days when Peats Ridge got cancelled due to bad weather conditions.

We were due to produce and run the Dome Stage [at Peat's Ridge] that year –
we already had the truck packed when the "we're really sorry but ..." call came
through – so we figured we might as well put on some sort of party anyway'
(Matt Woodham, organiser, quoted in Carr 2009:1). That festival accidentally
discovered a niche for young local rock bands otherwise marginalised at larger
concert-format events. But idiosyncrasy rarely works twice; competitors to the
Parkes Elvis Festival failed because Elvis came to just one town. Equally many
began at strange times: midsummer in the scorching inland, when it seemed
folly to even tempt providence. Or in strange places – in a paddock outside an
isolated country town; even outback deserts. But that is part of the fun, and these
idiosyncrasies have survived, grown beyond expectations and attracted national
attention. At the same time others have deliberately sat down and debated what
might be successful; Wangaratta came up with a jazz festival and chose to foster
improvisation rather than settle for 'safe' programming, and Bermagui gained
a classical music festival – what were then innovative choices. Moreover they
complemented different musical festivals in nearby towns. There is no blueprint
beyond good ideas, enthusiasm and commitment. Multiple routes to success exist
but 'thinking outside the box' is one of them.

Small towns are thoroughly capable of producing creativity, despite
assumptions that creativity – and the creative industries – are metropolitan
phenomena, and that 'best practices' are to be found in the largest cities, from
where they may trickle down (Gibson 2010, van Heur 2010). Festivals alone
demonstrate that this is no longer tenable, and that many small towns have been
able to gain significant economic and social benefits by developing and trading
on improbable, even wholly fictitious and sometimes 'unworthy' events and
associations. Indeed music festivals, diverse and creative in themselves, are only
one part of a wider festival scene, that embraces the Deniliquin Ute Muster, a
'kombi' muster at Old Bar (NSW), goat races at Barcaldine (Queensland) and
the 'running of the sheep' at Boorowa (NSW). 'Utes in the Paddock' (NSW),
where a '7m metal marsupial is spectacularly silhouetted against the burnt blue
outback sky' (Davies 2009: 6), the Tin Horse Highway (WA) and Silverton (SA)'s
Mad Max Museum are further tiny components of the quirky and original rural
creativity that has gradually transformed image and reality in regional Australia.
Just as in England, where the media have been astounded at festivals and creativity
existing in seemingly improbable places (Voase 2009), so too in Australia have
metropolitan commentators slowly begun to acknowledge rural creativity, evident
in such festivals as Bermagui's Four Winds. Creativity is exemplified both in and
beyond regional festivals, and has been invaluable.

Small, struggling towns in rural Australia have promoted hundreds of festivals,
both as community-building exercises and because they can attract visitors.
Few have been anywhere near as successful as Parkes, despite an unpromising
theme and an inauspicious beginning, demonstrating how a small place can stage
a festival in a relatively remote location, on a theme of no local relevance, and
succeed despite itself. Indeed Parkes succeeded against long odds: droughts and

floods, early local hostility, a fringe-of-town location, a satirical national press, an uninterested local press, an oppressive climate and a dead headline performer. In Parkes the constant repetition of phrases such as: 'it is a real morale booster when we are in drought' emphasises how fortuitous that festival has been. But festivals can boost morale at any time when well staged, well attended and with a positive impact on the local economy.

Festivals are, on the one hand, the cultural expressions of local people, emerging as local projects, dependent on local support, at one level occasions for expressing collective belonging to a group or place (Ekman 1999; Derrett 2009), but they are also the relationship between these people and the wider world, the participants and the audiences. Yet festivals invariably reflect the interests of just some local people. They are sites where certain people project visions of place and music that may have limited local relevance, where mere empty space is required (especially in the rave era), where tastes are those of a minority, and where commerce dominates decisions about anything resembling local identity. Most festivals have experienced pressures to become more commercially astute, both when they have sought access to arts funding and national support, or to acquire larger markets. As that has occurred (and for most, arguably, that has not been the case), festivals have grown, management has become more professional and powerful, but local ownership and identity is challenged (Davies 2011), while festivals may also be pressed to retain their creativity and individuality (Quinn 2005). Festivals taking aesthetic risks gain credibility among specialist audiences, but those aimed at engaging a broader spectrum of the community (or where places host a number of festivals catering to different segments of the population) go further in alleviating a sense of exclusion. For this reason alone, the incorporation of festivals into regional development policy-making requires consideration of questions of cultural expression, vitality and inclusion. Hence the Four Winds Festival at Bermagui sought to reconcile concerns for quality programming with strategies to involve the wider community. Evolution, innovation and credibility are the concomitants of successful festivals, and the means of warding off life cycles that end in death.

Yet, as the intentions of so many festival-goers indicate, having fun is the rationale for what usually amounts to a weekend's entertainment. Frivolity and escapism are never far from the surface of most festivals, and deep consideration of aesthetics or inclusion may be optional extras. Deserts (or at least 'outbacks'), paddocks, woolsheds and wineries commonly draw crowds to festivals, generating a sense of difference from the norm, but 'fun, family and friends', the familiar, are a large part of the rationale. That a lieder concert in Inverell might lose some of its audience when a country star was in town suggests either a remarkable diversity in musical tastes or, more probably, that the 'show' in any form and format is at the heart of the experience for many. Street parades, dressing up, and joining in can be the highlight of many festivals, however irrelevant vintage cars are to the theme of the festival. Likewise the outdoors, itself part of the allure of festivals, offers the ambience and alternative sounds of wind, birds and other native animals.

While the musical content is important it is just one influence on participation and enjoyment. Over and over again, but perhaps particularly at Parkes and at Tamworth, and at festivals close to metropolitan centres, most people were simply there for something different, fun and relaxation, a good day or weekend out in the country, some brief experience of 'country hospitality' and the music. Marketing tactics that broaden a festival's appeal beyond the music alone into the 'experience' and ambience are invaluable. As Bowen and Daniels (2004:155) argue, to succeed festivals must create 'a fun and festive atmosphere that offers ample opportunity to socialize and have new ... experiences'. But, as longitudinal data from Parkes showed, many wanted repeated experiences: fun, reunion and nostalgia combined. Visitors seek both active and passive entertainment.

Not only are festival visitors varied in what they seek to experience and participate in, but they have varied enthusiasms and knowledge. Some are ardent fanatics – opera buffs or globe trotters in search of Elvis festivals – but the majority are simply casual fans, seeking a few hours or days' entertainment – with like-minded people, family and friends, in a pleasant environment, where other activities such as shopping, eating, drinking and conversation are just as important. A music festival provides the context for diverse activities and various forms of enjoyment. Yet all festivals have their aficionados – regular returnees for whom the festival annually cements bonds with other members of their neo-tribe, or just their friends. And festivals are not necessarily interchangeable: opera buffs might dislike Parkes and country music; blues fans be suspicious of opera, even in a paddock. In such evidently successful cases as Parkes and Tamworth there has been sustained dissent over the relationship between the town and festivals that were not to everyone's taste. Both towns have spent decades seeking a degree of festival and musical diversity. Both towns took time to support events that seemed foolish or inappropriate. Establishing and ensuring community support is no mean feat. For most festivals 'seeing off the competition' and establishing an assured regional presence is the most difficult task.

Festival-Led Development: a Hybrid Affair

In this book we have sought to understand the economic qualities of music festivals as culturally, spatially and temporally produced, to explore how the regional development potential of music festivals is embedded in a wider cultural politics of place and identity – and to reflect on music festivals in light of debates about what kind of regional economic development strategies rural places ought to pursue. Through understanding music festivals as simultaneously 'cultural' and 'economic' phenomena, it becomes possible to see where they fit into regional development. They bring tourists and income, and have become part of strategies to attract in-migrants and put towns more permanently into the national consciousness. Music festivals catalyse networks and reciprocities with local councils, tourism agencies, charities, non-profit organisations, music associations and clubs. Festivals are fulcrums of relationships: business, professional, social. And sometimes those relationships extend to other festivals: cooperation rather than competition. The organisers of the Elvis Festival at Parkes went to Tamworth to learn how to expand successfully, while Tamworth's tourism managers went to Nashville with the same intent. The economic networks of festivals are complex. But because festivals by definition are sites of cultural expression they also necessarily involve complex questions of aesthetics, social equality, diversity and belonging – questions not just tangential to those of hard-nosed economics, but integral to the commercial success of festivals.

This book has sought to show how staging festivals is a hybrid affair, where culture and commerce combine to generate both social and economic benefits. Economic development planners and local councils, where they have been slow to support local endeavours, might therefore take festivals more seriously. Although 'touchy-feely' social and cultural aims and values might (rightly) underpin most festivals, even the most radical, avant-garde or uncommercial festivals invariably require audiences, support services, staging and audio equipment (all things reliant on some element of planning, and part of a broader festival economy). Even when not regarded by musicians or arts promoters as 'commercial', music festivals are 'economic' in the broadest sense, because they have audiences, use buildings, facilities and equipment and entail some kind of service or entertainment provision. Thus Opera in The Paddock, with a wholly non-commercial intent, necessarily spends $1000 on lighting, and more on fireworks, pays musicians and attracts visitors who spend money en route on petrol, food and accommodation, all supporting local business. All festivals have both demand and supply-side economic impacts on localities (even if inadvertently so). While 'hard-nosed' modelling of multiplier impacts is a valuable 'reality check' to measure the fiscal 'success' of individual festivals, festivals are necessarily *always* cultural phenomena, and debates regarding culture, identity and inclusion/exclusion are much more than mere externalities. Indeed, the entire viability of music festivals is jeopardised when economics downplays or ignores issues of social impact, elitism, inclusiveness or aesthetic quality. Conceptualising how music festivals – across the full spectrum from commercial concert-format events to small non-profit affairs – exactly contribute to regional development requires consideration of their multiple connections. A qualitative approach goes beyond whether music festivals are worth it on a single bottom line of costs versus income, and beyond events management and visitor segmentation studies to consider the meaning, significance and embeddedness of festivals in places – a triple-bottom-line incorporating economic, social and environmental dimensions. The very nature of the festival matters – the management structure, the philosophy and history (whether having grown organically from a small number of committed locals, or commercial concerts 'parachuted' into a rural locale), the ethics underpinning how even seemingly trivial decisions are made over which food stalls to allow in or where to source PA and toilet hire.

As festivals evolve they are perceived and evaluated in different ways. Even the most esoteric have community connections. Environmental issues were of trivial significance in early days, especially as festivals started small, whereas they are now of sometimes critical importance and have influenced locations and structures, while even the stalls at festivals have taken on environmental themes and marketed local produce. Intangible benefits are there but much harder to track. Musicianship and performance skills are enhanced. Small towns become attractive as subsequent tourist destinations. At Tamworth, a country music festival became the means to claim 'country' as its own, with additional benefits through pitching the town as a year-round tourist destination, with country music museums, venues and memorials, as well as semantic slippages that enabled the town to claim it was quintessentially 'country', meaning rural, and in turn, therefore, quintessentially Australian. Such regional tourism promotion and place marketing involve forays into the world of imagery, symbolism and culture – with associated risks, from alienating locals who cringe at the 'hick' elements of country music to simplifying depictions of local people and promoting caricatured clichés such as 'country values' that are in reality little more than cultural conservatism. While Bermagui's Four Winds Festival has resulted in at least one family moving to the town, evidence for other new migration is rarely more than apocryphal, though festivals usually (often intentionally) present small towns in their best light. Festivals have probably influenced return visits even if not on a full-time basis. In Dungog (NSW), where an annual Film Festival draws several thousand visitors, many regular festival-goers return at other times of the year (often not seeing or exploring enough during the busy festival) and some buy second homes or move permanently (Frew 2011b). The same is very likely in Port Fairy, Bellingen and Byron Bay but impossible to measure.

Regional development means little unless cultural diversity is embraced and local people feel included. In Tamworth, beyond glossy brochures with cowboys, guitars and horses appealing to conservative norms of 'country' are layers of diversity that have been enabled by that festival's decentralised management structure; Aboriginal country musicians, country punk, 'indie' country women performers and a whole host of other niche pursuits (from gum leaf playing to bush balladeering) co-exist and jostle for attention. Nationalistic jingoism and cartoon cowboy marketing can perhaps be excused when the reality of the festival's management structure offers something far more inclusive. Even so, trying to attract more younger visitors led Tamworth to book high profile pop acts that broadened appeal, but threatened the credibility of the festival; stalwarts complained of losing touch with the 'roots' of the festival and country style. It is impossible to please everyone.

Diversification goes some way to cater for diverging tastes, although families and the middle class are more likely to be targeted. There are festivals to suit every taste and almost every instrument, from bagpipes to gum leaves. And yet there is scope for expansion; Australia has no Gilbert and Sullivan or Michael Jackson festival. Many are more popular with performers than audiences, who welcome the exposure, the honing of their skills, and the opportunity to be paid and sell CDs where their incomes from live performances exceed dwindling revenue from record sales. As Simon Daly, the founder of the Falls Creek Festival, has said

> Live music has never been so strong. The punters are the biggest winners of all. They have so many opportunities to see live music in different ways. That's a great thing. With CD sales and album sales dropping away it's great for the artists too, that so many people are going out to see live music. (Quoted in Shedden 2007)

Festivals are both social opportunities and commercial opportunities for new artists to reach new audiences, to sell CDs and to revitalise their music, and – but not always – for local youth to become more involved in music.

Context matters. There is both a measurable geography of festivals in terms of which towns have numerous and/or successful festivals, and an argument that the regional development implications of a given festival only make sense in that locality. Country music festivals are not surprisingly more common in inland rural agricultural regions; jazz and blues festivals more common on the coast (though not exclusive to it, as Wangaratta demonstrates); classical music festivals often located in out of the way, distinct, unique, memorable locations, from deserts to paddocks to natural amphitheatres with ocean views – but more particularly in sea-change towns, organised by relatively new urban migrants. But more than this, there is an intimate geography of the location of festivals within towns – whether at one central concert venue (Woodford) or separated festival sites (as at Splendour in the Grass), or scattered across many pubs and clubs (as at Goulburn, Parkes and Tamworth). Each have their quirks from a management perspective; scattered venues are more complicated to coordinate, but filter spending benefits around, maximising the 'trickle down'. Parkes only really took off after the festival was moved from suburbia to a central location. Conversely Byron Bay has increasingly sought to dispatch festivals to larger sites on the edge of town or beyond it.

The existing economic base, demographic profile, infrastructure, history and cultural proclivities of a festival's host village or town also count: Parkes had Elvis fans and a Gracelands club. Bermagui had classical music enthusiasts; a farm outside Inverell was home to a prominent opera singer. Most classical festivals had powerful local advocates. Byron Bay, a small ex-whaling town and abattoir centre, became Australia's most famous music, festival and alternative culture centre – an equivalent to Woodstock and Glastonbury where 'alternative' culture and festivals have come together in spectacular, but contested, ways. In Byron Bay the very same cultural milieu that gave birth to multiple alternative festivals in the 1970s and 1980s later became a threat when festivals grew, changed direction, disrupted the peace and disturbed local ecology. Festivals were blocked by local council planning restrictions and made to feel unwelcome by the local community. Some places – those that are middle class, that have high property values or that purport to be 'green' places – may be more sensitive to festival incursions than others.

More simply there is an upper limit to the number of festivals, their size and level of acceptability within a community. Even then, Meredith is more anarchic, noisier and in a tinier place than Splendour in the Grass, and yet has the farmers and townsfolk on side, with less commercialism and less intensive security needed. The qualities, philosophies and communalities of festivals are all critical.

A Festival Future?

Ultimately music festivals are enjoyable, for the visitors, for the promoters and countless volunteers (despite the hours of organisation), and in most cases they 'lift spirits, transfer knowledge and enhance neighbourliness' (Derrett 2009:108). And neighbourliness extends beyond local people to more distant festival-goers. Many visitors see meeting local people as one of the pleasures of participation, and homestay schemes as at Tamworth and Parkes formalise this for mutual benefit. Above all visitors emphasise the relaxed ambience and atmosphere – being (usually) in the open air and away from the confines of urban life and concert halls, the routine of daily life and the chaos of the city. In the end it is for these pleasurable reasons that festivals have survived and thrived and, in contrast to death and taxes, they have become a vital and welcome part of regional life. Indeed that is why the numbers and size of festivals are growing, which ultimately raises questions about the limits to growth: certainly not all can survive. Just as there is a tourism life cycle for destinations that demands periodic reinvention and renewal, relocation or death (Butler 1980) so for festivals too longevity is earned rather than assumed. Volunteers burn out and committees need renewing; visitors eventually tire of revisiting without some new attractions each year; and host communities become weary with the noise, congestion and notoriety.

Maintaining a successful festival over many years can be demanding. Local volunteer committees need replenishing, not without difficulty. Although the most successful music festivals are those that have matured over many years, rarely have music festivals survived longer than a couple of decades. The longevity of Tamworth is a function of its unusual, decentralised organisational structure and the continuing commitment of Tamworth Council to oversee logistical arrangements while leaving music venues to manage their own affairs, a situation not easily replicated elsewhere. Parkes is likely to keep investing in the Elvis Revival Festival so long as crowds keep coming, though it took passionate individuals within the community and the local tourism bureau to see it through difficult times. The biggest challenge for the Forth Valley Blues Festival's Lea Coates is 'many changes to the rules and regulations around the staging of festivals, on all three government levels ... regulatory "red tape" is definitely the most frustrating part of putting this event together' (personal communication 2010). Many music festivals fade eventually, especially commercial pop music events, with waning enthusiasm, financial difficulties, changing tastes or the retirement or migration of key movers and shakers.

The continuity of festivals can also be threatened through competition from growing numbers, or because of unrealistic prices and wage demands, and financial losses. Festivals in Britain, such as the Phoenix Festival in Oxfordshire, have been cancelled through lack of support and 'excessive' demands from bands; fans prefer to go to festivals with reasonable prices (especially for drinks), short queues and adequate facilities. Some such as Wangaratta have managed to effectively balance tensions between place promotion and income generation, and artistic independence and creativity; others such as Goulburn, Bermagui and Inverell have steadfastly maintained artistic standards and perennially negotiate financial hurdles – perhaps a necessary burden. In other instances towns and regions lose festivals after fall-outs between organisers and local authorities: Byron Bay jettisoned Splendour in the Grass over environmental concerns, while the Wintersun Festival left the Gold Coast in 2010 for Port Macquarie amidst complaints that accommodation facilities on the Gold Coast were engaging in price-gouging – charging festival-goers dramatically increased rates in an otherwise quiet season (Murphy 2010; Tuttiett 2011). Gold Coast authorities in turn created a new festival, Cooly Rocks On, to fill the void left by Wintersun, and were confident it would prove lucrative, but reputation and credibility are difficult to create or clone.

Where events have survived over many years they have tended to be place-based celebrations with civic backing, or iconic festivals with deeply embedded reputations organised by non-profit organisations, as at the Meredith Music Festival, Bellingen's Global Carnival, and Woodford Folk Festival. The vast bulk of commercial music festivals rarely sustain both commercial viability and critical acclaim over a long period. This is scarcely surprising: levels of risk are much higher for concert based commercial events, where the illness of a star performer who pulls out at the last minute can wreck a festival and lead to a flood of requests for refunds; 'bad weather, rowdy crowds or unexciting performers can put the whole operation in jeopardy' (Kazi 2006:16). The Big Day Out – which plays in Australian capital cities rather than nonmetropolitan areas – like Splendour in the Grass and the Falls Festival is budgeted on a sell-out; according to producer Ken West, 'Every year you're not sure how it's going to go. I've got a love-hate relationship with that event. If we lose Queensland [because of cyclones] that means $6 million will fall over if it has to be cancelled. We're always dealing with very scary scenarios' (quoted in Kazi 2006:16). As writing this book came to a close, media reports cast new doubt over the future of music festivals (Davey 2011; Turner 2011; Westwood 2011). The largest commercial festivals were experiencing dwindling ticket sales (where instant sell-outs were previously the norm); offered two-for-one deals; or in the case of Good Vibrations, took a periodic hiatus. Those who still went to the larger commercial festivals were argued to be 'the shirtless and drugged-up' who outnumbered the music lovers. Costs are considerable. Some promoters cited over-saturation – hence Justin Hemmes from Good Vibrations argued the problem was 'every Tom, Dick and Harry thinking they can start up a festival' (Quoted in Feeney and Moore 2010). 'Brand identities' were becoming blurred as festivals jostled to tap into 'an authentic native spirit' of the host place (Westwood 2011:17). Big commercial festivals have become, in the words of Australian band Eskimo Joe's lead singer Kav Temperley, a 'blood sport' (quoted in Clarke 2011). Equally responsible are undersupply of quality music acts, that can attract distant audiences willing to pay high ticket prices, and the general economic climate bordering on recession.

Yet, these music festivals in precarious circumstances are usually commercial, concert-format events in large cities where line-up is everything, tickets are expensive and connections to the community sector weak. Big cities offer many other attractions (and festivals) and life could go on without them (cf. Prentice and Andersen 2005). The vast bulk of festivals discussed in this book – at Parkes, Goulburn, Inverell, Port Fairy, Bellingen, Forth Valley, Dorrigo, Wangaratta, Bermagui and beyond – look nothing like this. With the backing of councils and non-profit organisations, linked to charities and clubs, and attracting a mix of day trippers, enthusiasts, loyal fans and curious townsfolk simply out for the fun and the show, regional music festivals are on the whole far more resilient to capitalism's fluctuating boom and bust cycles. Indeed they have survived, and boosted towns, during drought and agricultural slumps.

Festivals are neither panacea to all manner of economic woes, nor mere commercialism. They capture many of the broader contradictions and tensions that emerge when the creative arts are more fully imagined as avenues of regional development. In regional Australia music festivals remain an under-acknowledged and yet potentially significant component of strategies to develop grass-roots economies, what Wearing et al. (2005:424) called a 'decommodified' tourism paradigm. They frequently advance laudable goals of inclusion, community and celebration: an alternative pathway to development (Gibson and Cameron 2005) that even reduces exposure to recession. And, as so many festival organisers noted, they allow residents not just to temporarily forget hard times in the bush but to raise local incomes in sometimes impoverished towns.

The biggest challenges for regional music festivals may be 'sleepers' – long-term vulnerabilities that creep up rather than catalyse commercial collapse. For example generational differences, the underlying demographic trend behind the ever-expanding market for festivals discussed in this book, is arguably the greatest future challenge. Keven Oxford described his East Coast Blues and Roots Festival as 'like a Big Day Out for the baby boomer generation' (quoted in Shedden 2000:17), while Parkes according to one survey respondent was 'schoolies for oldies'. People continually seek fun well beyond their youth, so there will continue to be a market (though that, like music tastes, might change with generations), but audiences are getting older. What will happen when baby-boomers, the core market for Parkes, East Coast Blues and Roots Festival, Four Winds, Opera in the Paddock and the Tamworth Country Music Festival, grow old, become immobile or have to curtail spending? With the bulk of baby-boomers approaching retirement, selected festivals may reap rewards of that generation's financial wealth and free time, as audiences but also as all important volunteers (Salt 2010). Festivals that over-rely on this market may well go the way of flower shows – once a mainstay of country life but fading with the retirement (and death) of committee members (and participants) (Edwards 2011). Equally unknown is the extent to which volunteerism and social capital may transfer through subsequent generations, or whether sponsors (and audiences) will continue to come in harsher economic times. Eventually festivals serving the changing tastes of Generations X and Y may fill the gap, but that remains uncertain – a market perhaps to be captured by more forward-looking, innovative places. In the meantime, across Australia's country towns people will continue doing their own thing, putting on festivals in a distinctly community-driven, do-it-yourself form of local development. In the words of Mary Nolan, on whose land the Meredith Music Festival takes place annually,

> I feel a sense of privilege in being able to be part of something like that – that whole thing of people coming together, and what those people do when they come together. That's the locals, the city and country. There's lots of little levels to it: the volunteers, the punters, and the music of course – the music.

With local connections, quirky folk, fans and escapists alike, music festivals – even in their most eclectic iterations – offer pathways to regional development that build on and give back to the communities that host them.

Bibliography

ABC News 2010. Splendour cash won't flow south. *ABC News* [Online, 30 July] Available at: www.abc.net.au/news/stories/2010/07/30/2968775.htm [accessed: 5 September 2010].

Albert, J. 2001. The secret festival. *The Australian*, 31 August, 15.

Alcoa Foundation 2010. Nanga Music Festival makes 'roadies' out of Alcoa volunteers, press release, 12 October.

Aldskogius, H. 1993. Festivals and meets: the place of music in 'summer Sweden'. *Geografiska Annaler*, 75B, 55–72.

Allen, J., O'Toole, W., Harris, R. and McDonnell, I. 2008. *Festival and Special Event Management*. Brisbane: Wiley.

Allen, M. 1988. *The Tamworth Country Music Festival*. Sydney: Horwitz Grahame.

Andersen, B. and White, C. 2010. Byron still Splendour's 'spiritual home'. *ABC News* [Online, 31 July] Available at: www.abc.net.au/news/stories/2010/07/31/2969725.htm [accessed: 5 September 2010].

Arcodia, C. and Whitford, M. 2006. Festival attendance and the development of social capital. *Journal of Convention and Event Tourism*, 8, 1–18.

Attali, J. 1985. *Noise: The Political Economy of Music*. Manchester: Manchester University Press.

Australian Elvis Presley Fan Club 2011. [Online] Available at: http://elvisclub. org/viewad.asp?id=50286971164100004 [accessed: 11 March 2011].

Barlow, M. and Shibli, S. 2007. Audience development in the arts: A case study of chamber music. *Managing Leisure*, 12, 102–19.

Barrett, R. 2011. Byron bid for a freeze on festivals. *The Weekend Australian*, 13–14 August, 5.

Baum, C. 2010. Frozen in time. *Sydney Morning Herald*, 16 March, 5.

Beer, A., Maude, A. and Pritchard, B. 2003. *Developing Australia's Regions: Theory and Practice*. Sydney: UNSW Press.

Beeton, S. 2006. *Community Development Through Tourism*. Melbourne: Landlinks Press.

Begg, R. 2011. Culturing commitment: serious leisure and the folk festival experience, in *Festival Places: Revitalising Rural Australia*, edited by C. Gibson and J. Connell. Bristol: Channel View, 248–64.

Bilton, R. 2010. Smells like teen spirit. *The Australian Magazine*, 10 July, 42.

Bowen, H. and Daniels, M. 2005. Does the music matter? Motivations for attending a music festival. *Event Management*, 9(3), 155–64.

Bowen, N. 1999. Drive up, drink on, pass out. *City Hub*, 14 January, 24.

The Brag 2010. Splendour debate, 9 August, 16.

Brennan-Horley, C., Connell, J. and Gibson, C. 2007. The Parkes Elvis Revival Festival: economic development and contested place identities in rural Australia. *Geographical Research*, 45(1), 71–84.

Buchanan, M. 2009. Hey buddy, can you spare a PlayStation? *Sydney Morning Herald*, 21 January, 5.

Butler, R. 1980. The concept of a tourist area cycle of evolution: implications for management of resources. *Canadian Geographer*, 24, 5–12.

Cameron, N. 1995. *Maleny Folk Festival: The Art of Celebration*. Maleny: Mimburi Press.

Carr, M. 2009. *High & Dry with Matt Woodham* [Online] Available at: http://musicfeeds.com.au/features/high-dry-with-matt-woodham/ [accessed: 9 August 2011].

Chhabra, D., Sills, E. and Cubbage, F. 2003. The significance of festivals to rural economies: estimating the economic impacts of Scottish Highland Games in North Carolina. *Journal of Travel Research*, 41, 421–27.

Clarke, J. 2011. Eskimo Joe frontman calls music festivals 'blood sport'. *Sydney Morning Herald*, 12 August, 14.

Clarke, M. 1982. *The Politics of Pop Festivals*. London: Junction Books.

Connell, J. and Gibson, C. 2003. *Sound Tracks: Popular Music, Identity and Place*, London: Routledge.

Connell, J. and McManus, P. 2011. *Rural Revival? Place Marketing, Tree Change and Regional Migration in Australia*. Farnham: Ashgate.

Connellan, B. and Mack, D. 2010. Splendour in the Grass 2010, *Honi Soit*, 5 August, 10–11.

Connelly, C. 2007. *In Search of Elvis*. London: Abacus.

Cox, K. 2003. Hopes ride the high road in the heart of country. *Sun-Herald*, 19 January, 42–43.

Crompton, J., Lee, S.K. and Shuster, T. 2001. A guide for undertaking economic impact studies: The Springfest example. *Journal of Travel Research*, 40, 79–87.

Cunningham, H. 2010. Magical moments come rain, hail or shine as director takes risks. *Sydney Morning Herald*, 6 April, 12.

Curtis, R. 2010. Australia's capital of jazz? The (re)creation of place, music and community at Wangaratta Jazz Festival. *Australian Geographer*, 41(1), 101–16.

Curtis, R. 2011. What is Wangaratta to jazz? The (re)creation of place, music and community at the Wangaratta Jazz Festival, in *Festival Places: Revitalising Rural Australia*, edited by C. Gibson and J. Connell. Bristol: Channel View, 280–93.

Darian-Smith, K. 2011. Histories of agricultural shows and rural festivals in Australia, in *Festival Places: Revitalising Rural Australia*, edited by C. Gibson and J. Connell. Bristol: Channel View, 25–43.

Davidson, L. and Schaffer, W. 1980. A Discussion of methods employed in analyzing the impact of short-term entertainment events. *Journal of Travel Research*, 18(3), 12–16.

Davey, M. 2011. The music festival is dead, long live a civilised gathering. *Sun-Herald*, 31 July, 30.

Davies, A. 2011. Local leadership and rural renewal through festival fun: the case of Snowfest, in *Festival Places: Revitalising Rural Australia*, edited by C. Gibson and J. Connell. Bristol: Channel View, 61–73.

Davies, K. 2009. The Outback gallery where utes rule, *The Sunday Telegraph*, 23 August, 6.

De Bres, K. and Davis, J. 2001. Celebrating group and place identity: a case study of a new regional festival. *Tourism Geographies*, 3, 326–37.

Delaney, B. 2003. Towns are alive with the sound of music. *Sydney Morning Herald*, 11 February, 11.

Deloitte Access Economics. 2011. *The Economic, Social and Cultural Contribution of Venue-based Live Music in Victoria*. Melbourne: Deloitte.

Derrett, R. 2003. Festivals and tourists in the Rainbow Region, in *Belonging in the Rainbow Region: Cultural Perspectives on the NSW North Coast*, edited by H. Wilson. Lismore: Southern Cross University Press, 287–308.

Derrett, R. 2009. How festivals nurture resilience in regional communities, in *International Perspectives of Festivals and Events: Paradigms of Analysis*, edited by J. Ali-Knight, M. Robertson, A. Fyall and A. Ladkin. Oxford: Elsevier, 107–24.

Di Stefano, M. and Lee, A. 2009. Honi goes to Splendour in the Grass. *Honi Soit*, 20 July, 12–13.

Drever, A. 2008. End of the Earthcore. *The Age*, 28 November, 6.

Duffy, M. 2000. Lines of drift: festival participation and performing a sense of place. *Popular Music*, 19, 51–64.

Duffy, M. 2009. *Music of Place: Community Identity in Contemporary Australian Music Festivals*. Saarbrucken : VDM Verlag.

Duffy, M. and Waitt, G. 2011. Rural festivals and processes of belonging, in *Festival Places: Revitalising Rural Australia*, edited by C. Gibson and J. Connell. Bristol: Channel View, 44–57.

Dunbar-Hall, P. and Gibson, C. 2004. *Deadly Sounds, Deadly Places: Contemporary Aboriginal Music in Australia*. Sydney: UNSW Press.

Dwyer, L., Agrusa, J. and Coats, W. 2001. Economic scale of a community event: the Lafayette Mardi Gras. *Pacific Tourism Review*, 5, 167–79.

Edwards, R. 2011. Birthday parties and flower shows, musters and multiculturalism: festivals in post-war Gympie, in *Festival Places: Revitalising Rural Australia*, edited by C. Gibson and J. Connell. Bristol: Channel View, 136–54.

Ekman, A. 1999. The revival of cultural celebrations in regional Sweden. Aspects of tradition and transition. *Sociologia Ruralis*, 39, 280–93.

Elder, B. 1999. The sundance kids. *Sydney Morning Herald*, 14 January, 2–3.

Elder, B. 2002. Bay watch. *Sydney Morning Herald*, 8–14 March, 21.

Elder, B. 2003. Around the world in three magical days. *Sydney Morning Herald*, 26 February, 18.

Elder, B. 2010. Boutique Bellingen has fun going global. *Sydney Morning Herald*, 28 September, 11.

Essex, S.J. and Brown, G.P. 1997. The emergence of post-suburban landscapes on the North Coast of New South Wales: a case study of contested space. *International Journal of Urban and Regional Research*, 21, 259–85

Falls Festival 2010. *2010 Falls Festival Sustainability Report* [Online] Available at: http://2011.fallsfestival.com.au/sustainability/ [accessed 25 February 2011].

Feeney, K. and Moore, T. 2010. Big days down and out? Music festivals under threat. *Brisbane Times* [Online] Available at: http://www.brisbanetimes.com.au/entertainment/music/big-days-down-and-out-music-festivals-under-threat-20101117-17xhi.html#ixzz1QXgGnI00 [accessed: 4 April 2011].

Formica, S., and Uysal, M. 1996. A market segmentation of festival visitors: Umbria Jazz Festival in Italy. *Festival Management & Event Tourism*, 3, 175–82.

Fraser, A. 2005. Wrong note, billygoat. *The Weekend Australian*, 10–11 September, 24.

Fraser, A. 2006. Gumboots were made for rocking. *The Australian*, 24 July, 16.

Fraser, A. 2009. Council rocks Splendour in the Grass festival. *The Australian*, 26 November, 9.

Frew, W. 1989. Our booming music city shrugs off its 'hick' image. *The Australian Financial Review* 1 January, 30.

Frew, W. 2011a. Grassroots festival grows into the big league. *Sydney Morning Herald*, 9 December, 14.

Frew, W. 2011b. Dungog proves itself to be the real star of the film festival. *Sydney Morning Herald*, 28 May, 11.

Frey, B. 1994. The economics of music festivals. *Journal of Cultural Economics*, 18, 29–39.

Fyfe, M. 2001. It ain't just country at Tamworth. *Sunday Age*, 21 January, 6.

Gebicki, M. 2003. Getting it together. *The Australian*, 11 October, 24–25.

Gelan, A. 2003. Local economic impacts: The British Open. *Annals of Tourism Research*, 30, 406–25.

Gelder, G. and Robinson, P. 2009. A critical comparative study of visitor motivations for attending music festivals: a case study of Glastonbury and V Festival. *Event Management*, 13, 181–96.

Getz, D. 2007. *Event Studies: Theory, Research and Policy for Planned Events*. Oxford: Butterworth-Heinemann.

Getz, D. 2010. The nature and scope of festival studies. *International Journal of Event Management Research*, 5, 1–47.

Getz, D., Andersson, T. and Carlsen, J. 2010. Festival management studies: developing a framework for comparative and cross-cultural research. *International Journal of Event and Festival Management*, 1, 29–59.

Giaoutzi, M. and Nijkamp, P. 2006. *Tourism and Regional Development: New Pathways*. Aldershot: Ashgate.

Gibson, C. 2003. Cultures at work: why 'culture' matters in research on the 'cultural' industries. *Social and Cultural Geography*, 4(2), 201–15.

Gibson, C. 2007. Music festivals: transformations in non-metropolitan places, and in creative work. *Media International Australia incorporating Culture and Policy*, 123, 65–81.

Gibson, C. 2010. Creative geographies: tales from the 'margins'. *Australian Geographer*, 41(1), 1–10.

Gibson, C., Allen, K., Lee, V., and Mirow, K. 2004. Experiential learning in the field: measuring the economic impacts of a music festival in regional Australia. *Geography Bulletin*, 36(3), 18–27.

Gibson, C. and Connell, J. 2003. 'Bongo Fury': tourism, music and cultural economy at Byron Bay, Australia. *Tijdschrift voor Economische en Sociale Geografie*, 94(2), 164–87.

Gibson, C. and Connell, J. 2005. *Music and Tourism*. Clevedon: Channel View.

Gibson, C. and Connell, J. eds. 2011. *Festival Places: Revitalising Rural Australia*. Bristol: Channel View.

Gibson, C. and Davidson, D. 2004. Tamworth, Australia's 'country music capital': place marketing, rural narratives and resident reactions. *Journal of Rural Studies* 20(4), 387–404.

Gibson, C., Waitt, G., Walmsley, J. and Connell, J. 2010. Cultural festivals and economic development in regional Australia. *Journal of Planning Education and Research*, 29(3), 280–93.

Gibson, C. and Wong, C. 2011. Greening rural festivals: ecology, sustainability, and human-nature relations, in *Festival Places: Revitalising Rural Australia*, edited by C. Gibson and J. Connell. Bristol: Channel View, 92–105.

Gibson, K. and Cameron, J. 2005. Alternative pathways to community and economic development: the Latrobe Valley Community Partnering Project. *Geographical Research*, 43, 274–85.

Gilbert, D. and Tung, L. 1990. Public organisations and rural marketing planning in England and Wales. *Tourism Management*, 11(2), 164–72.

Gilbert, J. and Pearson, E. 1999. *Discographies: Dance Music, Culture and the Politics of Sound*. London: Routledge.

Gorman-Murray, A., Waitt, G. and Gibson, C. 2008. A queer country? A case study of the politics of gay/lesbian belonging in an Australian country town. *Australian Geographer*, 39(2), 171–91.

Gradus, Y. and Lithwick, H. 1996. *Frontiers in Regional Development*. Lanham: Rowman and Littlefield.

Gregory, D. 2002. Resort mayor tells tourists to keep out. *Sun-Herald*, 29 September, 47.

Hall, C.M. 1989. The definition and analysis of hallmark tourist events. *GeoJournal*, 19, 263–68.

Hannan, M. 2003. From blockades to blue moon: musical cultures of Nimbin, in *Belonging in the Rainbow Region: Cultural Perspectives on the NSW Far*

North Coast, edited by H. Wilson. Lismore: Southern Cross University Press, 247–62.

Hede, A-M. and Rentschler, R. 2007. Mentoring volunteer festival managers: Evaluation of a pilot scheme in regional Australia. *Managing Leisure*, 12, 157–70.

Hemphill, P. 1970. *The Nashville Sound*. New York: Simon and Schuster.

Hicks, J. 2001. *Australian Cowboys, Roughriders and Rodeos*. Rockhampton: Central Queensland University Press.

Higham, J. and Ritchie, B. 2001. The evolution of festivals and other events in rural southern New Zealand. *Event Management*, 7(1), 39–49.

Hobsbawm, E. 1983. Introduction: inventing traditions, in *The Invention of Tradition*, edited by E. Hobsbawm and T. Ranger. Cambridge: Cambridge University Press, 1–14.

Hughes, H. 2000. *Arts, Entertainment and Tourism*, Butterworth Heinemann, Oxford.

Hughes, H.L. 1994. Tourism multiplier studies: a more judicious approach. *Tourism Management*, 15(6), 403–6.

Irwin, R., Wang, P. and Sutton, W. 1996. Comparative analysis of diaries and projected spending to assess patron expenditure behaviour at short-term sporting events. *Festival Management & Event Tourism*, 4, 29–37.

Jetty Research 2010. *Random Telephone Survey of Residents to Measure Impact of the 2010 CountryLink Parkes Elvis Festival*. Sydney: UTS.

Jones, M. 2009. *Sustainable Event Management: A Practical Guide*. London: Earthscan.

Jones, R. 1998. What price the field of dreams? *The Guardian*, 30 May, 2.

Kazi, E. 2006. Easy for music festivals to hit the wrong note. *The Australian Financial Review*, 27 January, 16.

Kelly, M. 2010. *Four Winds Festival* [Online] Available at: www.mikekelly. alp.org.au/news/2010/04/06/420000-for-four-winds-festival [accessed: 9 November 2010].

Kither, L. 1998. It's party time for a festival. *Sunshine Coast Daily*, 27 December, 2.

Kong, L. 1995. Popular music in geographical analyses. *Progress in Human Geography* 19(2), 183–98.

Konkes, C. 1999. Earth Beat. *The Australian*, 11 December, 1–2.

Lee, S. 2001. A review of economic impact study on sport events, *The Sport Journal*, 4(2).

Lewis, G. 1997. Lap dancer or hillbilly deluxe? The cultural constructions of modern country music. *Journal of Popular Culture*, 31(3), 163–73.

Lewis, J.L. and Dowsey-Magog, P. 1993. The Maleny 'Fire Event': Rehearsals Toward Neo-liminality. *Australian Journal of Anthropology*, 4, 198–219.

Li, J. and Connell, J. 2011. At Home with Elvis: home hosting at the Parkes Elvis Festival. *Hospitality and Society*, 1, 189-201..

Li, M., Huang, Z. and Cai, L. 2009. Benefit segmentation of visitors to a rural community-based festival. *Journal of Tourism and Travel Marketing*, 26, 585–598.

Little, J. 1999. Otherness, representation and the cultural construction of rurality. *Progress in Human Geography* 23, 437–42.

Long, P. and Perdue, R. 1990. The economic impact of rural festivals and special events: assessing the spatial distribution of expenditures. *Journal of Travel Research*, 28(4), 10–14.

McKay, P. 2004. Patriot games. *Sydney Morning Herald*, 31 January, D1.

Mackellar, J. 2007. Conventions, festivals and tourism: exploring the network that binds. *Journal of Convention and Event Tourism*, 8(2), 45–56.

Mackellar, J. 2009a. Dabblers, fans and fanatics: Exploring behavioural segmentation at a special-interest event. *Journal of Vacation Marketing*, 15, 5–24.

Mackellar, J. 2009b. An examination of serious participants at the Australian Wintersun Festival. *Leisure Studies*, 28, 85–104.

Mason, P. and Beaumont-Kerridge, J. 2004. Motivations for attendance at the 2001 Sidmouth International Festival: Fun, family, friends, fulfilment or folk?, in *Festivals and Tourism: Marketing, Management and Evaluation*, edited by P. Long and R. Robinson. Sunderland, Business Education Publishers, 33–46.

Matheson, C. 2005. Festivity and sociability: A study of a Celtic music festival. *Tourism, Culture and Communications*, 3, 149–63.

Mayerfield, T. and Crompton, J. 1995. Development of an instrument for identifying community reasons for staging a festival. *Festival Management and Event Tourism*, 2(3), 37–44.

Melourney, C. and Moran, J. 2010. Out of tune at country festival. *Sunday Telegraph*, 17 January, 3.

Morgan, C. 2003. Beethoven's rolling over in the tropics. *Sydney Morning Herald*, 3 July, 15.

Morgan, M. 2008. What makes a good festival? Understanding the event experience. *Event Management*, 12, 81–93.

Morrison, M. 2008. Vine romance: artists line up for picnic gigs. *Sydney Morning Herald*, 29 November, 11.

Moscardo, G. 2008. Analyzing the role of festivals and events in regional development. *Event Management*, 11(1–2), 23–32.

Moscardo, G., McCarthy, B., Murphy, L. and Pearce, P. 2009. The importance of networks in special interest tourism: case studies of music tourism in Australia. *International Journal of Tourism Policy*, 2, 5–23.

Murphy, D. 2010. Byron sings blues over giant venue. *Sydney Morning Herald*, 11 October, 5.

Nanga Music Festival 2009. *2009 Nanga Music Festival Evaluation Report*, mimeo.

Nature Conservation Council of NSW 2008. Submission to Development Application 10.2007.462.1 [Online] Available at: http://nccnsw.org.au/index.

php?option=com_content&task=view&id=2328&Itemid=950 [accessed: 6 August 2010].

Neuenfeldt, K. 1995. The Kyana corroboree: Cultural production of indigenous ethnogenesis. *Sociological Inquiry*, 65(1), 21–46.

Neuenfeldt, K. 2000. The Transformative Effects of CDs on the Australian Folk Festival Scene. *Transformations* [Online] Available at: http://www.cqu.edu.au/transformations [accessed 8 August 2011].

Neuenfeldt, K. 2002. From silence to celebration: Indigenous Australian performers at the Woodford Folk Festival. *The World of Music*, 43(2–3), 65–91.

New England Focus 2010. [Online] Available at www.focusmag.com.au/ne/featured/opera-in-the-paddock [accessed 7 March 2011].

Nicholson, R. and Pearce, D. 2000. Who goes to events: a comparative analysis of the profile characteristics of visitors to four South Island events in New Zealand. *Journal of Vacation Marketing*, 6, 236–53.

Nicholson, R. and Pearce, D. 2001. Why do people attend events? A comparative analysis of visitor motivations at four South Island events. *Journal of Travel Research*, 39, 449–60.

Ninan, A., Oakley, K. and Hearn, G. 2004. *Queensland Music Industry Trends: Independence Day?* QUT, Brisbane.

Northern Daily Leader 1976. Editorial, 23 January, 7.

Northern Daily Leader 1977. Welcome to 'hick' city, 28 January, 11.

Northern Daily Leader 1978. City crowded for weekend festival, 28 January, 1.

Northern Daily Leader 1979. Many suggestions to improve country music week in city, 2 February, 2.

Northern Daily Leader 1980. Country Music tag pays off, 17 January, 5.

Northern Territory Treasury 2007. *Economic Evaluation of the Darwin Festival*. Darwin: NT Treasury, Darwin Festival and Charles Darwin University.

Oakes, S. 2010. Profiling the jazz festival audience. *International Journal of Event and Festival Management*, 1, 110–19.

Olding, R. 2010a. Byron boomers prove you can't stop the music. *Sydney Morning Herald*, July 24–25, 5.

Olding, R. 2010b. A little bit of glamping to go with the glam rock on stage. *Sydney Morning Herald*, 31 July, 3.

Olding, R. 2011a. Vacancy signs light way to Tamworth. *Sydney Morning Herald*, 15–16 January, 9.

Olding, R. 2011b. Locals make festival fans heel at home. *Sydney Morning Herald*, 12 January, 3.

Packer, J. and Ballantyne, J. 2010. The impact of music festival attendance on young people's psychological and social well-being. *Psychology of Music*, 39, 164–81.

Peace, A. 2011. Barossa dreaming: imagining place and constituting cuisine in contemporary Australia. *Anthropological Forum*, 21, 23–42.

Pegg, S. and Patterson, I. 2010. Rethinking music festivals as a staged event: gaining insights from understanding visitor motivations and the experiences they seek. *Journal of Convention and Event Tourism*, 11, 85–99.

Peters, B. 2002. The Aspen Idea. *Opera News*, 66, 36–39.

Peterson, R.A. 1997. *Creating Country Music: fabricating authenticity*. Chicago: University of Chicago Press.

Phipps, P. 2011. Performing culture as political strategy: the Garma Festival, Northeast Arnhem Land, in *Festival Places: Revitalising Rural Australia*, edited by C. Gibson and J. Connell. Bristol: Channel View, 109–22.

Pike, A., Rodríguez-Pose, A. and Tomaney, J. 2006. *Local and Regional Development*. London: Routledge.

Premier of New South Wales 2007a. *Iemma Announces Establishment of $85 Million Major Events Corporation, John O'Neill Appointed Interim Chair.* [Online, 25 June] Available at: http://www.eventsnsw.com.au/Media-Centre/Media-Archive.aspx [accessed: 4 October, 2010].

Premier of New South Wales 2007b. *Events New South Wales – Leading From the Front*. [Online, 8 November] Available at: http://www.eventsnsw.com.au/Media-Centre/Media-Archive.aspx [accessed: 4 October, 2010].

Prentice, R. and Andersen, V. 2003. Festival as creative destination. *Annals of Tourism Research*, 30, 7–30.

Quinn, B. 1996. The sounds of tourism: exploring music as a tourist resource with particular reference to music festivals, in *Tourism and Culture Towards the 21st Century*, edited by M. Robinson, N. Evans and P. Callaghan. Sunderland: Centre for Travel and Tourism, 383–96.

Quinn, B. 2005. Changing festival places: insights from Galway. *Social and Cultural Geography*, 6, 237–25.

Quinn, B. 2010. Arts festivals, urban tourism and cultural policy. *Journal of Policy Research in Tourism, Leisure & Events*, 2(3), 264–79.

Rawlins, A. 1986. *Festivals in Australia: An Intimate History*. Spring Hill, Victoria: DTE Publishers.

Raybould, M., Digance, J. and McCullough, C. 1999. Fire and festival: authenticity and visitor motivation at an Australian folk festival. *Pacific Tourism Review*, 3, 201–12.

Reid, S. 2008. Identifying social consequences of rural events. *Event Management*, 11, 89–98.

Richard Trembath Research 1997. *1997 Opera in the Outback: Economic and Social Impact Study*. Adelaide: South Australian Tourist Commission.

Ritchie, J. 1984. Assessing the impact of hallmark events: conceptual and research issues. *Journal of Travel Research*, 23, 2–11.

Roberts, J. 2003. Flushed with peace and love. *The Australian*, 6 August, 17.

Ruting, B. and Li, J. 2011. Tartans, kilts and bagpipes; cultural identity and community creation at the Bundanoon is Brigadoon Cultural Festival, in *Festival Places: Revitalising Rural Australia*, edited by C. Gibson and J. Connell. Bristol: Channel View, 265–79.

Saleh, F. and Ryan, C. 1993. Jazz and knitwear: factors that attract tourists to festivals. *Tourism Management*, 14, 289–97.

Salt, B. 2010. Mapping volunteers points the way to healthy communities. *The Australian*, 4 November, 33.

Sarahanne 2011. *So you want to start a festival?* [Online] Available at: http://www. fasterlouder.com.au/features/27384/So-you-want-to-start-a-festival [accessed 8 August 2011].

SBS (Special Broadcasting Corporation) 2007. *Elvis Lives in Parkes*, SBS Documentary, Sydney.

Schwarz, E. and Tait, R. 2007. Recreation, arts, events and festivals: their contribution to a sense of community in the Colac-Otway Shire of Country Victoria. *Rural Society*, 17, 125–38.

Shedden, I. 1998. Tripping the rock fantastic. *The Australian*, 12 August, 11.

Shedden, I. 2000. Beyond the blues. *The Australian*, 8–9 April, 16–18.

Shedden, I. 2007. Grass greener on every side. *The Australian*, 29 December, 6.

Shedden, I. 2008. Heard it on the Grapevine. *The Australian*, 6 December, 6–7.

Shedden, I. 2010. Talent comes up trumps in Tamworth. *The Australian*, 25 January, 14.

Shedden, I. 2011a. A galaxy of cosmic sounds. *The Australian*, 28 June, 17.

Shedden, I. 2011b. Down to earth vision puts loo king on top of the heap. *The Australian*, 29 March, 7.

Slater, L. 2007. My island home is waiting for me: the Dreaming Festival and archipelago Australia. *Continuum: Journal of Media and Cultural Studies*, 21, 571–581.

Slater, L. 2010. 'Calling our spirits home': Indigenous cultural festivals and the making of a good life. *Cultural Studies Review*, 16, 143–54.

Slater, L. 2011. 'Our spirit rises from the ashes': Mapoon Festival and History's shadow, in *Festival Places: Revitalising Rural Australia*, edited by C. Gibson and J. Connell. Bristol: Channel View, 123–35.

Soppe, R. 2009. It'll be new to you, folks. *The Australian*, 24 December, 5.

Sorensen, R. 2007a. By the river, dancing with sitars. *The Australian*, 28 September, 14.

Sorensen, R. 2007b. Voices from across the world join in outback music. *Sydney Morning Herald*, 14 July, 8.

Stebbins, R. 1996. Cultural tourism as serious leisure. *Annals of Tourism Research*, 23, 945–950.

Steketee, M. 2001. Hope for healing springs at festival. *The Australian*, 8 September, 5.

Stevenson, A. 2001. Great linedancing Grandpas! If this is Hicksville, it sure is catching. *Sydney Morning Herald*, 24 January, 5.

Stone, C. 2009. The British pop music festival phenomenon, in *International Perspectives of Festivals and Events: Paradigms of Analysis*, edited by J. Ali-Knight, M. Robertson, A. Fyall and A. Ladkin. Oxford: Elsevier, 205–24.

Tamworth City Council 2004. *Tamworth Country Music Festival—Introduction.* [Online] Available at: http://www.tamworth.nsw.gov.au/default.asp?iNav-CatID=578&iSubCatID=774. [accessed: 6 March 2004].

Taylor, T. 1997. *Global Pop: World Music, World Markets.* London: Routledge.

Thomas, B. 1994. Pop go the country clichés. *Sun-Herald,* 16 January, 134.

Thomas, B. 2002. Blue days at Byron. *Sun-Herald,* 10 March, 10.

Thrane, C. 2002. Music quality, satisfaction and behavioural intentions within a jazz festival context. *Event Management,* 7, 143–50.

Tindall, P. 2011. Economic benefits of rural festivals and questions of geographical scale: the Rusty Gromfest surf carnival, in *Festival Places: Revitalising Rural Australia,* edited by C. Gibson and J. Connell. Bristol: Channel View, 74–91.

Tomljenovic, R. Larsson, M. and Faulkner, H. 2010. Predictors of satisfaction with festival attendance: A case of Störsjoyran Rock Music Festival. *Tourism,* 49, 123–32.

Tonts, M. 2005. Competitive sport and social capital in rural Australia. *Journal of Rural Studies,* 21(2), 137–49.

Tourism Bellinger 2006. *Bellinger Magic.* Bellingen: Tourism Bellinger.

Tourism NSW 2010. *Travel to Northern Rivers Year Ended December 2010.* [Online] Available at: www.tourism.nsw.gov.au [accessed: 8 August, 2011].

Tourism Tamworth 2007. *Tamworth Country Music Festival Visitor Research 19th–28th January 2007.* Sydney: Micromex Research.

Treloar, J. 1996. Tamworth is country. *Tamworth City Times,* 26 January, 2.

Turner, B. 2011. Saving the show: How FNQ kept the music alive. *Australian Financial Review,* 21 July, 43.

Tuttiett, H. 2011. *Price-Gouging Blamed for Wintersun Loss.* [Online] Available at: http://www.goldcoast.com.au/article/2011/03/08/297675_gold-coast-news.html [accessed: 7 May 2011].

US Embassy 2010. *From the Ambassador's desk.* [Online] Available at: http://canberra.usembassy.gov/ambassador/from-the-ambassadors-desk/elvis.html [accessed: 12 March 2011].

van Heur, B. 2010. Small cities and the geographical bias of creative industries research and policy. *Journal of Policy Research in Tourism, Leisure & Events,* 2, 189-192.

Van Zyl, C. and Botha, C. 2003. Motivational factors of local residents to attend the Aardklop National Arts Festival. *Event Management,* 8, 213–22.

Voase, R. 2009. Why Huddersfield? Media representations of a festival of contemporary music in the 'unlikeliest' of places. *Journal of Tourism and Cultural Change,* 7, 146-156.

Waitt, G. 2008. Urban festivals: geographies of hype, helplessness and hope. *Geography Compass,* 2, 513–537.

Walmsley, D.J. 2003. Rural tourism: a case of lifestyle-led opportunities. *Australian Geographer,* 34, 61–72.

Warren, A. and Evitt, R. 2010. Indigenous hip-hop: overcoming marginality, encountering constraints. *Australian Geographer,* 41(1), 141–58.

Waterman, S. 1998. Carnivals for élites? The cultural politics of arts festivals. *Progress in Human Geography*, 22, 54–74.

Wearing, S., McDonald, M. and Ponting, J. 2005. Building a decommodified research paradigm in tourism: the contribution of NGOs. *Journal of Sustainable Tourism*, 13(5), 424–39.

Weeks, P. and Adams, J. 2006. Clubs and hallmark events: two Australian cases. *International Journal of Hospitality and Tourism Administration*, 7, 177–94.

Westwood, M. 2006. Wine flows for festival's refined taste, *The Australian*, 27 November, 17.

Westwood, M. 2011. Feast of festivals gets new menu, *The Australian*, 13 December, 17.

Wheat, S. 2000. Where there's muck there's brass. *Geographical*, 72(7), 23–25.

White, C. 2010. Splendour in the mud not dampening spirits. *ABC News* [Online, 14 August] Available at: www.abc.net.au/news/stories/2010/07/30/2968841. htm [accessed: 6 May 2011].

Whiteoak, J. 2003. Two frontiers: early cowboy music and Australian popular culture, in *Outback and Urban: Australian Country Music*, edited by P. Hayward. Gympie: Australian Institute of Country Music Press, 1–28.

Whitford, M. 2004. Event Public policy development in the Northern Sub-Regional Organization of Councils, Queensland, Australia: rhetoric or realization? *Journal of Convention and Event Tourism*, 6(3), 81–99.

Whyte, S. and Connellan, B. 2010. Record crowd at Splendour. *Sun-Herald*, 1 August, 28.

Williams, S. 2002. Country hits. *Australian Financial Review*, 30 November, 43–44.

Wilson, A. 2008. Blue note. *The Weekend Australian*, 11–12 October, 16–17.

Wood, E. and Thomas, R. 2009. Festivals and tourism in rural economies, in *International Perspectives of Festivals and Events: Paradigms of Analysis*, edited by J. Ali-Knight, M. Robertson, A. Fyall and A. Ladkin. Oxford: Elsevier, 149–58.

Woodford Folk Festival 2010. *Woodford Visitor Survey 2009/10*. Woodford: Woodford Folk Festival.

Wright, J. 2009. Folk behind Woodford Folk Festival have a feel for the crowd. *The Courier-Mail*, 6 November, 8.

Xie, P.F. 2003. The Bamboo-beating dance in Hainan, China: authenticity and commodification. *Journal of Sustainable Tourism*, 11, 5–16.

Yu, Y. and Turco, D. 2000. Issues in tourism event economic impact studies: The case the Albuquerque Balloon Fiesta. *Current Issues in Tourism*, 3(2), 138–49.

Zuel, B. 2005. Vintage rock. *Sydney Morning Herald*, 1 January, 4.

Index